Office copy

C000272071

Please return to R

Pension Economics

Pension Economics

David Blake

John Wiley & Sons, Ltd

Published by   John Wiley & Sons Ltd, The Atrium, Southern Gate, Chichester,
West Sussex PO19 8SQ, England

Telephone   (+44) 1243 779777

Email (for orders and customer service enquiries): cs-books@wiley.co.uk
Visit our Home Page on www.wiley.com

Other Wiley Editorial Offices

John Wiley & Sons Inc., 111 River Street, Hoboken, NJ 07030, USA

Jossey-Bass, 989 Market Street, San Francisco, CA 94103-1741, USA

Wiley-VCH Verlag GmbH, Boschstr. 12, D-69469 Weinheim, Germany

John Wiley & Sons Australia Ltd, 42 McDougall Street, Milton, Queensland 4064, Australia

John Wiley & Sons (Asia) Pte Ltd, 2 Clementi Loop #02-01, Jin Xing Distripark, Singapore 129809

John Wiley & Sons Canada Ltd, 6045 Freemont Blvd, Mississauga, ONT, L5R 4J3, Canada

Wiley also publishes its books in a variety of electronic formats. Some content that appears in print
may not be available in electronic books.

Library of Congress Cataloguing-in-Publication Data

Blake, David, 1954–
    Pension economics / David Blake.
       p. cm.
    Includes bibliographical references and index.
    ISBN-13: 978-0-470-05844-2
    ISBN-10: 0-470-05844-7
    1. Old age pensions.   2. Pension trusts–Investments–Econometric models.
3. Portfolio management–Econometric models.   I. Title.

HD7105.3B55 2006
331.25′2—dc22   2006020144

British Library Cataloguing in Publication Data

A catalogue record for this book is available from the British Library

ISBN 13 978-0-470-05844-2 (HB)
ISBN 10 0-470-05844-7 (HB)

Typeset in 11/13pt Times by TechBooks, New Delhi, India
Printed and bound in Great Britain by TJ International Ltd, Padstow, Cornwall, UK
This book is printed on acid-free paper responsibly manufactured from sustainable forestry
in which at least two trees are planted for each one used for paper production.

For my mother

Thelma Blake

Contents

Preface

With many countries in the world facing an existing or looming pension crisis, there could not be a more opportune moment to launch a new series of books on pensions. Countries around the globe are fast waking up to the fact that they have a major challenge on their hands with their state-run pension schemes. The combination of a rapidly changing population and fertility rates well below replacement rates has led to a striking increase in the dependency ratios in many countries. At the same time, many private sector schemes are facing severe funding difficulties as a result of poor stock market returns, falling interest rates and increasing longevity.

Pensions problems are becoming highly complex, and although there are many people with expertise in pensions, their expertise tends to be one dimensional. They might be a pension lawyer with a deep understanding of pension rules and regulations, but their understanding of the role of pensions in lifecycle financial planning might be poor. They might be a pension actuary with an indepth knowledge of how to calculate pension liabilities in a number of different ways, but their understanding of the financial risks in pension funds might be inadequate. They might be a skilled investment manager, but have little comprehension of how pension liabilities respond to macroeconomic or demographic shocks. They might be a pension accountant familiar with all the global pension accounting standards, but have little understanding of how these standards affect corporate dividend and investment policy. All these professions might know very little about the social dimension of pensions in their own country or about the pensions systems operating in other countries.

What is clearly needed is a well-trained group of professionals capable of providing appropriate and sustainable pensions solutions to complex pension problems. In short, there is a need for a new class of professional, the *pension scientist*. This is someone who can competently deal with the multi-disciplinary nature of pension problems. The development of a common body of knowledge is the first step in this process.

The Pensions Institute was started by economists. But we soon became aware of the limits of our knowledge in the pensions field. We found that actuaries, accountants and lawyers were talking about pensions in a language that was at the same time both strange and familiar. It was strange because of the new terms they used. It was also strange because terms familiar to us had subtly different meanings to them. For us to be able to deepen our understanding of the complexities of pensions, we needed to begin to understand the way that these different professional groups thought about pensions.

In the process of doing this, we realised just how multi-disciplinary a thorough understanding of pensions needs to be. To use a mountaineering analogy, we felt as though we were talking to different groups of skilled mountaineers who had climbed different sides of the same mountain. While each group was an expert at climbing its own side, they knew very little about the other sides of the mountain. We felt that was time to look at the pensions mountain from all sides.

That is why at the Pensions Institute we have started to write a series of books that will look at pensions from each of the different side of the pensions mountain. The first two books in the series are:

- Pension economics
- Pension finance

In due course we hope to have the following additional books:

- Actuarial principles for pensions
- Pension accounting
- Pension law
- Comparative pensions systems and regulation
- Social policy and ageing populations

These books are aimed at those currently working as, or seeking to work as:

- a pension regulator
- a pension policymaker
- a pension scheme manager
- an employee benefit consultant

- a client relationship manager
- a pension lawyer
- a pension scheme auditor
- a pension accountant
- an investment manager
- an investment consultant
- a pension economist

David Blake, Director of the Pensions Institute and Professor of Pension Economics at Cass Business School, London

1
Introduction

1.1 WHAT IS PENSION ECONOMICS?

This book is about pension economics, and it is important to understand both what a pension is and what economics is all about.

What is a pension? A *pension* is a stream of payments that starts when someone retires and continues in payment until they die.[1] In other words, a pension provides lifetime income security in retirement for however long the retiree lives (Bodie, 1990). A pension therefore has two essential purposes. The first is *consumption smoothing* over an individual's lifecycle, i.e., a pension provides an income in retirement when someone is no longer working in exchange for contributions into a pension scheme when they are. The second is *insurance*, especially in respect of longevity risk – the uncertainty attached to an individual's length of life. Public policy might have two additional objectives for a pension scheme. The first is *poverty relief*: a society might wish its pensioners to have a minimum standard of living in retirement. The second is a *distributional objective*: a society might wish to distribute additional resources above the poverty level to certain members of society, such as women bringing up children and other carers (Barr, 2004).

There are only two ways of 'paying' for a pension. In the first case, young workers agree to pay (out of their labour income) the pension of retired people in return for the promise that the next generation of workers pays for their pension. This is called an *unfunded* or *pay-as-you-go* (PAYG) pension scheme or plan. In the second case, each generation of workers saves (out of their labour income) for their pensions in a *funded* pension scheme or plan. There are two key features of both types of pension arrangements: time and risk. Workers must pay now for something that they will get in the future, i.e., the pension provides the economic function of transferring income (and hence consumption) from work years to retirement years. There is some risk that the actual pension payments received will be less than those expected when the

---

[1] This is also the definition of a life annuity, so a pension is an example of a life annuity.

plan was first started. Indeed, there is some chance that the pension might not actually be paid at all on account of the pension scheme becoming insolvent. This is why people talk about a *pension promise*, rather than a *pension guarantee*.

What is economics? There are three parts to economics: microeconomics, macroeconomics and welfare economics.

Microeconomics deals with how individuals and firms allocate scarce resources, both in a single period and over time. It is about optimisation subject to constraints. Optimisation is the process of making decisions that maximise (or possibly minimise) the value of an objective function that is considered to be important to an individual or firm.

Individuals are assumed to maximise utility (their own sense of well-being or welfare) both within each period and over time, subject to their lifetime wealth constraint (which involves a combination of human and financial capital). Firms are assumed to maximise profits (or minimise costs) within each period and over time, subject to a technology constraint (or production function) that involves inputs of so-called factors of production, such as labour, physical capital and possibly land. Microeconomics also deals with government microeconomic policy. The government occasionally intervenes in the decision-making process of individuals and firms in an attempt to influence their behaviour. For example, it might wish to encourage people to save more for their pension, and use tax and other incentives to make pension saving more attractive than other forms of saving.

Macroeconomics deals with the collective or aggregate consequences of individual and firm decision making, as well as with the consequences of government macroeconomic policy. Individuals and firms operate in markets, such as the labour market, the capital market and the market for goods and services. If the markets in which individuals and firms operate are fairly competitive, then the actions of utility-maximising individuals and profit-maximising firms lead to the efficient allocation of resources. The government frequently intervenes in the way that the economy operates in order to achieve outcomes that it considers to be socially desirable, for example, promoting full employment or controlling inflation (the increase in the general price level). To do this it uses two key macroeconomic policies: fiscal policy and monetary policy.

Fiscal policy uses government spending (financed by taxes or government borrowing, which is a form of deferred taxation, since the money borrowed must eventually be repaid from future taxes) to try and achieve a macroeconomic objective, such as full employment. The government might employ directly some unemployed workers or it might buy goods and services from private sector companies who then employ additional workers to meet the increase in demand. Monetary policy involves changes in the interest rate or the money supply to achieve another macroeconomic objective, such as controlling inflation. By restricting the money supply or raising interest rates, the level of aggregate demand in the economy can be reduced to a level that creates excess capacity in the economy, thereby restricting the ability of firms to raise prices and workers to demand pay rises. Macroeconomic policy is not typically used to influence pension decisions.

Welfare economics deals with the economic wellbeing of different members of society. This will depend on the distribution of resources (i.e., income and wealth) to different members of society and on the ability of society to share risks between different members of society. Welfare economics therefore deals with issues of equity as opposed to efficiency, and with the consequences of different economic policies for equity and risk sharing. Different types of pension scheme have different risk and distributional implications.

So what is pension economics? *Pension economics* deals with the allocation of scarce resources over the lifecycle between the time an individual is in work and the time he is in retirement. There are microeconomic, macroeconomic and welfare implications of this.

1.2   TYPES OF PENSION SCHEME

It is worth making the point at the outset that pensions and retirement are inventions of the late nineteenth and early twentieth centuries in developed economies. Before this, people in what are now developed economies did not retire; they continued working until they dropped, often ending their lives in the 'poor house'. Bismarck created the world's first state pension system in Germany in the 1880s. During the twentieth century, state and occupational pension schemes developed in the other countries of Europe and in developed economies as far apart as the USA and Australia. However, in many parts of Africa, Asia and Latin America, even today the idea of retirement and pensions remains a dream. The history of state and occupational pension schemes in the UK is explained in Blake (2003a, ch. 1–3) and Hannah (1986).

For those people living in developed countries, it is conventional to talk of *three pillars* of support in old age.

The *first pillar* is provided by the state as part of its *social security system*. There are two main types of social security system, Beveridgean and

Bismarckian. A *Beveridgean system* provides just sufficient support to keep people off the breadline; if people want to enjoy a higher standard of living, they are expected to make their own alternative arrangements. The UK and USA have Beveridgean social security systems. A *Bismarckian system* provides much more generous support, often at a level that does not require individuals to make additional arrangements. Germany, Italy and France have Bismarckian social security systems. The first pillar is financed by collecting tax (part of the social security tax that the government raises) from workers and paying it out immediately to pensioners. In other words, it is known as an unfunded system, since no fund of pension assets is accumulated. Clearly the level of social security tax collected will be lower in the former than the latter systems.

Most first pillar schemes are (non-financial) defined benefit in nature. Recently, countries such as Sweden and Poland have experimented with *non-financial* (or *notional*) *defined contribution* (NDC) schemes for their first pillar (see Holzmann and Palmer, 2006). These are unfunded schemes in which members have individual defined contribution (DC) accounts in which the returns that are credited to the contributions are not related to the returns on financial assets, but to some non-financial variable, such as the growth rate in the country's GDP or the growth rate in national average earnings (denoted g below). The contribution rate is a fixed proportion of earnings. At retirement, the notional capital in the member's account is converted to a life annuity, using an *annuity factor*[2] that reflects both the cohort life expectancy of the member and the rate of return on the scheme over the expected term of the annuity.

The system is kept in financial balance to ensure that the present value of system assets ($\text{PV}(A)$), i.e., the accruing notional capital, always equals the present value of system liabilities ($\text{PV}(L)$), i.e., the expected pension payments. This is achieved by using an adjusted rate of return $g + \rho$, where $\rho = [(\text{PV}(A)/\text{PV}(L)) - 1]$. The effects of demographic and economic shocks are therefore accommodated endogenously within the scheme and within each cohort, since the credited return on the scheme, $g + \rho$, adjusts the member's notional capital during both the

---

[2] An annuity factor shows the present value of one unit of pension payable annually for the life of the pensioner. The discount rate for calculating this present value is related to return on the non-financial variable used by the scheme during the accrual stage, such as the growth rate in the country's GDP or the growth rate in national average earnings. The estimated length of life of the pensioner is set equal to the life expectancy of the member's birth cohort (i.e., all people born in the same year as the pensioner). The annuity factor is divided into the notional capital to get the total annual pension. Present values are explained Box 1.1.

accrual and payment stages and the annuity paid at retirement reflects changes in birth cohort life expectancy.

Box 1.1   The Time Value of Money

A unit of money (say $1) is more valuable today than it will be if it is received in one year's time and $1 in one year's time is more valuable than it will be if it is received in two years' time. Money becomes less and less valuable, the further into the future it will be received. So if we are to receive $1 today, $1 in a year's time and $1 in two years' time, we cannot just add the three dollars together and say we have $3. We have less than this in present value terms.

Present value

The present or current value of a sum of money to be received in the future is found by discounting. To do this we need to know the interest rate or discount rate. Suppose it is possible to borrow or lend at a riskless rate of interest of 10%. Then $1 to be received in one year's time has a present value of:

$$\frac{\$1}{(1.1)} = \$0.91$$

This is because if we had $0.91 today, we could save it for one year, earning 10% interest, and have exactly $1 in a year's time:

$$\$0.91 + 0.1 \times \$0.91 = \$1$$

Similarly, the present value of $1 to be received in two years' time is:

$$\frac{\$1}{(1.1)^2} = \$0.83$$

This is because if we had $0.83 today and saved it for a year, we would have $0.91 in a year's time and if we then saved the $0.91 for another year we would have exactly $1 in two years' time.

The present value of the three dollars is therefore $2.74.

NDC schemes therefore have four properties (Palmer, 2006):

- At any time, the present value of an individual's lifetime benefit equals the individual's account balance.

- To maintain a fixed contribution rate, total NDC system assets must equal or be greater than total liabilities.
- The NDC benefit is constructed as a life annuity, reflecting life expectancy at retirement.
- Financial balance requires the accounts be valued at the rate $g + \rho$.

NDC schemes can be interpreted as exhibiting intergenerational fairness, since each generation pays the same contribution rate as a proportion of earnings and receives a pension based on its own economic performance over its lifecycle and its own mortality prospects.

The *second pillar* is provided by the companies in the form of *occupational pension schemes* or *plans*. Companies are said to *sponsor* such schemes. Typically, occupational pension schemes are funded, i.e., a fund of pension assets accrues from the contributions or premiums paid by the employer (the scheme sponsor) and worker (the scheme member) and from the investment returns on these contributions. The pension is paid from the accrued fund once the member retires. Sometimes (and this is more common in smaller companies than larger companies), the accrued fund is given to a life assurance company which then provides a life annuity to the retiree.

There are three classes of pension scheme member: the *active member*, who still works for the company and is still making contributions; the *retired member*, who has retired from the company and is drawing a pension; and the *deferred member*, a worker who is no longer working for the company and has not yet retired, but has accrued rights to a pension on the basis of his previous service for the firm and associated membership of the scheme – the pension then becomes payable when the deferred member retires from his last job.

Although most occupational pension schemes are funded, the calculation of the pension benefits can differ widely between different types of scheme. There are three main types of occupational scheme: *defined benefit* (DB), *defined contribution* (DC) and *hybrid*.

Until recently, the most common type of scheme was a DB scheme. In such a scheme it is the benefit that is defined and the scheme promises to pay a pension, based on this defined benefit, whatever the size of the fund backing this promise. The simplest DB scheme offers a fixed monetary pension at retirement, irrespective of earnings or subsequent inflation. Such schemes are common in Germany and the USA (where they are known as *fixed benefit* or *fixed amount plans*).

Table 1.1   Value of pension benefits as a proportion of salary

Year of employment	Present value of new benefits earned (%)	Value of accrued benefits (%)
1	0.32	0.32
10	0.98	6.88
20	3.10	32.58
30	9.18	115.68
40	26.08	365.14

Assumptions: The plan pays a benefit equal to 1% of final salary per year of service. Plan participants enter the plan at age 25, retire at age 65, and live until age 85. The employee's salary grows at the rate of inflation, which is 5% per year. The interest rate used for discounting nominal annuities is 9% per year.
Source: Bodie (1990, table 1).

However, the most common type of DB scheme is a *salary-related scheme*. The most common of these is the *final salary scheme*, in which the pension paid is related to the salary earned in the final year of employment (or the average of the final three or five years of employment) of the scheme member. The actual pension is some fraction of the final salary, where the fraction is calculated as the product of the accrual rate (e.g., 1%) and the number of years of service.

Table 1.1 shows the value of pension benefits as a proportion of final salary. The table shows that benefits are *backloaded*: the present value of benefits earned in each year is greater in later years than earlier years. For example, the present value of benefits earned in the 10th year of membership is 0.98% of final salary, while that earned in the 40th year is equal to 26.08%. The backloading is caused by two factors: the time value of money and inflation. An older worker is closer to retirement than a younger worker and so the present value of an additional unit of pension benefit is higher for the older worker.

Inflation increases backloading for two reasons. First, by increasing the nominal interest rate, it magnifies the time value effect. Second, by increasing nominal wages, it will magnify the uprating component of the benefit earned each year. With each additional year of employment, an additional year of service is earned and the nominal salary is higher.

More recently, *average salary schemes* have been introduced: the pension is based on the average salary earned during the member's career. A number of industry-wide schemes in Holland, for example, have switched from final salary to career average. In career average revalued earnings (CARE) schemes, the average salary calculation corrects for general price or wage inflation that occurred over the member's career. CARE schemes therefore lie in between average salary and final salary schemes in terms of the generosity of pension benefits.

Another type of DB scheme is the *retirement balance scheme*. The benefit is defined in terms of a lump sum rather than a pension and it is typically measured as the multiple of an accrual amount (a specified percentage of career average salary) and years of service. If final rather than average salary is used, such schemes are known as *final salary lump sum* or *pension equity schemes*. They are common in Japan and Australia. They are not proper pension schemes, however, unless the lump sum is used to buy an annuity, and hence provide lifetime income security.

A DB scheme will show a *surplus* if the value of the assets in the pension fund exceeds the value of the liabilities, namely the present value of the future promised pension payments. A DB scheme will show a *deficit* if the value of the liabilities exceeds the assets. Pension regulators or supervisors (appointed by the government) generally impose strict rules on the elimination of both surpluses and deficits. Surpluses are typically eliminated through *sponsor contribution holidays*, i.e., the sponsor stops making contributions to the fund until the surplus has been eliminated. Deficits are eliminated through a series of deficiency payments, i.e., additional contributions from the sponsor, that extinguish the deficit within a specified recovery period, such as 5–10 years or the average remaining service life of the company's workforce (typically around 15 years).

Increasingly, DB schemes are being replaced with DC schemes. In such schemes, it is the rate of contributions into the scheme that is defined. The contributions might be a fixed annual amount or they might be a fixed percentage of salary. The pension will depend on the value of the fund accrued by the time of retirement. No particular level of pension is promised with a DC scheme. If the value of the fund is low, either as a result of low contributions or poor investment performance, then the pension will be low as well. If, on the other hand, the value of the pension is high, the pension will be correspondingly high. By definition, DC schemes show neither surpluses nor deficits.

Hybrid schemes have a mixture of DB and DC components. The main examples are as follows (Wesbroom and Reay, 2005):

- *Sequential hybrid scheme*. The scheme might have a DC element (commonly called a *nursery DC scheme*) for those below a certain age (e.g., 45) and a DB element for those above it. Such a scheme offers good portability for younger workers who tend to be more mobile and a more predictable pension for older workers.

- *Combination hybrid scheme.* The scheme offers a DB pension in relation to salary up to a limit (which might be the basic salary) and a DC pension in respect of salary above this limit (which might be the variable element of salary).
- *Underpinning arrangements.* There are two main types. The first is a DC scheme with a DB underpin. Such a scheme provides a minimum pension, based on what a corresponding DB scheme with the same salary experience and service would have paid, in case the investment performance is very poor. The second is a DB scheme with a DC underpin. This type of scheme is intended to provide a 'value-for-money' guarantee for early leavers. The value of the final salary benefit is guaranteed not to be less than a DC benefit calculated on the basis of a multiple of the member's contributions accumulated with interest.
- *Cash balance scheme.* This is a defined benefit scheme in which the benefit is defined as an individual account within the scheme. The scheme specifies the rate of contribution and the rate of investment return (independent of the performance of the underlying assets in the scheme, but typically linked to the return on bonds) that will be credited to the member's account. The accumulated lump sum at retirement is used to buy an annuity. To the member, a cash balance scheme resembles a DC scheme. It is the most common hybrid arrangement in the USA (see Rappaport *et al.*, 1997). It is also sometimes known as a *shared risk scheme.*
- *Targeted benefit scheme.* This is a DC scheme but the aim is to deliver a target pension, so the contributions will have to be adjusted over time if the fund falls short of or exceeds the target.

The *third pillar* is any additional savings for retirement that the individual chooses above that provided by the state or the company for whom the individual works. These savings will typically be held in deposit accounts or in mutual funds invested in equities or bonds. If the individual chooses to do this via a formal pension scheme, it will almost invariably be in the form of a DC scheme, known as a *personal pension scheme* or an *individual retirement account.* Other assets can also be used to provide income in retirement. The best example of this is the domestic home. When they retire, individuals sometimes sell their home and buy a smaller one in order to increase their spending power in retirement; this is known as trading down. An alternative is to borrow against the equity in the home and allow the interest to roll up. The initial loan and the rolled-up interest are repaid at the time of death of the occupant out of the proceeds from selling the home. This is called *home equity release*.

Increasingly there is a *fourth pillar* of support in old age, and that is post-retirement work. Sometimes this is by choice. Some individuals do not like the idea of being fully employed one day and then having no work to do the next. Such individuals prefer a gradual entry into retirement. For other individuals, there might be no choice but to take a part-time job to make ends meet.

A pension is not the only issue that elderly people need to deal with. Health problems, medical expenses and the possible need for *long-term care* are issues that many people need to confront as they get older. In the UK, around 20% of old people need long-term care for up to two years before they die and the average annual cost of this is equal to the average annual salary in the UK. The bulk of a typical person's lifetime medical expenses occur in the last six months of their life. A pension scheme is not designed or intended to cover these costs. Either people rely on the state to pay these costs or, increasingly, they have to sell their other assets, including their home, to pay for their long-term care costs. While insurance policies covering long-term care costs exist, very few people take them out.

1.3   CONCLUSIONS

Pension economics is a relatively new branch of economics dealing with the micro, macro and welfare implications of different types of pension scheme. Pensions themselves are a relatively recent innovation and involve the input of the state, companies and individuals. For a discussion of different consequences of different types of scheme, see Blake (2000). For details of the UK pension system, see Blake (2003b). For details of other social security systems, see Gruber and Wise (2004).

QUESTIONS

1. What is a pension?
2. What is a life annuity?
3. What is pension economics?
4. Explain the differences between Beveridgean and Bismarckian approaches to social security.
5. Explain the four pillars.

6. Explain the difference between DB and DC schemes.
7. Explain the main types of DB scheme.
8. Explain why DB benefits are backloaded.
9. Explain the main types of hybrid scheme.
10. Explain NDC schemes.
11. Explain the time value of money.
12. What other issues apart from their pensions do elderly people have to deal with?

REFERENCES

Barr, N. (2004) *The Economics of the Welfare State*, Oxford University Press, Oxford.

Blake, D. (2000) Does it matter what type of pension scheme you have?, *Economic Journal*, **110**, F46–F81.

Blake, D. (2003a) *Pension Schemes and Pension Funds in the United Kingdom*, Oxford University Press, Oxford.

Blake, D. (2003b) The UK pension system: key features, *Pensions*, **8**, 330–375.

Bodie, Z. (1990) Pensions as retirement income insurance, *Journal of Economic Literature*, **28**, 28–49.

Gruber, J. and Wise, D. (2004) *Social Security Programs and Retirement around the World*, University of Chicago Press, Chicago.

Hannah, L. (1986) *Inventing Retirement: The Development of Occupational Pension Schemes in Britain*, Cambridge University Press, Cambridge.

Holzmann, R. and Palmer, E. (eds) (2006) *Pension Reform: Issues and Prospect for Non-Financial Defined Contribution Schemes*, World Bank, Washington, DC.

Palmer, E. (2006) What is NDC?, in Holzmann, R. and Palmer, E. (eds), *Pension Reform: Issues and Prospect for Non-Financial Defined Contribution Schemes*, World Bank, Washington, DC, pp. 17–33.

Rappaport, A., Young, M., Levell, C. and Blalock, B. (1997) Cash balance pension plans, in Gordon, M., Mitchell, O. and Twinney, M. (eds), *Positioning Pensions for the Twenty-First Century*, University of Pennsylvania Press, Philadelphia, pp. 29–44.

Wesbroom, K. and Reay, T. (2005) Hybrid Pension Plans: UK and International Experience, Research Report 271, Department for Work and Pensions, Leeds.

2
Individual Pension Decision Making

This is the first component of pension microeconomics. The traditional model for examining individual pension decision making is the lifecycle model of Ando and Modigliani. We use the model to examine both savings decisions across the lifecycle and the retirement decision. The lifecycle model has been tested empirically and we examine some of these empirical studies. We also look at a version of the lifecycle model with induced retirement, developed by Feldstein and estimated using UK data.

2.1 THE LIFECYCLE MODEL

We will analyse individual pension decision making using the *lifecycle model* (LCM) of Ando and Modigliani (1957) and Modigliani and Ando (1963), and extended by Merton (1969, 1971). The LCM is based on the idea of a rational and well-informed representative individual who plans his consumption over his entire lifecycle, based on his forecasts of his lifetime earnings. According to the LCM, the principal motivation for saving is to accumulate assets in order to support habitual consumption in retirement. It builds on the empirical observation that per capita aggregate consumption (which we can think of as the consumption of the typical or representative individual) is smoother (i.e., less volatile) than per capita aggregate income (which we can think of as the income of this representative individual).

In a lifecycle context this suggests that individuals will try to smooth their consumption over time. The simplest case is where an individual's life is divided into two parts, a period of youth and work, and a period of old age and retirement. In the absence of a pension system, the individual will experience a significant fall in living standards if he has not saved adequately for retirement. It will be hard for the individual to borrow from others to support his consumption in the future, if he has no prospect of future earnings with which to repay the loan. Realising this and naturally not welcoming it, the individual will plan to reduce consumption expenditure below income when income is relatively high (i.e., when the individual is young and in work) in order to enjoy higher consumption than income when income is relatively low (i.e., when the individual is old and retired). This is called saving for retirement and as a consequence of this saving, consumption will be smoother than income. The savings for retirement lead to the accumulation of financial assets that are drawn down once the individual has retired.

To illustrate the LCM in a world without uncertainty and a zero interest rate, consider a 25-year-old who will work for 40 years and be retired for 10 years. He earns $25,000 each year so his total *human capital* or wealth (the present value of his lifetime earnings from work) will be $1,000,000 (when the interest rate is zero, we can simply sum up the annual earnings over the 40 years of the working life). The $1,000,000 of human capital has to be consumed over the individual's 50 years of remaining life. Since he values smooth consumption over his lifecycle, he can spend $20,000 a year and die with all his assets exhausted. To achieve this spending pattern, he saves $5000 a year whilst in work. At retirement he will have accumulated a pension fund of $200,000, which can be drawn down at the rate of $20,000 a year.

In the above example, the individual had no inherited wealth and leaves no bequests. Suppose instead he inherits $250,000 in financial assets. His total wealth is the sum of his human and financial wealth, namely $1,250,000. He will now be able to spend $25,000 a year and die with zero assets. So with the LCM, consumption is a function of total wealth and is financed either from income or the sale of financial assets.

The LCM can be extended to allow for borrowing as well as lending. This can be done by dividing the lifecycle into three stages: a period of youth, a period of middle age and a period of old age. The first period of youth begins when the individual first gets a job once full-time education has ended. The individual might want to buy physical assets such as a home and start a family. The costs of doing this will typically exceed the individual's income and so he has to borrow from the future to finance the excess of consumption expenditure over income. During mid-life, once these high expenditure levels have tailed off and the individual's income exceeds consumption, he can pay off his past borrowings and begin to save for retirement by accumulating a fund of financial and physical assets. During the final stage of life, the retirement stage, the individual spends more than his income, by dissaving or drawing down the financial assets accumulated during mid-life until death. Consumption expenditure might actually be lower than in the pre-retirement stage (travel costs to work are no longer incurred, for example), but income is usually significantly lower than in the pre-retirement stage (pensions are lower than final salary for most people).

An even more general model of the LCM assumes the individual lives for a large number of periods and maximises the discounted value of the utility from consumption over all these periods; we assume a positive interest rate but no uncertainty. Formally, the individual maximises (for $t = 0, \bar{D}$):

$$\Lambda_t = U(C_t) + \left(\frac{1}{1+\rho}\right) U(C_{t+1}) + \left(\frac{1}{1+\rho}\right)^2 U(C_{t+2})$$

$$+ \cdots + \left(\frac{1}{1+\rho}\right)^{\bar{D}} U\left(C_{t+\bar{D}}\right) = \sum_{s=t}^{\bar{D}} \left(\frac{1}{1+\rho}\right)^{s-t} U(C_s)$$

$$(2.1)$$

subject to the *lifetime* (or intertemporal) *budget constraint* that lifetime consumption must equal lifetime income:

$$\sum_{s=t}^{\bar{D}} C_s \left(\frac{1}{1+r}\right)^{s-t} = A_t + \sum_{s=t}^{R} W_s \left(\frac{1}{1+r}\right)^{s-t}$$

$$= A_t + \bar{W}_t \qquad (2.2)$$

where Λ_t is the discounted value of lifetime utility, $U(C_t)$ is utility from consumption C_t in period t (see Figure 2.1), W_t is income in period t, ρ is the rate of time preference, A_t is the current level of non-human

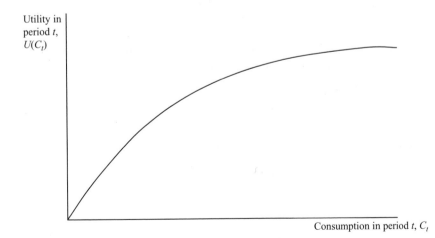

Figure 2.1   Utility function exhibiting positive but decreasing marginal utility

(mainly financial) wealth, r is the market rate of interest on financial wealth, $\bar{D}$ is the length of life (assumed fixed) and R is the length of the working life ($<\bar{D}$).

Box 2.1 explains the notion of utility.

Box 2.1   Utility

Utility measures the enjoyment or benefit an individual receives from consuming a good or service. However, utility does not increase linearly with the amount of good or service consumed. Rather, utility tends to increase but at a decreasing rate as the amount of a good or service increases. Individuals are said to have positive, but decreasing, *marginal* utility for the goods and services consumed: the first strawberry eaten tastes better than the second one.

Economists represent utility using a *utility function*. This is a functional transformation of consumption that exhibits positive but diminishing marginal utility. If the utility of consumption at time t, C_t, is denoted by $U(C_t)$, then the first derivative or slope of $U(C_t)$ measures the marginal utility of consumption:

$$U'(C_t) = \frac{\partial U(C_t)}{\partial C_t} > 0$$

and the second derivative or curvature measures the degree to which marginal utility decreases as consumption increases:

$$U''(C_t) = \frac{\partial^2 U(C_t)}{(\partial C_t)^2} < 0$$

Figure 2.1 shows this graphically. A common functional form for a utility function is the logarithmic utility function $U(C_t) = \ln(C_t)$. With this functional form:

$$U'(C_t) = \frac{1}{C_t} > 0$$

and

$$U''(C_t) = -\frac{1}{(C_t)^2} < 0$$

The term

$$\sigma[C_t] = -\frac{U'(C_t)}{U''(C_t)C_t}$$

is known as the *intertemporal substitution elasticity* (ISE). The ISE measures the willingness to substitute consumption across time, i.e., to engage in consumption smoothing. When ISE is low (i.e., below unity, which occurs when $U''(C_t)$ is high, i.e., when the utility function exhibits a lot of curvature, or when C_t is high), the willingness to engage in consumption smoothing over time is high. A 1% increase in wealth today will lead to a less than 1% increase in consumption today, which allows for some of the increase in wealth to be consumed in future periods. When the utility function is highly curved, an increase in consumption results in a lower increase in utility than when the utility function is less curved, and this lowers the value of an increase in consumption today relative to an increase in consumption in the future. The same is true when current consumption, C_t, is high, since this means $U'(C_t)$ is low and a further increase in current consumption is not highly valued. With logarithmic utility, $\sigma[C_t] = 1$, which means that a 1% increase in wealth today will lead to a 1% increase in consumption today and in all future periods.

The *rate of time preference* (sometimes called the personal or subjective discount rate or the degree of impatience) measures the individual's preference between current consumption and future consumption. Individuals with a high rate of time preference 'live for today' rather than 'plan for the future'. They discount the future very heavily: from equation (2.1) future utility such as $U(C_{t+1})$ decreases (is discounted) relative to current utility $U(C_t)$, the higher the value of ρ. The rate of time preference can be interpreted as the personal interest rate of the individual. The market interest rate, r, is the weighted average of the rates of time preference of all the individuals in the economy (or society as a whole), where the weights will reflect the distribution of wealth in the economy (i.e., the different values of A_t for different members of society). Individuals with above average rates of time preference ($\rho > r$) will tend to borrow funds (at the current market interest rate r) from individuals with below average rates of time preference ($\rho < r$) to increase further their current consumption, recognising that they must at some future stage repay these borrowings in order to avoid violating their lifetime budget constraint (2.2).

We can look at this in another way. A low rate of time preference (signalling a high degree of patience) indicates a high value to human capital in the mind of the individual. The individual believes that his capacity to repay any borrowings is strong because he is confident about his natural talent and/or about his ability to acquire the skills needed to get a job with a sufficiently high salary. In contrast, a high rate of time preference (signalling a high degree of impatience) indicates that the individual discounts future earnings very heavily and places a low value to human capital. The individual has low confidence in his ability to repay borrowings from future income. Accordingly, current consumption will depend fairly heavily on current income. It will be high (relative to current income) and have the same or similar volatility as current income. In short, individuals with very high rates of time preference do not value lifetime consumption smoothing and will have accumulated a much smaller fund of financial assets at retirement than an individual with the same pattern of income during the working life and a low rate of time preference.

The principal feature of the LCM is that current consumption, C_t, depends on the value of lifetime wealth, which is the sum of financial wealth (i.e., non-human wealth, A_t) and human wealth or capital (the present value of lifetime labour income, $\bar{W}_t$). If the lifetime budget constraint (2.2) is satisfied, then the above optimisation problem leads to the following utility-maximising LCM current *consumption* (C_t) *function* if the utility function is logarithmic (i.e., $U(C_t) = \ln(C_t)$):

$$C_t = b(A_t + \bar{W}_t) \tag{2.3}$$

where human capital is given by (assuming wages grow at a constant rate $g < r$):

$$\bar{W}_t = \sum_{s=t}^{R} W_s \left(\frac{1}{1+r} \right)^{s-t}$$

$$= \sum_{s=t}^{R} W_t \left(\frac{1+g}{1+r} \right)^{s-t} \tag{2.4}$$

$$= \left(\frac{\left(\frac{1+g}{1+r} \right)^{R+1-t} - 1}{\left(\frac{1+g}{1+r} \right) - 1} \right) W_t$$

(see Blake, 2000, p. 199) and where b is the *marginal propensity to consume*[1] from total wealth. In the case where the length of life, $\bar{D}$, is finite (which would be true for a single individual), then $b = \bar{D}^{-1}$, i.e., consumption is spread evenly over the remaining lifetime. In the case of an infinite horizon (which would hold for an infinitely lived family),

---

[1] The marginal propensity to consume from total wealth is the proportion of an additional dollar of total wealth spent on consumer goods.

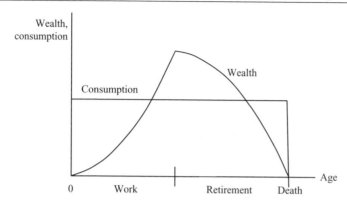

Figure 2.2   The lifecycle profile of wealth and consumption

$b = \rho$, i.e., consumption is proportional to total wealth, with the constant of proportionality equal to the rate of time preference. These results are proved in Merton (1969, 1971). Current savings equal the difference between current income and current consumption given by equation (2.3).

Figure 2.2 shows the typical shape of the *wealth–age profile* (or age–savings profile) in the LCM. It exhibits a hump shape. The LCM predicts that consumption is stable over the lifecycle. As a consequence, savings are predicted to be positive for working individuals and negative for retired individuals (Modigliani, 1986).

2.2   PENSIONS AND SAVINGS

Pensions play a very important role in lifecycle savings. Blinder (1981) employs a very simple model in which individuals save purely to finance retirement consumption. Capital markets are assumed to be *perfect* (which permits unlimited amounts of borrowing at the risk-free interest rate) and there are no taxes. Suppose individuals face the choice of saving personally for retirement or saving through an organised and mandatory pension scheme. We consider two cases, an unfunded state scheme and a private funded pension scheme organised by the employer.

2.2.1   Unfunded State Pension

A state pension system, since it is unfunded and operates on a pay-as-you-go basis, will reduce individual and national savings dollar for dollar. This is because each $1 taken from a worker and given to a pensioner in the state scheme will increase the pensioner's consumption.

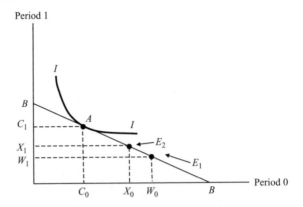

Figure 2.3 Reduced savings in an unfunded state pension scheme
Source: Blinder (1981). Reproduced by permission of Alan Blinder

But it will not change the worker's consumption. Instead it will simply reduce the worker's savings.

This is shown in Figure 2.3 in a two-period world of work or youth (period 0) and retirement or old age (period 1). Suppose the initial endowment point is E_1, with income of W_0 when young and W_1 when old. The *intertemporal budget constraint* is *BB*, which has a slope of $-(1 + r)$ where r is the risk-free interest rate. If the worker's *intertemporal indifference curve* (along which utility is constant) is *II*, the optimal consumption point is *A* (the tangency point between the intertemporal budget constraint and the intertemporal indifference curve).

Suppose a mandatory unfunded state pension scheme (or social security scheme) is now introduced and the worker's disposable income is reduced by the contribution $W_0 - X_0$. The endowment point moves to E_2, but the optimal consumption point remains at *A*. In this case, total savings are reduced by the introduction of the pension scheme from $W_0 - C_0$ to $X_0 - C_0$. Consumption and utility are unchanged. When the worker retires, he will receive a pension from the next generation of workers based on his contributions whilst in work. The value of this promised state pension is known as his state pension or social security wealth.

2.2.2   Private Funded Pension

In a private funded pension scheme (known as an occupational pension scheme if it is sponsored by the employer), every $1 placed in a private funded pension scheme will exactly displace $1 of private savings. Such schemes therefore have no effect on national savings, the sum of all workers' discretionary and pension savings.

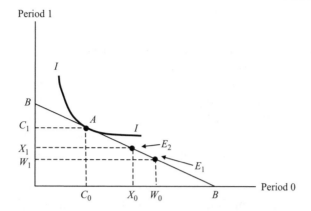

Figure 2.4 Inframarginal pension savings in a private funded pension scheme
Source: Blinder (1981). Reproduced by permission of Alan Blinder

This is shown in Figure 2.4. The introduction of the mandatory funded private pension scheme reduces the worker's disposable income by the contribution $W_0 - X_0$ to the scheme which earns r. The endowment point moves to E_2, but the optimal consumption point remains at A. In this case, pension savings are *inframarginal* (i.e., submarginal or situated below a margin or edge). Total savings $W_0 - C_0$ are unchanged by the introduction of the pension scheme. All that happens is that the mandatory pension savings fully displace discretionary savings. Consumption and utility are unchanged.

Suppose we now introduce a capital market constraint, namely that it is impossible to borrow against mandatory pension savings. Figure 2.5

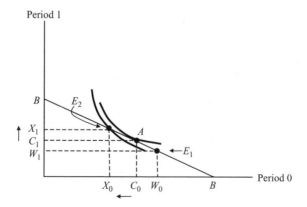

Figure 2.5 Forced oversaving
Source: Blinder (1981). Reproduced by permission of Alan Blinder

shows the case in which this constraint is binding. The individual's optimum point moves from A (an interior solution) to E_2 (a corner solution) as a result of the mandatory pension savings. Total savings increase from $W_0 - C_0$ to $W_0 - X_0$, but total utility falls. This is a situation of forced oversaving (of $C_0 - X_0$). Non-pension savings are zero. Any increase in the level of mandatory pension savings, since they are marginal (i.e., situated at the margin), will increase national savings dollar for dollar.

Now introduce another distortion, tax breaks on private pension savings, so that pension savings earn a higher after-tax return (r) than discretionary savings ($r(1 - \tau)$, where τ is the proportional tax rate). In Figure 2.6, pension savings are inframarginal and there is a pure income effect as the optimum shifts from A_1 to A_2. Consumption rises in both periods from (C_0, C_1) to (γ_0, γ_1), since net income rises, and this increases utility. Total savings fall, but retirement savings rise as a result of the value of the tax break BD (see vertical axis).

Figure 2.7 shows the corner solution of forced pension oversaving. Consumption in youth falls from C_0 to γ_0. Retirement consumption rises from C_1 to γ_1. Depending on how large the pension is, utility might rise or fall. In this case, utility rises. So it is possible for a worker to gain from a suboptimal pension plan. Again, non-pension savings are zero.

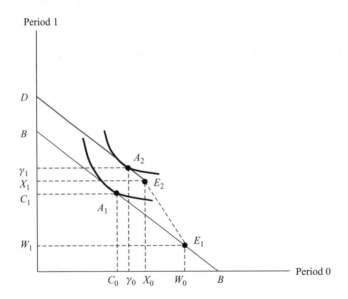

Figure 2.6 Inframarginal pension saving when there are tax breaks

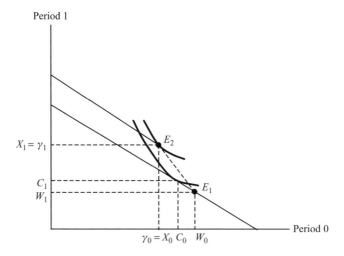

Figure 2.7 Forced oversaving when there are tax breaks
Source: Blinder (1981). Reproduced by permission of Alan Blinder

Any increase in the level of mandatory pension savings will increase national savings dollar for dollar.

2.3 PENSIONS AND RETIREMENT DECISIONS

The analysis up until now has assumed that the existence of a pension scheme had no influence on the worker's pattern of labour supply. However, in practice, it is possible that the existence of a pension scheme, whether funded or unfunded, might influence the decision about when to retire.

2.3.1 No Pension

Figure 2.8 shows the labour–leisure choice for a worker with no pension, subject to the condition that the worker either does not work at all and chooses A (receiving a_t in social security and/or income from his assets or, if he has retired, a pension) or has to work between a minimum and maximum number of hours per week between B and C (see Blinder, 1981). The slope of the line segment indicates the after-tax wage rate, W_t.

Three things happen as the worker ages. First, preferences change, usually favouring leisure over work. Second, a_t usually rises as individuals get older. Third, wages might fall. All these factors lead to the

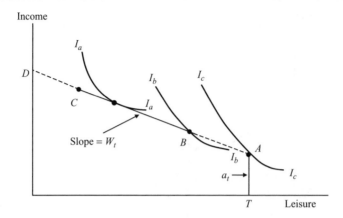

Figure 2.8 Labour–leisure choice
Source: Blinder (1981). Reproduced by permission of Alan Blinder

worker's optimal choice moving over time in favour of shorter hours, i.e., the indifference curve $I_a I_a$ shifts down to the right. Once it reaches $I_b I_b$ at B, the worker has no further move but to jump abruptly to A (on indifference curve $I_c I_c$, i.e., to retire.

The implication of this is that workers are more likely to retire if they are older, sicker, wealthier, have lower wages or can get a higher retirement pension. Correspondingly, retirement is likely to be delayed for those on higher salaries and having more flexible hours (i.e., B is further to the right).

2.3.2   Private Funded Pension

Now introduce a private funded pension scheme which pays a fixed pension P when the worker retires. Figure 2.9 shows what happens to the budget constraint. *TAD* is the budget constraint before retirement (the same as in Figure 2.8). To receive the pension, the worker must retire from his main job. It is still open to the worker to take another, probably lower-paid job on a part-time basis, paying w_t. The budget constraint now becomes *TEHG*. The effective combined budget constraint is *CFH* plus *E*.

As the indifference curve moves through time (and a_t rises over time), the individual might decide to step down to a lower paid job working shorter hours (so the optimum will be along *FH*). Alternatively, he might

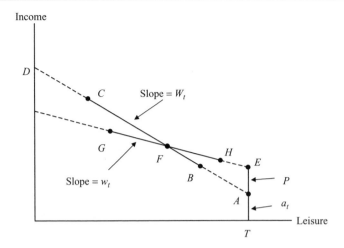

Figure 2.9 Taking a part-time job after retirement with a private funded pension scheme
Source: Blinder (1981). Reproduced by permission of Alan Blinder

decide to retire completely from the labour force (point E). Complete retirement is more likely if the pension is larger, the difference between W_t and w_t is larger, and the higher the minimum hours that need to be worked in the part-time job.

In final salary pension schemes, if the worker works an extra year, the pension is increased. The pension is P_t if he retires this year and $P_{t+1} > P_t$ if he retires next year. He therefore loses the present value of $P_{t+1} - P_t$ if he retires this year. If this is large enough, he might decide to delay retirement. The pension is also increased if the worker has a high salary at retirement or a high salary in the last few years prior to retirement, if the pension is based on the average salary over these years. Retirement might be delayed to achieve this.

Bodie *et al.* (1992) show how workers whose pension funds fall short of the level needed to deliver an acceptable pension in retirement can extend their working lives to make up the deficiency.

2.3.3   Unfunded State Pension

An unfunded state pension system tends to encourage or induce early retirement (Feldstein, 1974; Crawford and Lilien, 1981). This is because the state pension is typically subject to an earnings test. An earnings test

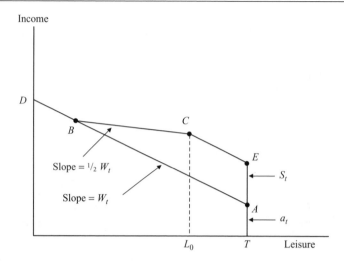

Figure 2.10 Taking a part-time job after retirement with a state pension system and an earning test
Source: Blinder (1981). Reproduced by permission of Alan Blinder

implicitly taxes post-retirement earnings above a threshold by reducing the state pension payable. Suppose the state pension is S_t. Figure 2.10 shows the case where a worker's pension is reduced by $1 for every $2 earned if more than $T - L_0$ hours a week are worked, where $L_0 = X/W_t$ with X the level of threshold earnings. The budget constraint is *TECBD* (below B the worker receives no pension). The earnings test imposes a strong disincentive to work beyond C.

The state pension system usually increases the pension if retirement is delayed beyond the state pension age. But the increase in the pension is sometimes less than actuarially fair, and this too encourages early retirement.

2.3.4   Unfunded State Pension with Private Funded Pension

When a worker has both a state and private pension, then the budget constraint is *TAFG* in either Figure 2.11 or Figure 2.12 (depending on whether the private pension is small or large) if he stays in his main job after state pension age. If he retires from his main job and takes a part-time job after state pension age, the budget constraint is *TEfg*. Points F and f show where the exempt amount of earnings is achieved. Since $w_t < W_t$, the slope of Ef is less than that of AF and F involves lower hours worked than f.

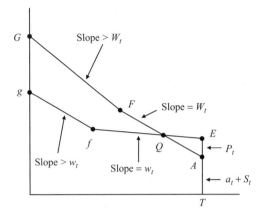

Figure 2.11 Post-retirement budget constraint with a state pension and a small private pension
Source: Blinder (1981). Reproduced by permission of Alan Blinder

If the worker has a small private pension, Figure 2.11 applies. The intersection of the two budget constraints (Q) lies along AF. The composite budget constraint is $TEQFG$ with the following possibilities:

- Full retirement (E).
- A part-time job after retirement (QE).
- Remaining in the main job and drawing the state pension (a tangency with the indifference curve to the left of Q).

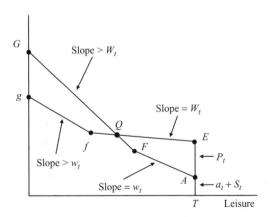

Figure 2.12 Post-retirement budget constraint with a state pension and a large private pension
Source: Blinder (1981). Reproduced by permission of Alan Blinder

With only moderately convex indifference curves, it is conceivable that a worker at some age jumps from full time work (*GF*) to full retirement (*E*), without taking a part-time job.

If the worker has a large private pension, Figure 2.12 applies. The intersection of the two budget constraints (*Q*) lies along *GF*. The composite budget constraint is *TEQG*. Moving from full-time work to complete retirement is more likely now, especially if $w_t \ll W_t$.

2.4 EMPIRICAL STUDIES TESTING THE VALIDITY OF THE LIFECYCLE MODEL

Despite the theoretical attractions of the LCM, the early empirical studies did not offer a great deal of support for the model.

A number of studies have found evidence inconsistent with the LCM's predictions that wealth built up during the working life is run down during retirement. Darby (1979), Kotlikoff and Summers (1981) and Laitner and Juster (1996) found that 'life cycle assets' in the USA (arising from accumulated savings) accounted for at most 30% of total US assets (the remainder having been inherited). Mirer (1979), Danziger *et al.* (1982–83), Poterba (1994) and Horioka *et al.* (1996) found that the elderly in the USA and Japan do not decumulate wealth sufficiently rapidly (indeed they appear to accumulate wealth in the USA) to be consistent with the lifecycle model (under certainty with no bequest motive). Friedman and Warshawsky (1990) found that the demand for annuities in retirement was too low if the lifecycle model with lifetime uncertainty was valid.[2] This may be because annuity yields are actuarially unfair (for both adverse selection and moral hazard reasons), so that precautionary savings are higher than would otherwise be the case in the presence of uncertain lifetimes. Involuntary bequests would be an unintended consequence of this.

Similar inconsistencies with the lifecycle model have been found using flow rather than stock data: Taylor (1971) found that the responsiveness of discretionary savings to a rise in social security contributions was −2.16, when it should be −1 (see Figure 2.3); Threadgold (1978), using UK data, found that private pension savings tended to increase total savings; Pitelis (1985), also using UK data, found that the

---

[2] Annuities protect individuals against outliving their resources and Yaari (1965) has shown that it is optimal for individuals to annuitise all their wealth in retirement in the absence of a bequest motive. Davidoff *et al* (2005) show that even if annuities markets are incomplete, it is optimal for individuals to annuitise a sizeable proportion of their wealth.

responsiveness of discretionary non-pension savings to a rise in private pension savings varied between 0.8 and 1.25, whereas it should be -1 if there was perfect substitution between them.

Further evidence is available from cross-section studies. Most of these found that increasing social security wealth tends to reduce savings, while increasing private pension wealth tends to increase savings. Kotlikoff (1979) and Leimer and Richardson (1992), using US data, found that social security wealth replaced between 0.6 and 0.67 of private wealth (rather than 1 if the lifecycle model was valid). Takayama (1990) found that a rise in social security wealth reduced the Japanese savings ratio. However, some studies found no significant relationship between consumption and social security wealth, e.g., Blinder *et al.* (1983), Kurz (1984) and David and Menchik (1985). Green (1981), using UK data, found that increased occupational pension savings increased discretionary non-pension savings with coefficients in the range 0.48–1.19 (rather than -1 if there was perfect substitution).

Jappelli and Modigliani (2005) counter that these studies, showing that savings rise rather than fall in retirement, do not define savings appropriately. The standard definition of savings adopted by these studies is the difference between disposable cash income (gross cash income less income tax) and consumption. This definition of savings ignores the contributions to pension schemes during the working life, but includes the cash pension received in retirement. Jappelli and Modigliani argue that the relevant definition of income is earned income (from labour and property) and therefore that the relevant definition of savings is the difference between earned income (net of income tax) and consumption. The relevant definition of savings during the working life therefore requires all contributions to pension schemes (whether public or private, mandatory or voluntary) to be added to cash income received to derive earned income (since these contributions are paid from earned income and therefore must be added back to cash income). It also requires that in retirement the pension received is subtracted from cash income, since the pension is not part of earned income. The standard definition of savings is lower than the lifecycle definition of savings during the working life and higher than the lifecycle definition during retirement. The wealth–age profile (see Figure 2.2) using the standard definition of savings is therefore 'too flat'. The effect of the adjustment suggested by Jappelli and Modigliani is to increase savings during the working life compared with the standard definition and to reduce it during retirement, thereby recovering the hump-shaped pattern to lifetime savings predicted by the LCM.

2.5   THE FELDSTEIN LIFECYCLE MODEL WITH INDUCED RETIREMENT

The earliest time series studies of the effect of (state) pension wealth on consumption and savings behaviour were those of Feldstein (1974, 1976, 1979, 1982). He used the *lifecycle model with induced retirement* to identify a *savings replacement* (or *wealth substitution*) *effect* and a *retirement effect*. With the first effect, as we saw in the simple model of Blinder (1981) above, state pensions reduce the need to save privately for retirement. With the second effect, state pensions induce workers to retire earlier than they otherwise would and this increases the need to save privately for retirement in order to maintain living standards. The net effect of these two opposing influences is an empirical matter and Feldstein's own time series estimates on US data over the period 1930–74 (even when corrected for the computer programming error identified by Leimer and Lesnoy, 1982) indicated that social security wealth had a small but statistically significant effect in reducing private savings (increasing consumption). He found similar results in other countries (Feldstein, 1980).

Feldstein's work generated a substantial debate. One strand was theoretical and revolved around the appropriate model to test the underlying hypothesis. Barro (1974, 1978), for example, argued that Feldstein's model ignored private intergenerational transfers (such as bequests to children from parents concerned about the burden of their own retirement benefits). The effect of these would be to offset exactly the impact of mandatory social security payments, so that *Ricardian equivalence* holds.[3] Barro, using a consumption function similar to Feldstein's but with additional variables (the government surplus, the unemployment rate and the stock of durable goods), found the effect of social security wealth on consumption was statistically insignificant.

Early UK time series studies also found that there was no statistically significant effect on savings of pension wealth whether the pension wealth measure was state pension wealth alone, occupational pension wealth alone, or state and private pension wealth combined (Hemming, 1978; Hemming and Harvey, 1983; Browning, 1982).

Another strand of the debate initiated by Feldstein concerned the measures that were used to proxy pension wealth. His social security

---

[3] If Ricardian equivalence (named after the economist David Ricardo) holds, individuals will use private transactions to exactly offset the imposition of mandatory controls on their behaviour.

wealth measure was a rather crude approximation to the underlying true variable, which is the actuarial value of the social security pension that individuals expect to receive in retirement. Feldstein made the following simplifying assumptions: the ratio of benefits to disposable income remains constant over time at the historical average of 0.41; the number of future beneficiaries equals the number of current covered workers adjusted for differences in labour force participation by age; and the number of females receiving widow's benefits in future is proportional to the number of current male covered workers and pensioners.

UK studies also made some unsatisfactory assumptions concerning pension wealth. Hemming (1978) made an early attempt to use appropriate actuarial methods (discounting future anticipated cash flows weighted by survival probabilities), but his series was too short to draw meaningful conclusions and, subsequently, official estimates were revised downwards. Hemming and Harvey (1983) made the following assumptions: pension wealth is a scalar multiple of current pension benefits; financial wealth is equal to the present value of an annuity determined by the current level of pre-tax interest income discounted by 10% with no allowance for real earnings growth; housing wealth is inferred from rateable values; and the possibility of being an early leaver and so getting less than the maximum pension of two-thirds of final salary is ignored. Browning (1982) made the following assumptions: real state pensions grow at a constant rate (less than the discount rate), even though real state pensions are constant over time, although the numbers claiming them grow over time; a rectangular age distribution over the ages 0 to 72; private pension wealth equals the market value of pension funds (so that the surplus is assumed always to be zero); unfunded schemes equal the size of funded schemes, so that private pension wealth is assumed to equal twice the market value of pension funds.

Cross-section studies have been used to determine the effect of pension schemes on inducing retirement. Disney *et al.* (1994) and Meghir and Whitehouse (1997), in studies using UK data, found that workers with occupational pension rights tended to remain longer in particular jobs, but also tended to retire earlier than those without them; also the earlier the age at which workers began to accrue these rights, the more likely they were to take early retirement. The income and wealth effects of occupational pension assets therefore appear to dominate the intertemporal substitution effect, which would tend to delay retirement since greater work leads to a higher final salary pension. For workers without occupational pension rights, the most likely causes of permanent job exit prior to normal retirement age are redundancy and ill-health. There are also offsetting effects present with unfunded state pension schemes, but they are rather different from those operating with funded private pension schemes. On the one hand, Sheshinski (1978), Boskin (1977) and Boskin and Hurd (1978) argue that if higher social security taxes are needed to pay the state pensions of the growing elderly population, this provides a disincentive effect that could lead to a reduction in labour force participation and earlier retirement. On the other hand, Blinder *et al.* (1980) argue that state pensions do not necessarily have the effect of encouraging earlier retirement, since delayed retirement after state pension age can result in a more than actuarially fair increase in the state pension. The effects differ with different social security systems, of course, and the net effect remains an empirical question for each system.

The psychological research literature also offers insights. Cagan (1965), for instance, identified a *recognition effect* in individual behaviour. When someone is obliged to join a pension scheme, they begin to recognise for the first time the importance of saving for old age and this encourages them to save even harder. Similarly, Katona (1964) identified a *goal-gradient effect* in individual behaviour, whereby effort is heightened the nearer individuals are to their goal.

2.5.1   The Consumption Decision

Blake (2004) used post-war UK data to estimate a version of Feldstein's LCM consumption function (2.3) for a single representative agent.[4] The advantage of this approach is that it is possible to use aggregate data for the economy (which is readily available) to estimate the parameters of the representative agent's consumption function. However, a representative agent model provides a valid representation of microeconomic behaviour only under certain restrictive conditions concerning the distribution of income in the economy, namely that it is constant over time or at most a function of deterministic, time-dependent variables (Stoker, 1986). Blundell *et al.* (1993) have shown that, once these 'aggregation factors' have been taken into account, a time series-based representative agent model is not necessarily outperformed in terms of forecasting ability by microeconomic models involving panel data. A study by Goodman *et al.*

---

[4] The data are annual for the period 1948–1994. Most of the wealth data are taken from Blake and Orszag (1999). The exception is human capital, which is estimated as the expected present value of lifetime earnings for the whole adult population.

(1997, chapter 3) indicates that the distribution of income in the UK was fairly stable over the post-war period (with a Gini coefficient[5] of around 0.26) until 1985, after which inequalities (particularly at the extremes of the distribution) increased before stabilising again by 1993 (when the Gini coefficient was 0.34). When a variable measuring the annual Gini coefficients over the sample period was included in the model, it was found to be statistically insignificant, indicating that the changes in the income distribution since 1985 were not sufficient to invalidate the representative agent model.

The consumption function in equation (2.3) states that current consumption depends only on current total wealth, not on the composition of wealth and not on any other variable. But this is likely to hold only in a world of perfect capital and labour markets, where, for example, individuals can borrow against illiquid and non-tradeable assets such as pension wealth or human capital, and workers never experience involuntary unemployment.

In practice, we must allow for the following possibilities: that the components of wealth may have differential effects on consumption; that other characteristics of wealth may influence consumption (e.g., rates of return on the wealth components); that individuals are liquidity constrained; that these constraints may change over time as a result of, say, financial deregulation; and that other factors may influence consumption.

We accounted for these possibilities in the following way:

- *Including the components of wealth as separate regressors.* We decomposed total personal wealth $(A + \bar{W})$ into eight categories: net financial wealth (A_F), housing wealth (A_H), consumer durable wealth (A_D), basic state pension wealth[6] (A_B), state earnings related pension wealth (A_S), occupational pension wealth (A_O), personal pension wealth (A_P) and human capital $(\bar{W})$.
- *Including as regressors the real returns on total wealth and its components:*[7] $r_W, r_F, r_H, r_D, r_B, r_S, r_O$ and r_P.

---

[5] The Gini coefficient is a measure of income inequality developed by the Italian statistician Corrado Gini. It lies between 0 and 1, where 0 corresponds with perfect equality (where everyone has the same income) and 1 corresponds with perfect inequality (where one person has all the income, and everyone else has zero income).

[6] For more information on this and the other types of pension scheme in the UK, see Blake (2003).

[7] Internal rates of return were used for r_B, r_S, r_O, while r_W is the weighted average of the eight components of wealth. A constant real discount rate of 3% was used to estimate the value of human capital (the same discount rate as is used by the Government Actuary's Department to estimate the value of state pension wealth).

- *Liquidity constraints.* The effect of liquidity constraints is to introduce current income into the consumption function; they can account for the observed 'excess sensitivity' of consumption with respect to current income that is inconsistent with the lifecycle model (Hall, 1978; Flavin, 1985; Zeldes, 1989; Cushing, 1992). Take, for example, equation (2.3) aggregated over all consumers who are not liquidity constrained. Liquidity-constrained individuals are restricted to consuming their current income. If such individuals receive a fraction of total personal disposable income W_t equal to c, then the aggregate consumption function will take the form:

$$C_t = b(A_t + \bar{W}_t) + cW_t \qquad (2.5)$$

- *Lifecycle factors.* Equation (2.5) explains the optimal consumption behaviour of a representative agent with no bequest motive. In this framework, consumption is independent of the individual's age. Different investigators have accounted for lifecycle factors in a variety of ways. Some include the proportions of the population who are respectively young (the youth dependency ratio (*YOUTHDR*)) and old (the elderly dependency ratio (*AGEDR*)) (e.g., Modigliani, 1970; Feldstein, 1980). Others include life expectancy (*LIFEXP*) (e.g., Hamermesh, 1985). Some have attempted to discover a bequest motive. Hurd (1987), for example, has tested for this using cross-section data by examining whether the savings of the elderly who have children is higher than the savings of the elderly without children. He finds no evidence for a bequest motive. However, this motive is impossible to test in an aggregate time-series context.

- *Labour market status.* Clearly an individual's labour market status (employed or unemployed, in work or retired) can affect consumption behaviour. A number of investigators include the unemployment rate (*UN*). Campbell and Mankiw (1991), for example, test whether the increase in unemployment in the 1980s might have tended to counteract the positive impact of financial deregulation on consumption. Alternatively, if there is a trade-off between consumption and leisure, then real wages or hours worked should be included in the model, with rises in these two variables being associated with higher consumption; the unemployment rate can be used as a proxy for changes in hours worked (Barro, 1974, 1978; Burkhauser and Turner, 1982; Bayoumi, 1995).

- *Inflation rate.* Because 'nominal rather than real interest rate payments are considered to be income in the national accounts, hence in inflationary times consumers are forced to increase saving simply to keep their debt position stable' (Bayoumi, 1993, p. 1434). Hendry and von Ungern-Sternberg (1981) and Hendry (1994) use a variable that results from multiplying the value of liquid assets by the inflation rate ($\dot{P}_F$). A high value for $\dot{P}_F$ would be expected to induce individuals to increase their savings in order to maintain the real value of their liquid assets.

- *Spillover effects from other sectors.* Some investigators have included the savings of the corporate (*SC*) and government (*SG*) sectors since these might be substitutes for personal sector savings (complements for personal sector consumption). Examples are Feldstein (1974), who used corporate retained earnings, and Barro (1974, 1978), who used the government surplus. Another possibility is to include the surplus in occupational pension schemes (*SURPLUS*), on the grounds that some of the surplus might be shared with pensioners, but in any event increases the wealth of the shareholders of companies running surpluses.

The long-run elasticities[8] for three versions of the model are presented in Table 2.1. The long-run elasticity of total wealth is about one-third, while there are positive elasticities for housing wealth, basic state pension wealth and SERPS wealth of about 0.07– 0.08, 0.04 and 0.10, respectively, and negative elasticities of about −0.09 and −0.007, respectively, for occupational and personal pension wealth. The long-run income elasticity lies between 0.5 and 0.8. However, the key point is the significant positive effect of state pension wealth on consumption (corresponding to a negative effect on savings) and the significant negative effect of private pension wealth on consumption (corresponding to a positive effect on savings).

These results can be compared with those from a study of national savings by Edwards (1996), who used a panel of 36 OECD, Latin American and East Asian countries (but excluding the USA and UK). His main conclusions were that private savings were negatively related to the elderly dependency ratio, government savings and social security spending. Our results for the UK indicate that the elderly dependency ratio is

---

[8] The elasticity of A with respect to B shows the percentage change in A in response to a 1% change in B.

Table 2.1 Long-run elasticities of consumption with respect to wealth and additional variables

Regressors	Dependent variable		
	$C(1)$	$C(2)$	$C(3)$
$A + \bar{W}(t\text{-ratio})$	0.3447 (8.18)	—	—
A_H	—	0.0712 (11.18)	0.0811 (7.76)
A_B	—	0.0441 (2.54)	0.0444 (2.47)
A_S	—	0.1066 (5.58)	0.0977 (5.10)
A_O	—	−0.0883 (4.67)	−0.0860 (4.10)
ΔA_P	—	−0.0072 (9.47)	−0.0066 (6.46)
r_W	0.0054 (1.04)	0.0044 (4.80)	—
r_F	—	—	0.0003 (3.91)
r_B	—	—	0.0063 (2.33)
W	0.5030 (9.78)	0.7727 (21.13)	0.7693 (20.58)
$YOUTHDR$	0.0528 (1.19)	—	—
ΔUN	−0.0015 (5.11)	—	—
$AGEPR$	—	−0.0819 (4.73)	−0.0702 (3.64)
$\dot{P}_F$	−0.0068 (2.21)	—	—
SG	0.0035 (8.32)	0.0021 (5.63)	0.0023 (5.41)
SC	—	—	0.0180 (2.02)
$SUR PLUS$	—	0.0018 (2.40)	0.0013 (1.68)

Note: Δ means change in.
Source: Blake (2004, table 3)

not a significant determinant of consumption or personal savings (suggesting that the shares of income consumed and saved do not change as British people get older, in contrast with evidence from panel data), that government savings partially displace personal savings and that social security wealth also partially displaces personal savings.

A study by Poterba *et al.* (1996) found that raising contribution limits for tax-exempt Individual Retirement Accounts (IRAs) and 401(k) pension plans in the USA between 1983 and 1986 led to a one-for-one increase in personal savings. However, a study by Gale and Scholz (1994) covering the same period found that the increased contribution limits on IRAs merely shifted taxable forms of saving into tax-favoured IRAs with little increase overall in national savings. These two studies therefore suggest that the increase in personal savings might be substantially offset by the reduction in government savings needed to finance the tax breaks. We find exactly the same result when personal pensions (the equivalent of IRAs and 401(k) plans) were introduced in the UK in 1988.

The results can also be compared with some cross-section studies for the UK. Alessie *et al.* (1997), using a cohort analysis, while accepting that the high statutory downpayments on durables in the UK until June 1982 imposed a binding constraint on relatively young households, found that the sharp increase in consumer expenditure between 1985 and 1988 could not be explained by the additional steps towards full financial liberalisation that took place between 1984 and 1986. We find a similar result. Attanasio and Weber (1994) argued that the main cause of the consumer boom between 1985 and 1986 appeared to be upward revisions in expected lifetime labour income by the younger cohorts of the population who were mainly responsible for the boom. House price increases were important determinants of consumption after 1982, but could not on their own explain the consumption surge after 1985. We also find that housing wealth is an important determinant of consumption, although we could not find a statistically significant role for human capital. However, our principal explanation for the strong growth in consumption during the 1980s lies in the significant growth of state pension (especially SERPS) wealth and, to a lesser extent, in the growing occupational pension fund surpluses of the 1980s.

2.5.2   Retirement Behaviour

While there are still standard retirement ages (typically between 60 and 65), increasingly there is flexibility over the actual retirement age. At the same time, it is also the case that retirement is no longer a strict discrete choice variable: some people are less than fully employed prior to normal retirement age; others continue to work after this age. In addition, it is possible to induce retirement. So the retirement decision is a very complex one and is therefore very difficult to model precisely in an aggregate time series model.

Blake (2004) investigated retirement behaviour by examining the factors influencing the labour force participation rate of the elderly (*AGEPR*). Table 2.2 shows the long-run elasticities from the models that he estimated. The table indicates that a 1% rise in aggregate wealth lowers the elderly participation rate by just under 0.5%. This effect appears to arise principally from human capital ($\bar{W}$), the largest single component of aggregate wealth. $\bar{W}$ does not appear to have an independent effect on consumption, but it does have a significant positive effect on inducing retirement. Recall that the representative agent in this model is part young, part middle-aged and part old. If the part that is

Table 2.2 Long-run elasticities of the age participation rate on wealth and other variables

	Dependent variable	
Regressors	*AGEPR*(1)	*AGEPR*(2)
$A + \bar{W}$(t-ratio)	−0.4413 (1.53)	—
A_H	—	0.1534 (3.89)
A_O	—	−0.4839 (14.50)
A_P	—	0.0682 (10.17)
$\bar{W}$	—	−0.5148 (3.09)
W	0.9520 (2.17)	0.7058 (4.11)
YOUTHDR	2.0485 (10.81)	—
LIFEXP	−10.8196 (5.94)	—

Source: Blake (2004, table 4)

young, say, experiences an increase in human capital, this induces the part that is old to retire earlier. Occupational pension wealth (A_O) also has a significant positive effect on inducing retirement (with a long-run elasticity of −0.48). This is consistent with cross-section evidence for the UK, e.g., Disney *et al.* (1994) and Meghir and Whitehouse (1997). However, rising housing wealth and personal pension wealth have the effect of delaying retirement. This again appears to be evidence against the lifecycle hypothesis. The effect of income on elderly participation is strongly positive, with an elasticity varying between 0.7 and 0.95. Two other variables are significant in the equation involving aggregate wealth. An increase in youth dependency has a strong effect in delaying retirement. On the other hand, greater longevity (possibly linked to greater morbidity) is associated with lower labour force participation after retirement. Interestingly, state pension wealth appears to have no net effect on the retirement decision, suggesting that for the UK, the Sheshinski, Boskin and Hurd effect and the Blinder, Gordon and Wise effect (discussed above) are exactly offsetting.

2.5.3 Discussion

In terms of state pension wealth, we find similar results to those found by Feldstein (1974, 1976, 1979, 1982), namely that state pensions have a strong savings replacement effect and reduce the need to save privately for retirement. However, they have no induced retirement effect (or at least an effect in reducing the elderly participation rate). Private occupational pensions, in contrast, have a direct effect in increasing savings (reducing consumption), but an indirect effect in lowering savings via their effect on lowering the elderly participation rate (which helps to raise consumption). The net effect on savings is positive, however. Private personal pensions also have a direct effect in increasing savings, and this is reinforced by the positive effect that personal pensions have in raising the elderly participation rate. From Tables 2.1 and 2.2, the long-run elasticities of savings with respect to occupational and personal pension wealth, taking into account their long-run impact on the elderly participation rate, are 0.0577 and 0.0127, respectively.

Certain important policy implications emerge from this analysis. First, if governments wish to increase national savings or delay retirement, they should consider establishing individual retirement accounts for state pension schemes. This has been recommended by, inter alia, Feldstein (1978, 1997). National savings increased sharply in Chile following the privatisation of pension provision in 1981 (Holzman, 1997), although, as Gale and Scholz (1994) have shown, any tax breaks used to encourage private pensions will tend to reduce public savings. Feldstein and Bacchetta (1991) have also shown that policies that raise domestic savings also succeed in raising the domestic capital stock; at most one-third of any increment leaks abroad. Second, as capital market imperfections are increasingly eliminated, consumers will find that they can borrow against their 'illiquid' pension assets in the same way that they found they could borrow against their 'illiquid' housing assets from the beginning of the 1980s. This will have a striking impact on consumption and make it much more difficult for the authorities to influence consumption using conventional policy tools. It could even offset the positive savings effect from private funded pension schemes.

2.6   CONCLUSIONS

The lifecycle model has been the principal model for examining savings and retirement decisions for the last half century. Individuals recognise that there will come a time when they are too old for work and will therefore need to have saved enough during the working life to enjoy an acceptable standard of living in retirement.

Organised pension schemes fit neatly into the LCM framework. Contributions to an unfunded state pension scheme will reduce private discretionary savings and hence national savings by the same amount, since individuals no longer need to save privately for their retirement.

Contributions to a mandatory private funded state pension scheme will, in general, have no effect on total savings; discretionary savings will fall by the same amount as the mandatory contributions.

The existence of a pension scheme can also influence the retirement decision. The existence of significant pension wealth can induce people to retire early. This seems to be true of the unfunded state pension scheme. Benefits are backloaded in occupational schemes, especially in the private sector, and this can encourage later retirement. People with insufficient pension assets can decide to work longer to make up for this deficiency.

The early empirical studies failed to offer strong support for the LCM, but this has been put down to an incorrect definition of savings. Nevertheless, the empirical evidence does show that: state pensions reduce the need to save privately for retirement, although their effect on inducing early retirement is weak; private occupational pensions increase savings and encourage earlier retirement; and private personal pensions also increase savings but encourage later retirement.

QUESTIONS

1. Explain the lifecycle model.
2. Use an example to derive the hump-shaped pattern of savings across the lifecycle.
3. What is discounted lifetime utility?
4. Explain the intertemporal budget constraint.
5. Explain utility and marginal utility.
6. Explain the intertemporal substitution elasticity.
7. What does the rate of time preference measure?
8. What determines whether individuals are likely to be borrowers or lenders?
9. Define human capital.
10. If utility of consumption is logarithmic, how will optimal consumption be determined if capital and labour markets are perfect?
11. What is an intertemporal indifference curve?
12. What effect will the introduction of an unfunded state pension scheme have on individual and national savings?
13. What effect will the introduction of a private funded pension scheme have on individual and national savings?
14. Explain the difference between marginal and inframarginal.
15. When can there be forced oversavings?

16. Examine the effects of tax breaks on private pension savings.
17. Explain the retirement decision when there is no pension scheme.
18. Explain the retirement decision when there is a private funded pension scheme.
19. Explain the retirement decision when there is an unfunded state pension scheme.
20. Examine the effect of earnings tests on incentives to work after retirement.
21. Review the empirical evidence testing the validity of the LCM.
22. What is the appropriate definition of savings in the LCM?
23. Explain the Feldstein LCM with induced retirement.
24. What other factors have been shown to influence consumption in the presence of imperfect capital and labour markets?

REFERENCES

Alessie, R., Devereux, M.P. and Weber, G. (1997) Intertemporal consumption, durables and liquidity constraints: a cohort analysis, *European Economic Review*, **41**, 37–59.

Ando, A. and Modigliani, F. (1957) The life cycle hypothesis of saving: aggregate implications and tests, *American Economic Review*, **53**, 55–84.

Attanasio, O.P. and Weber, G. (1994) The UK consumption boom of the late 1980s: aggregate implications of microeconomic evidence, *Economic Journal*, **104**, 1269–1302.

Barro, R.J. (1974) Are government bonds net wealth?, *Journal of Political Economy*, **82**, 1095–1117.

Barro, R. (1978) *The Impact of Social Security on Private Saving*, American Enterprise Institute, Washington, DC.

Bayoumi, T. (1993) Financial deregulation and household saving, *Economic Journal*, **103**, 1432–1443.

Bayoumi, T. (1995) Explaining Consumption: A Simple Test of Alternative Hypotheses, Discussion Paper 1289, Centre for Economic Policy Research, London, December.

Blake, D. (2000) *Financial Market Analysis*, John Wiley & Sons, Chichester.

Blake, D. (2003) *Pension Schemes and Pension Funds in the United Kingdom*, Oxford University Press, Oxford.

Blake, D. (2004) The impact of wealth on consumption and retirement behaviour in the UK, *Applied Financial Economics*, **14**, 555–576.

Blake, D. and Orszag, M. (1999) Annual estimates of personal wealth holdings in the UK since 1948, *Applied Financial Economics*, **9**, 397–421.

Blinder, A. (1981) *Private Pensions and Public Pensions: Theory & Fact*, W. S. Woytinsky Lecture No. 5, Institute of Public Policy Studies, University of Michigan.

Blinder, A., Gordon, R. and Wise, D. (1980) Reconsidering the disincentive effects of social security, *National Tax Journal*, **33**, 431–442.

Blinder, A., Gordon, R. and Wise, D. (1983) Social security bequests and the life cycle theory of saving: cross-sectional tests, in Modigliani, F. and Hemming, R. (eds), *The Determinants of National Savings and Wealth*, St. Martin's Press, New York, pp. 89–122.

Blundell, R., Pashardes, P. and Weber, G. (1993) What do we learn about consumer demand patterns from microdata?, *American Economic Review*, **83**, 570–597.

Bodie, Z., Merton, R. and Samuelson, W. (1992) Labor supply flexibility and portfolio choice in a life cycle model, *Journal of Economic Dynamics & Control*, **16**, 427–449.

Boskin, M.J. (1977) Social security and retirement decisions, *Economic Inquiry*, **15**, 1–25.

Boskin, M.J. and Hurd, M.D. (1978) The effect of social security on early retirement, *Journal of Public Economics*, **10**, 361–377.

Browning, M.J. (1982) Savings and pensions: some UK evidence, *Economic Journal*, **92**, 954–963.

Burkhauser, R. and Turner, J. (1982) Social security, preretirement labour supply and saving: a confirmation and critique, *Journal of Political Economy*, **90**, 643–664.

Cagan, P. (1965) *The Effect of Pension Plans on Aggregate Savings*, National Bureau of Economic Research, New York.

Campbell, J.Y. and Mankiw, N.G. (1991) The response of consumption to income: a cross-country investigation, *European Economic Review*, **35**, 723–767.

Crawford, P.C. and Lilien, D.M. (1981) Social security and the retirement decision, *Quarterly Journal of Economics*, **46**, 505–529.

Cushing, M.J. (1992) Liquidity constraints and aggregate consumption behaviour, *Economic Inquiry*, **30**, 134–153.

Danziger, S., Van Der Gaag, J., Smolensky, E. and Taussig, M. (1982–83) The life cycle hypothesis and the consumption behaviour of the elderly, *Journal of Post-Keynesian Economics*, **5**, 208–227.

Darby, M. (1979) *The Effects of Social Security on Income and the Capital Stock*, American Enterprise Institute, Washington, DC.

David, M. and Menchik, P. (1985) The effect of social security on lifetime wealth accumulation and bequests, *Economica*, **52**, 421–434.

Davidoff, T., Brown, J.R. and Diamond, P.A. (2005) Annuities and individual welfare, *American Economic Review*, **95**, 1573–1590.

Disney, R., Meghir, C. and Whitehouse, E. (1994) Retirement behaviour in Britain, *Fiscal Studies*, **15**, 24–43.

Edwards, S. (1996) The Chilean Pension Reform: A Pioneering Programme, NBER Working Paper No. 5811.

Feldstein, M. (1974) Social security, induced retirement and aggregate capital accumulation, *Journal of Political Economy*, **82**, 905–926.

Feldstein, M. (1976) Social security and savings: the extended life cycle theory, *American Economic Review, Papers and Proceedings*, **66**, 77–86.

Feldstein, M. (1978) Do private pensions increase national savings? *Journal of Public Economics*, **10**, 277–293.

Feldstein, M. (1979) Social security and private saving: another look, *Social Security Bulletin*, **42**, 36–39.

Feldstein, M. (1980) International differences in social security and savings, *Journal of Public Economics*, **14**, 225–244.

Feldstein, M. (1982) Social security and private saving: reply, *Journal of Political Economy*, **90**, 630–642.

Feldstein, M. (1997) The case for privatisation, *Foreign Affairs*, **76**, 24–38.

Feldstein, M. and Bacchetta, P. (1991) National savings and international investment, in Bernheim, B. and Shoven, J. (eds), *National Saving and Economic Performance*, University of Chicago Press, Chicago.

Flavin, M. (1985) Excess sensitivity of consumption to current income: liquidity constraints or myopia?, *Canadian Journal of Economics*, **18**, 117–136.

Friedman, B. and Warshawsky, M. (1990) The cost of annuities: implications for saving behaviour and bequests, *Quarterly Journal of Economics*, **105**, 135–154.

Gale, W. and Scholz, J. (1994) IRAs and household saving, *American Economic Review*, **84**, 1233–1260.

Goodman, A. Johnson, P. and Webb, S. (1997) *Inequality in the UK*, Oxford University Press, Oxford.

Green, F. (1981) The effect of occupational pension schemes on saving in the United Kingdom: a test of the life cycle hypothesis, *Economic Journal*, **91**, 136–144.

Hall, R.E. (1978) Stochastic implications of the life cycle – permanent income hypothesis: theory and evidence, *Journal of Political Economy*, **86**, 971–987.

Hamermesh, D. (1985) Expectations, life expectancy and economic behaviour, *Quarterly Journal of Economics*, **100**, 389–408.

Hemming, R. (1978) State pensions and personal savings, *Scottish Journal of Political Economy*, **25**, 135–147.

Hemming, R. and Harvey, R. (1983) Occupational pension scheme membership and retirement saving, *Economic Journal*, **93**, 128–144.

Hendry, D.F. (1994) HUS revisited, *Oxford Review of Economic Policy*, **10**, 86–106.

Hendry, D.F. and von Ungern-Sternberg, T. (1981) Liquidity and inflation effects on consumers' expenditure, in Deaton, A.S. (ed.), *Essays in the Theory and Measurement of Consumer Behaviour*, Cambridge University Press, Cambridge.

Holzman, R. (1997) Pension reform, financial market development and economic growth: preliminary evidence from Chile, *IMF Staff Papers*, **44**, 149–178.

Horioka, C., Kasuga, N., Yamazaki, K. and Watanabe, W. (1996) Do the Aged Dissave in Japan?: Evidence from Micro Data, University of Kobe Institute of Social and Economic Research, Discussion Paper No. 402.

Hurd, M. (1987) Savings of the elderly and desired bequests, *American Economic Review*, **77**, 298–312.

Jappelli, T. and Modigliani, F. (2005) The age–saving profile and the life-cycle hypothesis, *The Collected Papers of Franco Modigliani, Volume 6*, MIT Press, Cambridge, MA, pp. 141–172.

Katona, G. (1964) *Private Pensions and Individual Savings*, Survey Research Center, Institute for Social Research, University of Michigan.

Kotlikoff, C.J. (1979) Testing a theory of social security and life cycle accumulation, *American Economic Review*, **69**, 396–410.

Kotlikoff, L. and Summers, L. (1981) The role of intergenerational transfers in aggregate capital accumulation, *Journal of Political Economy*, **89**, 706–732.

Kurz, M. (1984) Capital accumulation and the characteristics of private intergenerational transfers, *Economica*, **51**, 1–22.

Laitner, J. and Juster, F.T. (1996) New evidence on altruism: a study of TIAA-CREF retirees, *American Economic Review*, **86**, 893–908.

Leimer, D. and Lesnoy, S. (1982) Social security and private saving: new time series evidence, *Journal of Political Economy*, **90**, 606–642.

Leimer, D. and Richardson, D. (1992) Social security, uncertainty adjustments and the consumption decision, *Economica*, **59**, 311–336.

Meghir, C. and Whitehouse, E. (1997) Labour market transitions and the retirement of men in the UK, *Journal of Econometrics*, **79**, 327–354.

Merton, R.C. (1969) Lifetime portfolio selection under uncertainty: the continuous-time case, *Review of Economics and Statistics*, **51**, 247–257.

Merton, R.C. (1971) Optimum consumption and portfolio rules in a continuous-time model, *Journal of Economic Theory*, **3**, 373–413.

Mirer, T. (1979) The wealth–age relation among the aged, *American Economic Review*, **69**, 435–443.

Modigliani, F. (1970) The life-cycle hypothesis of saving and intercountry differences in the savings ratio, in Eltis, W.A., Scott, F.G. and Wolfe, J.N. (eds), *Induction, Growth and Trade: Essays in Honour of Sir Roy Harrod*, Clarendon Press, Oxford, pp. 197–226.

Modigliani, F. (1986) Life-cycle, individual thrift, and the wealth of nations, *American Economic Review*, **76**, 297–313.

Modigliani, F. and Ando, A. (1963) The life cycle hypothesis of saving: aggregated implications and tests, *American Economic Review*, **53**, 55–84.

Pitelis, C.N. (1985) The effects of life assurance and pension funds on other savings: the post-war UK experience, *Bulletin of Economic Research*, **37**, 213–229.

Poterba, J. (1994), Introduction, in *International Comparison of Personal Saving*, Poterba, J. (ed.), University of Chicago Press, Chicago.

Poterba, J., Venti, S. and Wise, D. (1996) Personal Retirement Savings Programs and Asset Accumulation: Reconciling the Evidence, NBER Working Paper No. 5599.

Sheshinski, E. (1978) A model of social security and retirement decisions, *Journal of Public Economics*, **10**, 337–360.

Stoker, T. (1986) Simple tests of distributional effects on macroeconomic equations, *Journal of Political Economy*, **94**, 763–795.

Takayama, N. (1990) How much do public pensions discourage personal savings and induce early retirement in Japan, *Hitotsubashi Journal of Economics*, **31**, 87–104.

Taylor, L. (1971) Saving out of different types of income, *Brookings Papers on Economic Activity*, **2**, 383–407.

Threadgold, A.R. (1978) Personal Savings: The Impact of Life Assurance and Pension Funds, Bank of England Discussion Paper No. 1, October.

Yaari, M. (1965), Uncertain lifetime, life insurance and the theory of the consumer, *Review of Economic Studies*, **32**, 137–150.

Zeldes, S.P. (1989) Consumption and liquidity constraints: an empirical investigation, *Journal of Political Economy*, **97**, 305–346.

3
Corporate Pension Decision Making

Corporate pension decision making is the second component of pension microeconomics. We consider reasons why companies offer pensions to their workers as part of a compensation package in an employment contract. We also investigate why companies also sometimes have mandatory retirement clauses in these contracts. We examine the nature of pension liabilities from the point of view of the firm and show that the answer depends on whether the firm views its workers as being hired in a spot labour market or whether the firm considers that it has an implicit long-term contract with its workers. We look at tax and pension policy and end by examining the key agency relationships in company pension schemes and funds.

3.1   THE PROVISION OF PENSIONS BY CORPORATIONS

Corporate pension schemes started in developed countries in the late nineteenth century, but did not achieve wide coverage until the second half of the twentieth century.

A number of reasons have been suggested to explain this growth (Logue, 1979):

- The increasing awareness about poverty in old age in the late nineteenth century led to the introduction of state (i.e., social security) pension systems in the early part of the twentieth century and prompted a demand for private pension schemes that was met by the more altruistic employers.
- Companies also grew very rapidly during this period, becoming more complex and geographically dispersed. The establishment of pension schemes helped the management of such companies to monitor and control their workforce.
- Tax laws made the establishment of funded private pension schemes advantageous to companies and employees. In a number of countries such as the UK and USA, an *EET (Exempt–Exempt–Taxed) tax*

system was established. Pension contributions by both the employer and employee are tax deductible, investment returns on the contributions are free from income and capital gains tax, and only the pension itself is taxed once in payment (although there is frequently a tax-free cash lump sum available if the scheme member chooses to commute part of the pension in exchange).

- Pensions became a recognised part of the collective bargaining deals between employers and trades unions.
- Increasing life expectancy of the workforce required companies to plan for the retirement of their workforce in a more systematic way than hitherto, since they could no longer depend on natural mechanisms to eliminate unproductive workers.
- Investment opportunities, investment costs and the quality of investment management were believed to be more favourable for pension funds than for individuals investing on their own.
- Periodic incomes policies (for example, those implemented during war time or during high inflation periods such as the 1970s), which restrict direct wage increases, were circumvented by giving indirect wage increases in the form of additional pension benefits.

We will now examine the first three explanations in more detail.

3.2   THE ROLE OF PENSIONS IN EMPLOYMENT CONTRACTS

The three main reasons that have been put forward as to why companies offer pension schemes to their workers are (Logue, 1979):

- Pensions as altruism – a reward for long service.
- Pensions as deferred pay.
- Pensions as contingent claims.

3.2.1   Pensions as Altruism

The *altruistic view* of pensions dates back to the Victorian notion of civic responsibility. As Lee Welling Squires (1912) wrote: 'From the standpoint of the whole system of social economy, no employer has a right to engage in any occupation that exhausts the individual's industrial life in 10, 20 or 40 years; and then leave the remnant floating on society at large as a derelict at sea'. However, this view was also tinged with a brutal economic realism. A. Kaye Butterworth, general manager of the North Eastern Railway Company, argued that 'the pension . . . is an act of business common sense . . . not philanthropy . . . Unless you have something like an efficient pension fund, the directors would be under a constant compulsion to keep on the men' (evidence to the Departmental Committee on Railway Superannuation Funds, Cd. 5484, 1911). Underlying these arguments was a notion of 'human depreciation' and the early private pension schemes were based on the formula of a fixed monetary amount (not related to earnings) multiplied by years of service (thereby rewarding loyalty).

To begin with, however, there was no contractual right to a pension, as the following company disclaimer cited in Logue (1979) makes clear . . . 'This pension plan is a voluntary act on the part of the company and is not deemed to be or construed to be a part of any contract of employment . . . The company reserves the right to alter, amend, or annul or cancel the plan or any part of it at any time. The right of the company to discharge any employee at any time shall not be affected by this plan, nor shall such employee have any interest in any pension after discharge'.

The implication of this is that, as Logue (1979, p. 18) says: 'both management and labor viewed pensions as gratuities provided by enlightened employers, who believed that employees, like machines, not only depreciate but also are improvident and must be cared for financially in their old age. The only difference between the attitudes of labor and management was that organised labor viewed pensions as rights to be bargained and contracted for and management expressed a preference for allotting them on a discretionary basis'.

3.2.2 Pensions as Deferred Pay

During the second half of the twentieth century, the altruistic view was replaced by the *deferred pay* view. The pension became an entitlement rather than a gratuity.

Blinder (1981) and Wise (1985) argue that pension schemes can be used as a device for creating incentives in employment contracts. This is because pensions are deferred pay and so pension schemes can be designed to help achieve an efficient long-term relationship between the employer and the employee. The employer will want to influence recruitment, retention, work effort, training and the timing of retirement:

- The employer will want to recruit and retain high quality staff. It is costly to recruit and hire workers, so the employer will want to have low subsequent quit rates. It is also difficult to assess the true ability of workers before they join the firm. Since the employer knows much more about the ability of his own workers, he can save costs by retaining good workers.

- The employer will want to encourage his workers to work hard, to act honestly and not to shirk.
- Firms also invest in the human capital of workers, teaching them skills that might be specific to the firm, but might also be transferable. Employees need to be persuaded to stay with the firm long enough to cover its investment costs.
- Finally, at the end of the effective working life, workers who are no longer sufficiently productive need to be encouraged to retire.

The pension scheme can be designed in a way that helps to achieve all these things. For example, the scheme can have *vesting rules* that stipulate the number of years an employee must work for an employer before becoming entitled to pension benefits. This is clearly designed to reduce labour turnover, since workers who leave the scheme before the vesting date lose all their accrued benefits. Lazear (1985) shows that the design of pension benefits can improve labour productivity and even encourage investment in human capital, both of which help to increase employee earnings and hence the ultimate pension. Lazear (1983) argues that benefit enhancement can be used both to advance and retard retirement.

Pensions Neutrality in a World of Perfect Capital Markets

Blinder (1981) showed that in a world with perfect capital markets,[1] no uncertainty, no taxes, worker compensation equal to worker *marginal product*[2] and no compulsory retirement, then pensions and wages are perfect substitutes for each other. Blinder called this result the *neutrality of pensions*. Utility maximisation requires the *marginal rate of substitution between leisure and work*[3] to equal the wage rate.

---

[1] In perfect capital markets, individuals can borrow and lend unlimited amounts of money at the same constant riskless interest rate.

[2] The marginal product is the value of the output produced by a worker in the last hour worked during the working day. This must be worth at least the hourly wage that the employer pays the worker, otherwise the employer will be making a loss by employing him for that hour.

[3] The marginal rate of substitution between leisure and work is the value expressed in units of utility of giving up one hour of leisure in order to work for one additional hour. This must be worth at least the hourly wage paid to the worker, otherwise the worker will not voluntarily work the extra hour. If, on the other hand, it is worth less than the hourly wage, the worker will be willing to work longer hours, and will stop working when the marginal rate of substitution between leisure and work just equals the wage rate.

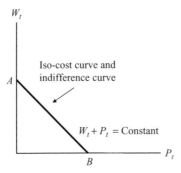

Figure 3.1 Pensions neutrality with perfect capital markets

A compensation package of high wages and low pension contributions is equivalent to one of low wages and high pension contributions so long as the value of the two compensation packages equals the worker's marginal product: this is called the *compensating wage principle*. If a worker's wages are cut by $1 and that $1 is paid into the worker's pension scheme, the worker can if he wishes reduce his private savings by $1 or even borrow $1 in order to give himself the same potential current purchasing power as before. The decisions about how much to work and how much to save are unaffected by the existence or not of a pension scheme as a component of the employment contract, so long as the total compensation stays the same. Under the compensating wage principle, *economic pension liabilities* will equal the present value of the wages that workers sacrifice in exchange for a pension at retirement (equivalently the present value of their pension savings). Figure 3.1 shows wages at time t (W_t) on the vertical axis and the value of the pension promise at time t (P_t) along the horizontal axis. Along AB, the compensation package $W_t + P_t$ is constant, so AB represents the *iso-cost curve*[4] of the employer. But in a perfect capital market, AB is also the individual's indifference curve, and any point along AB gives the individual the same total utility. The individual will therefore be indifferent to which combination of $W_t + P_t$ he is offered by his employer.

There are a number of reasons in the real world why this indifference will not hold. They include imperfect capital markets, risk, tax breaks, firm-specific human capital, and selection or sorting effects. These

---

[4] The employer's costs are constant along this curve.

factors can remove or reinforce the desirability of pensions as part of the compensation package.

Imperfect Capital Markets

The two most common types of market imperfection are when the borrowing rate exceeds the lending rate, and when banks will not lend to people with assets below a certain level.

When capital markets are imperfect, pension savings and private savings are no longer perfect substitutes and the pensions neutrality result no longer holds. Suppose a worker is suddenly forced to join a defined contribution pension scheme and has P_t deposited in his risk-free pension fund which cannot be withdrawn before retirement at time R, but which generates a return of r_L (the lending rate). Suppose the worker borrows P'_t from a bank to be repaid at retirement from the pension fund, but has to pay r_B (the borrowing rate $> r_L$) on the amount borrowed. The total repayments at retirement $(P'_t(1 + r_B)^{R-t})$ cannot exceed the value of the pension fund at retirement $(P_t(1 + r_L)^{R-t})$, so the worker cannot borrow enough to finance the same level of pre-retirement consumption as before the pension scheme was introduced. In the worst case, the worker might not be able to borrow against the future pension at all.

It is important to realise that although capital market imperfections can destroy the neutrality of pensions, they need not.

First, the capital market constraint might be a non-binding one. If mandatory pension savings is less than voluntary savings, the imposition of a pension scheme will not change total savings and the fact that capital markets are imperfect will be irrelevant. The curve ACD in Figure 3.2

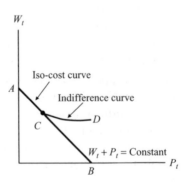

Figure 3.2 Pensions non-neutrality with imperfect capital markets
Source: Blinder (1981). Reproduced by permission of Alan Blinder

shows the indifference curve for a worker facing a borrowing constraint. To the left of C, the constraint is non-binding. To the right of C, the increasingly large pension component to his compensation package increasingly restricts his consumption flexibility and he needs to be compensated with a higher wage component: in other words, the trade-off between wages and pension is no longer linear. A small pension component is neutral, while a large pension component is not neutral.

Second, the compensation package is a matter of voluntary negotiation between employer and employee. It pays the employer not to offer a pension plan to the right of C.

Third, there are other capital market imperfections, such as transactions costs and uninsurable specific risks, whose impact is actually lowered in a pension scheme. The pension scheme can bring economies in transactions costs and diversification benefits which lower the cost to the individual, e.g., in the provision of annuities.

So for many workers, capital market imperfections might not be very significant.

Risk

Pension scheme members face three key risks before retirement: the risk of death before retirement, the risk of being fired before retirement, and the risk of scheme insolvency (usually linked to the insolvency of the sponsoring employer). As a consequence of these risks, the expected value to the worker of $1 of contributions is, say, $\phi < 1$. If the employer has the same expectations as the worker, ϕ is also the expected value of $1 of contributions. In this case, the pension neutrality result holds if both the worker and the employer are *risk neutral*.[5] In Figure 3.3, AE is both the iso-cost of the employer and the indifference curve of the worker in the case of uncertainty (as opposed to AB, the iso-cost and indifference curves when there is no uncertainty): pensions are less valuable to workers than wages, but also less costly to employers.

However, if the worker is *risk averse*[6] rather than risk neutral (while the employer remains risk neutral), the worker will value the $1 pension contribution as $\phi_W = \omega\phi < \phi$, where $\omega < 1$ is the risk discount factor

---

[5] Risk-neutral individuals make decisions taking into account what they expect to happen in the future, but disregarding any risks involved.

[6] Risk-averse individuals do not like risk and are prepared to pay a risk premium to someone who is willing to take the risk away from them.

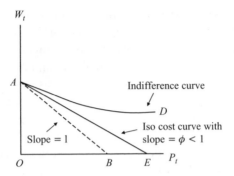

Figure 3.3 Pensions non-neutrality with uncertainty
Source: Blinder (1981). Reproduced by permission of Alan Blinder

for the worker which is an increasing function of P_t. The worker's indifference curve is AD and the optimal pension is zero.

Imperfect capital markets and risk are reasons why individuals and firms are either neutral or opposed to pensions. We now consider some positive reasons for pensions.

Tax Breaks

One of the key advantages of a pension scheme is the ability to defer taxes, until a time when the tax rate is lower (even if the income tax rate has not changed, retired people pay no social security or payroll tax). Savings in a private account are made from taxed income and the interest on the savings is taxed. $1 in a private savings account is worth $(1 - \tau)(1 + r(1 - \tau))^{R-t}$ at retirement if τ is the income tax rate. By contrast, savings in a pension scheme are generally made from pretaxed income, the interest is not taxed and the pension is taxed at retirement at a lower rate $\tau' < \tau$.[7] $1 in a pension scheme is therefore worth $(1 - \tau')(1 + r)^{R-t}$. Table 3.1 shows the tax advantages of pension schemes in the case where $\tau' = \tau - 0.1$.

The worker's marginal valuation of $1 of pension rises to $\phi_W = \kappa \omega \phi$, where κ is the tax factor reported in Table 3.1. Since κ is much greater than 1, it is possible for $\phi_W > 1$ for workers who are young or in high tax brackets. The demand by workers for pensions will be high when $\kappa \omega > 1$, i.e., when workers are highly taxed but not very risk averse.

---

[7] See Section 3.5.

Table 3.1   Accumulated value at retirement of $1 saved in a pension fund relative to that of $1 saved outside a pension fund*

Years to retirement	Tax rate $r = 4\%$		Tax rate $r = 8\%$	
	$\tau = 0.20$	$\tau = 0.40$	$\tau = 0.20$	$\tau = 0.40$
10	1.22	1.36	1.31	1.58
20	1.32	1.59	1.52	2.12
30	1.42	1.86	1.76	2.87
40	1.53	2.17	2.05	3.89

*Computed as $\kappa = \left[\frac{1-\tau+0.1}{1-\tau}\right]\left[\frac{1+r}{1+r(1-\tau)}\right]^{(R-t)}$.

Source: Blinder (1981). Reproduced by permission of Alan Blinder

Figure 3.4 shows how the optimal pension is determined when there are tax breaks. The worker's indifference curve, which was *AD* before the tax break, becomes *AF* after the tax break. The optimal division of the compensation package between W_t and P_t will be determined by the tangency condition between an indifference curve such as *AF* and an iso-cost curve such as *AE*. This is shown in Figure 3.5. The line through these tangency points is called the *contract curve*. It shows the optimal mix of W_t and P_t at different levels of total compensation $W_t + P_t$.

Firm-Specific Human Capital

Figure 3.6 shows how the pension scheme can be used to ensure the firm recovers any training costs it has incurred. The figure shows both the marginal product MP_t of a worker over his career and his compensation

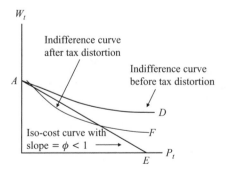

Figure 3.4   The effect on indifference curves of the tax break
Source: Blinder (1981). Reproduced by permission of Alan Blinder

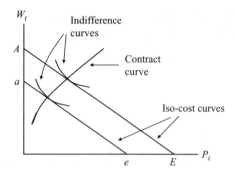

Figure 3.5 The contract curve for the compensation package with tax breaks
Source: Blinder (1981). Reproduced by permission of Alan Blinder

package $W_t + P_t$ also over his career. To induce a worker to join the firm, the employer has to pay the worker more than his marginal product when he is young (i.e., before age t_0). The employer also has to pay for the worker's training costs during this period. To recover these training costs, the worker has to receive compensation below his marginal product between ages t_0 and t_2. But the employer needs to ensure that the worker stays with the firm this long. Once trained, the employee has an incentive to leave the company for a higher paid job elsewhere, since he knows that after t_0, he will get paid less than his marginal product. Tying the employee in via a long-term employment contract will not work as such contracts are in practice unenforceable as well as generally illegal.

The firm needs to offer a financial incentive to persuade the worker to remain with the company. One way of doing this is to pay part of the worker's total compensation package, P_t, into a pension fund. This

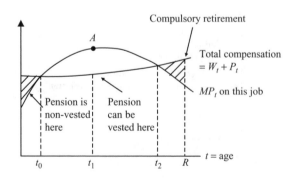

Figure 3.6 The role of the pension scheme in managing the worker's career
Source: Blinder (1981). Reproduced by permission of Alan Blinder

remains non-vested until age t_1 when the firm has recovered its costs, where t_1 is determined to ensure the following equality holds:

$$\sum_{t=0}^{t_1} \frac{W_t + P_t - MP_t}{(1+r)^t} = 0 \qquad (3.1)$$

At this age, the pension could be vested and the employer could move to a compensation package equal to marginal product, i.e., jump to A in Figure 3.6.

However, there are good reasons for both the employer and worker not to accept this. From the employer's point of view, the worker will be a valued, senior employee, at least for a while. The worker also has a strong incentive to stay with the firm. This is because, after a certain age t_2 in Figure 3.6, the worker's marginal product will fall below the value of the compensation package. He will have become too old for additional training to be effective, but convention has it that he is not expected to take a pay cut to reflect this.[8] The firm now does have an incentive to get rid of the worker, but is concerned that widespread use of this practice would give it a bad reputation.

The employer and employee have an incentive to agree the following implicit contract. The employer agrees to underpay the worker between t_1 and t_2, and, in return, agrees to overpay the worker between t_2 and retirement age R, such that the following equality holds:

$$\sum_{t=t_1+1}^{R} \frac{W_t + P_t - MP_t}{(1+r)^t} = 0 \qquad (3.2)$$

If equations (3.1) and (3.2) both hold, the worker will have been paid (in wages and pensions) the total value of his marginal product over his career.

Workers who work beyond R lose money for the company, so they must be forced or induced to retire at R. This can be achieved by a compulsory retirement clause in the employment contract or by offering actuarially enhanced benefits at R, or by not offering increases in pension benefits (or offering actuarially unfair increases) after R.

The purpose of this long-term labour contract is to raise *labour productivity* (output per worker) over the worker's career. This will be reflected in reduced costs. However, there is also likely to be *diminishing*

---

[8] However, there is an increasing tendency for workers to move to less stressful and lower-paid jobs in the years leading up to retirement.

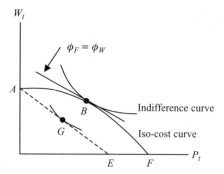

Figure 3.7 Optimal compensation package when there is diminishing returns
Source: Blinder (1981). Reproduced by permission of Alan Blinder

returns to labour: adding an extra worker to the production process when the capital stock is fixed will increase total output, but by less than was added by the previous worker. The firm's iso-cost curves will be concave like AF in Figure 3.7 (with slope ϕ_F), rather than linear as before (cf AE) and also further out from the origin. The optimal combination of wage (W_t) and pension (P_t) in the employee's compensation package will be at B, the tangency point between the firm's iso-cost curve and the employee's indifference curve (with slope ϕ_W), i.e., where $\phi_F = \phi_W$. The productivity gain leads to both a larger wage and a larger pension (cf B and G).

The long-term labour contract lies in stark contrast to the spot labour market contract in which workers are paid their marginal product during each period of their career whatever that happens to be, and there is no mandatory retirement.

Selection or Sorting Effects

The pension scheme can also be designed with specific features whose aim is to attract workers with characteristics desired by the employer for the job being offered. This is known as a *selection* or *sorting effect*. An employer who offers a package of low wages and high pensions will attract a different type of worker from an employer who offers a package of high wages and low pensions, even if the present value of each package is identical. Each employer might prefer the different worker types attracted by the compensation package he offers. Suppose there is a continuum of firms offering the same total compensation package $W_t + P_t$ but with different combinations of wage (W_t) and pension (P_t).

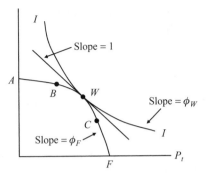

Figure 3.8   The optimal combination of wage and pension
Source: Blinder (1981). Reproduced by permission of Alan Blinder

A worker will choose the firm whose compensation package exactly matches his own preferences. This will be at the combination where a marginal utility of an extra dollar of pension equals the marginal utility of an extra dollar of wages, i.e., $\phi_W = 1$. The worker will then choose the firm whose compensation package equals $\phi_F = \phi_W = 1$ as at W in Figure 3.8. This procedure is known as *optimal sorting*.

In reality, such a continuum of choices might not be available and the worker might be forced to choose a suboptimal combination, such as B or C. At B, the worker would like a bigger pension ($\phi_W > 1$), but this is still preferable to A (no pension). At C, the worker would like a smaller pension ($\phi_W < 1$), but this too might be better than no pension. With a limited range of compensation packages, each firm will attract a select group of workers such that the marginal rate of substitution between pensions and wages, ϕ_W, for the median worker will equal the firm's marginal rate of transformation between pensions and wages,[9] ϕ_F.

Ippolito (1997), for example, found that employers who offer DC pension schemes in which they match the contribution made by the employee attracted workers who tended to save more. Such workers have low rates of time preference (i.e., discount the future less heavily and have more patience) and Ippolito argues that such individuals have characteristics valued by certain employers.

So, although pensions can be interpreted as deferred pay, it is likely that in the real world, pensions will not be neutral in the compensation package. They are imperfect substitutes for wages and can change the

---

[9] The marginal rate of transformation between pensions and wages shows the rate at which pensions can be traded against wages, keeping total employer costs constant.

lifetime profile of labour supply. For a recent summary of this literature, see McCarthy and Neuberger (2003).

3.2.3   Pensions as Contingent Claims

With this explanation, the pension scheme is designed to provide both incentives in the form of rewards and insurance to cover risks (Merton, 1985). To be effective, it requires that pension entitlements are not vested immediately. It also needs to recognise how the rewards and risks of the pension scheme are shared between the employer and employees.

In terms of rewards, how the successes of a company are shared between the employer and the employees in respect of the pension scheme depends on the particular scheme in operation. For example, in a DC scheme, the reward could be in the form of increased employer contributions. If, on the other hand, the scheme is DB, the reward could be in the form of a benefit formula improvement, such as a higher accrual rate. Similarly, if the investment performance of the pension fund assets is strong and a surplus in the pension fund emerges, then the employer can reduce his future contributions into the scheme. The employer, in effect, has a *call option*[10] on the assets of a DB scheme, and, in the event of a surplus emerging, can exercise the option and extract the surplus (Sharpe, 1976; Blake, 1998).

In terms of risks, again how these are shared depends on the type of scheme. With a DC scheme most of the key risks (e.g., investment risk) are transferred to the employees.

By contrast, with a DB scheme, the company bears the risk that fluctuations in the value of the pension fund assets will lead to a deficit in the pension scheme. The scheme members have a *put option*[11] on the assets of a DB scheme, and in the event of a deficit emerging can exercise the option and force the company to make deficiency payments to eliminate the deficit (Sharpe, 1976; Blake, 1998).

The company has some control over how any deficit is managed or even honoured. One way is for the company to pay off the deficit gradually over time from its future cash flows, although this clearly will be unattractive to shareholders who face dividend cuts in the short term and, possibly, cut-backs on the company's investment programme in the long

---

[10] A call option gives the holder the right to buy some asset or commodity at a predetermined price if the option is exercised.

[11] A put option gives the holder the right to sell some asset or commodity at a predetermined price if the option is exercised.

term. Prior to the deficit being cleared, the pension fund is an unsecured creditor of the company, and effectively holds a risky debt claim.

Another way is through its policy on hiring and firing, e.g., firing workers just before their pension entitlements vest and replacing them with younger, unvested workers. This has the effect of reducing the liabilities.

In the most extreme case, the company will recognise that it actually holds a put option against the pension fund. It can exercise the option by becoming insolvent and walking away from the pension fund (and indeed from its obligations to other creditors). Different classes of scheme member will be affected differently by this, since the risks are not shared equally between members. Members already retired usually get their pensions in full, whereas younger, more recently recruited members usually end up with very little.

In each of the last two cases in which the employer passes the buck back to the scheme members, it is the younger members, rather than the older members (so long as their pension entitlements are vested) who face the greatest risk.

3.3   THE NATURE OF CORPORATE PENSION LIABILITIES

Are corporate pension liabilities implicit liabilities or explicit liabilities of the company?

Ippolito (1985a, 1997) and Lazear (1979, 1983, 1985) interpret occupational pensions as part of the optimal long-term *implicit contract*[12] between the firm and the worker that can have an important effect on the productivity of the firm. In particular, they can influence quitting and retirement behaviour and can help to discourage workers from shirking or engaging in malfeasance on the job. It is conventionally argued that only a DB scheme can be used in this way. A DB scheme is a form of deferred compensation, the value of which is linked to the economic success of the company. Workers are committed to supplying high levels of effort over the long run and do not gain from either quitting or collective shirking. However, Lazear (1985) shows that the same results can be achieved using a DC scheme and a long-term labour contract offering *efficiency wages*.[13]

---

[12] An implicit contract refers to a relationship between two parties that is conducted without a formal contract.

[13] Efficiency wages are the wages above the strictly competitive level needed to retain the worker in his current job and include an additional amount (known as a rent) which is designed to incentivise the worker to work hard. The worker knows that if he moves to a new job, he will only get the

There are two aspects to these implicit contracts. The first is the view that the value of the pension is higher if the pension scheme is valued on an *ongoing* rather than a *discontinuance* or *termination* basis. The second is the view that, despite being a *promise* rather than a *guarantee*, there is an implicit obligation on the part of the firm to pay the promised pension in full, despite the company's other liabilities.

The ongoing valuation is based on the *projected benefit* assumption, namely that the DB pension benefits are projected to the normal retirement age of the worker and then discounted at the riskless rate. So a worker who joins a scheme R years before retirement with a salary of W_0 (that grows at the exponential rate g) will have accrued benefits after M years of work of:

$$A_{PS} = aMW_0 e^{gR} e^{-r(R-M)} \tag{3.3}$$

where r is the risk-free interest rate (and is equal to the return on assets in the pension scheme if they are also risk-free), a is the annual pension accrual rate, and we are projecting wages until retirement.[14]

The increase in the value of the benefits after working an additional year is:

$$\frac{dA_{PS}}{dM} = \left(\frac{1}{M} + g + r\right) A_{PS} \tag{3.4}$$

The first two terms are known as the *service cost*: $1/M$ results from an additional year of service and g arises from an increase in the salary base. The third term is called the *financing cost* and arises because benefits are one year closer to being received (it is sometimes called the *unwinding of the liability discount*). It is not part of the service cost, since it would still arise even if the worker was no longer part of the scheme. It is offset by the return on the assets held in the pension scheme (and would be completely offset if the pension fund invested entirely in riskless assets).

This approach is consistent with the *projected benefits method* used by actuaries for valuing pension liabilities. This method projects benefits to be accrued over the worker's complete career and then apportions them annually over the career as a fixed percentage of salary. Underlying this approach, however, is an implicit contract that the worker will be retained by the firm for his whole career. In this case, the cumulative

---

competitive wage as the new employer will not know whether the worker is a hard worker or a shirker.

[14] Note that we use *continuous* compounding (e^{gM}) and discounting ($e^{-r(R-M)}$) rather than *discrete* compounding ($(1+g)^M$) and discounting ($(1+r)^{-(R-M)}$).

economic profits to the firm of the implicit long-term labour contract would always be valued at zero, i.e., the firm would not be making a profit on its young workers and a loss on its old workers.

By contrast, Bulow (1982) argues that pension liabilities should be treated in the same way as corporate bonds. The valuation of corporate bonds depends on three factors:

- The terms of the contract, such as the dates of the interest payments.
- The value of the assets backing the bond.
- The presence of bond covenants restricting the behaviour of the firm, e.g., to issue more senior debt.

What is clear is that all the terms of the corporate bond contract are *explicit*.[15]

Bulow argues that in reality workers do not have long-term guaranteed contracts. Rather the contracts are subject to frequent, and in extreme cases (i.e., when workers are employed in a daily *spot labour market*, as many workers on building sites are, for example) constant, renegotiation. In this case, the employer will not be able to pay young workers less than their marginal product in wages and pension benefits, and older workers will not receive compensation in excess of their marginal products. This approach is consistent with the *accrued benefits method* used by actuaries for valuing liabilities. This assumes no implicit contract. Instead, it assumes that each period, the firm and worker explicitly negotiate the total compensation package and not just salary, and that the valuation of the pension liabilities takes into account only the service that has been accrued to date and the salary that has been earned to date, and not future service or salary.

The benefits accrued after M years of work using the accrued benefits method will be:

$$A_{PQ} = aMW_0 e^{gM} e^{-r(R-M)} \tag{3.5}$$

Bulow argues that the accrued benefits method, which is based on earnings after M years of work, is a truer measure of the firm's economic pension liabilities than the projected benefits method, which would need 'an extraordinary set of implicit contracts' to be appropriate for valuing the firm's economic pension liabilities. For example, the worker who leaves the firm early ends up subsidising workers who stay on if the

---

[15] An explicit contract refers to a relationship between two parties where the meaning and intent of the relationship are stated clearly in writing. Usually, an explicit contract is also enforceable in law.

projected benefits method is used to value his pension liabilities, unless an implicit contract prevents this.

All this has nothing to do with how the firm determines its contributions into the scheme, only with how pension liabilities are measured and accounted for. If pension liabilities are measured and accounted for using the accrued benefits method, they become explicit and can be treated like bond contracts.

McGill *et al.* (2005) could find no evidence for the wage–pension trade-off in annual salary negotiations favoured by Bulow (1982). Instead, their evidence indicated that final salary pension benefits constitute a compensation premium designed to reward good workers for long and loyal service. The benefits determined by the plan are determined at entry for the entire period of future service and measured in units linked to the employee's salary at exit. The world-wide decline in final salary pension schemes since the mid-1990s might, however, indicate that companies are moving away from the McGill *et al.* interpretation to the one favoured by Bulow.

3.4   QUITTING AND MANDATORY RETIREMENT

3.4.1   Quitting

In the spot labour market model of Bulow, workers will invest no more in the firm than they can expect to take out if they leave. In this model, there is no penalty to *quitting* prior to retirement. In the long-term implicit contract model of Ippolito and Lazear, workers forego wages for a pension assuming that they stay with the firm until retirement. A key feature of the latter model is that workers receive less back in pension entitlement than they contribute if they quit before the normal retirement age.

This follows because pension benefits are backloaded in DB schemes. This can be shown using the accrued benefits method (3.5). The benefit accrual attributable to current service (as a fraction of current salary) is:

$$\left(\frac{dA_{PQ}}{dM} - rB \right) \Big/ W_0 e^{gM} = a\left(1 + gM\right) e^{-r(R-M)} \qquad (3.6)$$

This is the sum of the component due to the increase in the number of years worked (providing benefits of $aW_0 e^{gM}$) and the component due to a higher salary base for previously accrued benefits ($agMW_0 e^{gM}$), all discounted by the years remaining until retirement ($e^{-r(R-M)}$).

It is clear from equation (3.6) that over time the benefits rise as a percentage of salary. The worker gets small benefit accruals early in his career and large benefit accruals later in his career: in other words, pension benefits in DB schemes are *backloaded* (see Table 1.1). This can still be consistent with the worker's total compensation over his working life at the firm being equal to his marginal product over the period (in present value terms), although he gets less than his marginal product in his early years and more than his marginal product in his later years.

It is the backloading of benefits that gives rise to a difference between stay pension wealth and quit pension wealth (Ippolito, 1997, p. 15). *Stay pension wealth* (A_{PS}) is the value of the pension calculated under the projected benefits method (3.3) and *quit pension wealth* (A_{PQ}) is the value of the pension under the accrued benefits method (3.5). They are related as follows:

$$A_{PQ} = A_{PS}e^{-g(R-M)} \tag{3.7}$$

The difference between the two is the *pension capital loss from quitting*:

$$PCL_Q = A_{PS} - A_{PQ} \tag{3.8}$$

This can be enormous, especially in the early years of service (see Figure 3.9). It is important to note that the capital loss is not due to years of service (both the stay and quit pension are based on the same T years of service), but because the stay pension is based on the projected final salary, whereas the quit pension is based on current salary.

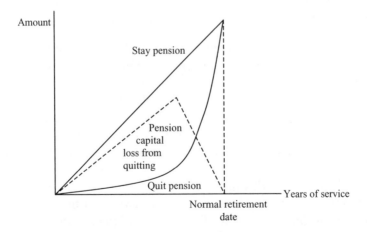

Figure 3.9 Pension capital loss from quitting
Source: Ippolito (1997). Reproduced with permission from Pension Plans and Employee Performance: Evidence, Analysis and Policy by R.A. Ippolito, Copyright 1997 Chicago University Press

3.4.2 Mandatory Retirement

At the other end of the age range, Lazear (1979) (see also Fabel, 1994, chapter 4) asked why there are *mandatory retirement* clauses in employment contracts, given that they can be interpreted as a form of age discrimination which is illegal or is becoming so in many countries.

A number of explanations have been put forward:

- It is a way of dealing with the reduced productivity of older workers. But why does the lower productivity of older workers not lead to a fall in their wages to match their lower productivity instead of their removal from the labour market?
- A cut in pay would be bad for the morale of older workers. But why would forcing people to retire at a certain age whatever their productivity be better for morale?
- It is hard to judge how much the productivity of older workers has fallen. But it is no easier to judge the productivity of workers of different ages.
- A uniform retirement policy avoids having to discriminate between employees. But employers continuously discriminate between employees, e.g., in respect of pay rises, promotion, etc.
- Mandatory retirement enables younger workers to be promoted. But why should a firm retire an efficient older worker who is being paid less than his marginal product in order to promote a younger worker so that he is paid precisely his marginal product?

Lazear does not accept that any of these explanations provides a valid reason for why mandatory retirement is preferred to a policy of systematically reducing wages in line with reduced marginal productivity.

Instead, Lazear offers the following explanation for why it is optimal for both the firm and workers to have a (long-term) employment contract that pays workers less than their marginal product when young and more than their marginal product when old, together with a mandatory retirement date which recognises that the employer will cease to be willing to pay the worker his current wage.

Workers are concerned about the present value of their lifetime income stream (human capital). Firms are concerned about the present value of the worker's lifetime marginal product stream. Other things equal, both the worker and the employer would be indifferent between an employment contract that paid the worker a constant wage over his career and one that paid less when young and more when old, so long as the present values of the two income streams were identical.

Lazear argues that other things are not equal and that the second contract allows both the worker and the employer to act in a way that raises the present value (PV) of the worker's marginal product over his lifetime. This is because deferring earnings might encourage the worker to put in more effort, whereas the first contract is more likely to lead to shirking by the worker or even to workers engaging in malfeasance on the job.

The optimality condition for retirement is that the value of the worker's marginal product is equal to his *reservation wage*[16] and this will determine the optimal retirement date. However, if workers are paid less than their marginal product when young and more than their marginal product when old, their wage rate at the optimal retirement date will exceed the value of the marginal product (VMP) and hence the reservation wage. Despite being the optimal retirement date (since at this date the PV of lifetime MP equals the PV of lifetime wages), the worker will not voluntarily retire at this date, since his actual wage exceeds his reservation wage.

There is therefore a *time inconsistency problem*.[17] The optimal employment contract raises the human capital of the worker which he prefers *ex ante*. He knows that the optimal contract requires him to retire at the optimal retirement date. But when the optimal retirement date arrives, the worker has an incentive to renege on the contract and continue working because his actual wage exceeds his reservation wage. Mandatory retirement is needed to ensure the worker leaves on the optimal date. Without it, the optimal employment contract which maximises the worker's human capital could not be implemented. So the worker is better off with a mandatory retirement clause. As Lazear points out, however, such a clause is only feasible in a long-term employment contract.

Figure 3.9 shows that stay pension wealth is maximised on the mandatory retirement date. As an alternative to having a mandatory retirement

---

[16] The minimum wage at which a worker is willing to work.

[17] Time inconsistency problems arise when a plan that is optimal at the start of a period ceases to be optimal over time (either as a result of new information or because there is an incentive to renegotiate the plan or renege on it). To reduce or eliminate this possibility, plans have to be made *incentive compatible*. As a simple example, workers are paid once a job has been completed rather than before, to deal with the time inconsistency problem of the reduced incentive to do a good job once the worker has been paid.

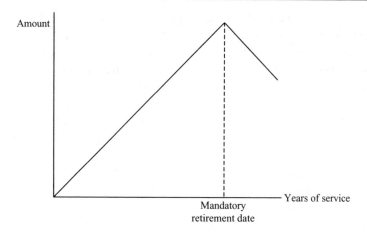

Figure 3.10 Pension wealth

clause with a mandatory retirement date, it is possible to induce retirement on the same date by imposing severe actuarial penalties for delaying retirement. People might be permitted to work beyond the desired date, but they are offered actuarially unfair increases for doing so. This, combined with the fact that life expectancy is finite (so that the pension when it is drawn is paid over a shorter period), will result in pension wealth falling after the mandatory retirement age (see Figure 3.10). In countries where age discrimination is illegal, this strategy can be used to deal with the time inconsistency problem.

3.5   TAX AND PENSION FUND POLICY

Munnell (1982) argues that the tax breaks offered to sponsors and members of funded pension schemes have been a significant cause of the growth of such schemes in the second half of the twentieth century. This is especially true in countries, such as the UK and USA, which operate an EET system of tax breaks. The sponsor in a funded scheme receives no tax relief when the pension is paid: this contrasts with an unfunded or pay-as-you-go scheme in which the company does get tax relief, since the pension payment, like wages, is a tax-deductible expense.

It is clear that an EET system provides the best incentives for encouraging the growth of funded pension schemes on a voluntary basis. It should come as no surprise that countries such as Germany, which operate a TTE system, do not have significant private pension assets, or

Table 3.2 The tax advantage of funding the pension scheme

	Current cash flows	Future cash flows
PAYG scheme		
Pay pensions when due	—	$-(1-\tau)P$
Funded scheme		
1. Borrow P/r	$+P/r$	$-(1-\tau)r \times P/r = -(1-\tau)P$
2. Transfer P/r to pension fund	$-(1-\tau)P/r$	—
3. Pension fund invests in bonds	—	$r \times P/r = +P$
4. Pay pensions when due	—	$-P$
Total cash flows	$+\tau P/r$	$-(1-\tau)P$
Cash-flow advantage of funded scheme over unfunded scheme	$+\tau P/r$	—

Source: Adapted from Brealey and Myers (1991, table 35.2). Principles of Corporate Finance by R. Brealey and S. Myers, Copyright © 1991, reproduced with permission of The McGraw-Hill Companies

that countries such as Australia, which operate a TTT system, only have significant private pension assets as a result of making membership of pension schemes mandatory.

Tepper and Affleck (1974), Black (1980) and Tepper (1981) show that the EET system of tax breaks gives companies a strong incentive to fully fund their pension schemes. Suppose the company is liable for an infinite stream of constant pension payments (P) and the interest rate is also fixed at r and the company faces a corporation tax rate of τ. If the company runs a PAYG scheme, its net annual cost is $(1-\tau)P$ as shown in Table 3.2.

Suppose instead the company decides to pre-fund its pension obligations by establishing a pension fund. Since the pension scheme is fully funded if the level of assets is P/r (i.e., the present value of all future pension payments),[18] the company could borrow this sum in the capital markets by issuing a bond. The after-tax cost to the company is $(1-\tau)P/r$, where τ is the corporation tax rate and the tax saving (which is the net economic value of establishing a pension fund) is $\tau P/r$. If the

---

[18] A pension scheme having financial assets valued at P/r and generating a return of r per year will always be able to pay out a pension equal to $r \times P/r = P$ per year.

pension fund invests in bonds,[19] paying an interest rate of r p.a., the pension fund receives an income of $r \times P/r = P$, just enough to pay the annual pension. The company also has to pay interest on the funds it has borrowed, which after tax is equal to:

$$(1 - \tau)r \times P/r = (1 - \tau)P \tag{3.9}$$

Both types of scheme involve future cash payments of $(1 - \tau)P$, but the funded scheme provides an immediate cash benefit of $\tau P/r$. So it is more advantageous for the company to borrow and transfer the proceeds to the pension fund to invest in bonds.

It is important to note that the benefit comes not from the decision to fund, but from the fact that the firm is able to borrow at the after-tax rate of interest, while the pension fund is able to earn the pre-tax rate of interest. To demonstrate this, suppose that the earnings of the pension fund were taxed at the corporation tax rate τ. In the case of the funded scheme, the company now contributes $P/r(1 - \tau)$ to the pension fund. The after-tax cost is:

$$(1 - \tau) \times \frac{P}{r(1 - \tau)} = \frac{P}{r} \tag{3.10}$$

which just offsets the amount borrowed. In this case, funding has no advantage over PAYG.

As an alternative to bonds, the company could finance the pension fund using external equity.[20] The after-tax cost to the investor remains $(1 - \tau)P/r$. However, the returns to the investor are the after-personal-tax (τ^*) stream of pension payments, discounted by the after-personal-tax rate on debt:

$$(1 - \tau)(1 - \tau^*)P \times \frac{1}{r(1 - \tau^*)} = \frac{(1 - \tau)P}{r} \tag{3.11}$$

so there is no net advantage to funding with external equity. The advantage of substituting pension scheme liabilities with corporate debt has been cancelled out by the substitution of personal leverage for the more tax-efficient corporate debt.

---

[19] Bonds are financial instruments that pay a fixed-interest payment (known as a coupon) per year together with a principal amount on the day that they mature. The bonds in this example are perpetual and so never mature or repay principal. They pay P per year indefinitely.

[20] Equity (also called shares) are financial instruments that pay an annual dividend indefinitely (i.e., equity does not mature). The amount of dividend is declared by the company and will be based on the profits made by the company in that year. Dividends are therefore variable, unlike the coupons on fixed-income bonds.

If the pension fund is financed from company profits which would otherwise be used to pay dividends, there is still a tax saving as the dividends would otherwise be taxed. The value to the shareholders is the tax saving $\tau^*(1 - \tau)P/r$, but in general this will be less than $\tau P/r$.

Black (1980) and Tepper (1981) argue that corporate defined benefit pension scheme liabilities are equivalent to corporate debt and that the pension fund's assets are corporate assets. Combine this with the EET system of tax breaks, and the optimal corporate pension policy should be one that maximises the tax shelter to the company's shareholders. This implies that a company should fully fund its pension plan and should invest the pension fund totally in bonds.

3.6   AGENCY COSTS IN PENSION SCHEMES AND PENSION FUNDS

All contractual relationships involve potential conflicts of interest. This is why *principal–agent problems* arise. An agency relationship arises when one party (the *principal*) contracts another party (the *agent*) to perform a specified service for the principal. The service typically involves the principal delegating a degree of decision-making authority to the agent (Jensen and Meckling, 1976, p. 308; Jensen, 1998). The principal's problem is to design a suitable incentive and monitoring system to ensure the contract is correctly executed, and this generally involves *monitoring costs*.

Problems arise in agency relationships because of moral hazard and because information is costly to acquire, is never complete and is *asymmetric* (some people have more information than others). The true behaviour of the agent cannot in general be observed by the principal. *Moral hazard* is the likelihood that the agent, once appointed, will not act in the best interests of the principal, but instead acts in a way that is suboptimal. For example, the agent might not put in his best efforts (i.e., shirks) or might act in a way that is careless or reckless. The agent will be aware that the principal is concerned about this possibility and might decide to incur *bonding costs* (both pecuniary and non-pecuniary) to demonstrate to the principal that he is not shirking or acting carelessly or recklessly (and so increase the benefits of 'sainthood'; Jensen and Meckling, 1976, p. 351). Even when monitoring and bonding costs are incurred, the agent might still not act in the very best interests of the principal and so there might still be a *residual loss* to the principal. Agency costs are the sum of the monitoring costs, bonding costs and the residual loss. And they 'are as real as any other costs' (Jensen and Meckling, 1976, p. 357).

There are a number of agency relationships surrounding a corporate pension scheme:

- A company is owned by its shareholders (principals), but the shareholders appoint managers (agents) to run the company in the best interests of the shareholders.
- If the company has a pension scheme, the managers will appoint a group of trustees (agents) to run the scheme in the best interests of the scheme members (principals).
- The trustees (principals) appoint fund managers (agents) to invest the scheme assets in the best interests of the members.
- In turn, the fund managers (principals) need to ensure that the managers (agents) of the companies in which they invest act in the best interests of the shareholders.

As is clear, there are complex *multiple-agency relationships* involved in a pension scheme. Both the company's shareholders and the scheme members have an agency relationship with the scheme's trustees and, through the trustees, a double-agency relationship with the fund manager and other providers of services to the pension scheme (such as investment consultants).

To deal with potential agency problems, the principal needs to establish either an *ex ante incentive compatible contract* (to encourage the agent to act in the best interests of the principal) or to have a credible threat of *ex post settling up* (i.e., to require the agent to compensate for any underperformance on the contract once it has been completed, using the threat of litigation if necessary). The principal will use whichever approach is cheapest (Fama, 1980). We will examine some pension-related examples.

3.6.1 Insider-Trustees

In the UK, pension scheme trustees have a responsibility to act independently. As the UK Pensions Regulator states in its guide *Pension Scheme Trustees* (2001, p. 17): 'As trustees, your duties are to the scheme and not to any group or individual that you are connected with, such as the employer, a trade union or a particular group of members, such as pensioner members. Sometimes you may find yourself faced with difficult decisions because of your other interests, such as whether to pay surplus funds to the employer'. This potential conflict of interest, in particular, affects *insider-trustees* (i.e., those appointed by the sponsor, such as executive directors of the sponsoring company). Their presence might allow the sponsoring company to exercise greater control over the pension fund than is in the interests of scheme members.

In the UK, the sponsor is entitled to appoint the majority of pension scheme trustees (there can be at most one-half member nominated trustees, but there are rarely sufficient volunteers to achieve this proportion) and can choose how many insiders to appoint. The trustees have the following very important powers:

- To appoint and remove professional advisers (actuaries, auditors, investment advisors, fund managers, custodians and lawyers).
- To decide the investment strategy of the pension fund.
- To establish and maintain a schedule of contributions, so that the schedule of contributions plus the scheme assets are sufficient to meet pension liabilities in full over a period not exceeding 10 years. If the pension scheme is less than 90% funded (and therefore classified as having a serious deficiency), the schedule of contributions must achieve the 90% funding level within 3 years.

The implications of tight control by a company over its pension scheme have been investigated by Cocco and Volpin (2005). They consider two hypotheses relating to insider-trustees: the agency hypothesis and the tax arbitrage hypothesis.

The *agency hypothesis* makes predictions about the agency costs of insider-trustees. Sharpe (1976) and Treynor (1977) were the first to recognise that highly leveraged companies (those with a high level of debt compared with shareholders' equity) had an incentive to undertake excessive risky investment projects. If these projects are successful, the shareholders get highly magnified returns (since the projects are partly financed with lower-cost debt). If the projects are unsuccessful, the shareholders can (given limited liability) walk away from the company and leave it to the banks and bondholders to sort out the mess.

The same is true in a pension scheme. If the scheme purchases riskier investments (such as shares rather than bonds) and these are successful, the company can fund the pension scheme at lower cost. Pension scheme deficits are equivalent to long-term debt (owed by the company to the pension scheme members), and members of an underfunded pension scheme are equivalent to debt holders of the sponsoring company (Besley and Pratt, 2003). In the case of pension scheme surpluses, insider-trustees have an incentive to terminate overfunded pension schemes and return the surplus to shareholders (Pontiff *et al.*, 1990; Petersen, 1992).

The agency hypothesis therefore makes three predictions:

- Agency prediction 1: Insider-trustees will have a higher pension fund weighting in shares, especially if the sponsoring company is highly leveraged.
- Agency prediction 2: Insider-trustees will make lower contributions into the pension scheme, especially if the sponsoring company is highly leveraged.
- Agency prediction 3: Insider-trustees will make lower contributions into the pension scheme, especially if the sponsoring company is highly leveraged, and this will be associated with higher dividend payments to shareholders (Webb, 2004).

There is an additional agency problem when companies are capital constrained and are unable to raise sufficient external funds to finance their investment programmes. In these circumstances, they will be forced to use internal funds instead. However, the need to make contributions to the pension scheme might lead financially constrained firms to reduce investment in the company (Rauh, 2006).

The *capital constraint hypothesis* (agency prediction 4) predicts that insider-trustees in financially constrained companies will reduce pension contributions in order to undertake investments that would not otherwise be made. If the investment is efficient, both the company and the pension scheme members gain. If the investment is inefficient, then there are agency costs involved.

The *tax arbitrage hypothesis* makes predictions about the role of insider-trustees in maximising the tax benefits to the company and its pension scheme. While the income and capital gains generated by the company are taxed, the income and capital gains generated by the pension scheme are tax exempt. Therefore the company has an incentive to integrate its company and pension scheme investment policies in order to engage in tax arbitrage. The company can minimise taxes by borrowing funds and increasing its leverage, and placing the borrowed funds in its pension scheme (Tepper and Affleck, 1974, and Section 3.5 above). This creates a debt tax shield without increasing the risk to the firm. The presence of insider-trustees facilitates the coordination of the company and pension scheme investment policies. Black (1980) shows that tax effects encourage the company to overfund the pension plan and invest in bonds, since overfunded pension plans are less likely to default on their pension promises.

The tax arbitrage hypothesis therefore has two predictions:

- Tax arbitrage prediction 1: Insider-trustees will have a higher pension fund weighting in bonds, especially if the sponsoring company is paying taxes.
- Tax arbitrage prediction 2: Insider-trustees will make higher contributions into the pension scheme when the sponsoring company faces a high tax rate.

Cocco and Volpin tested these hypotheses using data on 90 UK DB pension funds for 2002 (as reported in the 2003 annual reports). Their findings show overwhelming support for the agency hypothesis that insider-trustees act in the interests of the shareholders of the sponsoring company, rather than the pension scheme members. They find little support for the tax arbitrage hypothesis.

In particular, they find that the pension schemes of highly leveraged companies with a high proportion of insiders:

- Invest a higher proportion of pension scheme assets in equities.
- Contribute less to the pension scheme.
- Have a larger dividend payout ratio.
- Reduce pension contributions when the sponsoring company has a large investment programme, but there was no evidence that the lower contributions were correlated with better investment opportunities.

By contrast, Bodie *et al.* (1985) showed that profitable tax-paying companies behaved in a very different way. They were more likely to borrow to overfund their pension plans and invest in bonds, as predicted by Black (1980). However, there is a risk to overfunding the pension scheme: it can encourage hostile takeovers, the aim of which is to extract the pension fund surplus (Pontiff *et al.*, 1990).

3.6.2   Underfunding the Pension Scheme

Cooper and Ross (2002) argue that when a company sets up a pension fund for its workers, this acts as a *commitment device*, since it demonstrates to workers that the company will not be using the funds for other purposes. From the perspective of *optimal contract theory* (as well as that of *optimal tax planning*), the company has no incentive to underfund the pension scheme. Indeed, contract theory (see, e.g., Azariadis, 1975) implies that (large risk-neutral) firms will have a relationship with their (risk-averse) workers which is not only one of being a producer, but is also one of being a banker and an insurer. For example, they might lend money to the pension plan and will insure it against a deficit emerging.

These roles are easy to fulfil in a perfect markets context, when the company faces no restrictions on its borrowing and all risks can be hedged. In such an environment, it will be optimal for the company to offer fixed compensation (wages and pensions) over time to their workers, i.e., wages and pensions that are not dependent on the variability of the firm's output and sales revenue; this in turn leads to variable productivity. Risk-averse workers and pensioners who value smooth consumption profiles would not welcome the variability in their consumption that this dependence would imply. Risk-averse workers and pensioners also value the full funding of their pensions, and the company would agree to this and borrow if necessary if its own profits were not sufficient to make good a pension fund deficit. The loan contract between the company and the bank provides indirect insurance or commitment to the worker.

In practice, however, many companies deliberately underfund their pension schemes. A number of explanations have been put forward to explain why. They include market imperfections, bonding costs, a bargaining ploy and risk sharing. There are also strong incentives to underfund the pension scheme when pension fund insurance is available.

Market Imperfections

Cooper and Ross (2002) explain the presence of underfunded pension schemes in terms of *market imperfections*, such as borrowing constraints and high interest rates.

Some firms face borrowing constraints. These are designed to deal with the potential moral hazard problems of misusing the borrowed funds. This is a classic problem of asymmetric information, and was first studied by Myers and Majluf (1984). Such firms cannot credibly commit to being able to use the bank's funds to pay workers in youth and to fully fund the pension scheme. They will respond to this by partially funding (underfunding) the pension scheme with the funds they can borrow. Workers are also exposed to the risk of low productivity (arising from the low investment) and consequently low wages and/or pensions. In order to retain workers and stay in business, firms must offer higher subsequent wages and/or higher pensions to those younger workers who get low wages as a result of a negative productivity shock (i.e., *wage profiles*[21] will be upward sloping in age). In a sense this can be treated as a loan to the firm from the workers.

When firms face higher interest rates on borrowed funds than the returns available on pension assets, firms might prefer to use these borrowed funds in their main business rather than in their pension fund. This is again equivalent to borrowing from the workers. In compensation, workers need an upward sloping wage profile.

Montgomery *et al.* (1992), using data on US DB schemes, found that there was a one-for-one trade-off between wages and pension benefits in well-funded schemes, but that in companies with underfunded schemes the trade-off is greater than one-for-one, with workers expecting lower wage reductions to compensate for the weaker state of the pension promise.

Bonding Costs

Jensen and Meckling (1976, p. 308) argue that there are situations in which it is beneficial to the agent to deliberately incur *bonding costs*, which induce the agent not to take actions that damage the interests of the principal or that ensure the principal is compensated if such actions occur.

One example of this is for the managers to deliberately underfund their company's pension scheme. In the case where a company has a deficit in its pension scheme, this is equivalent to an unfunded debt obligation from the company to its managers and workers. This creates an incentive for the company's managers and its employees to take an interest in the welfare of the other bondholders in the company. This is because, via their pension schemes, they have claims on the assets of the company that are subordinate to the claims of most other creditors. As a consequence, managers who are contracted to run the company in the interests of shareholders have a reduced incentive to enhance shareholder value at the expense of bondholders.

As an example of how this might work, consider the case of a company planning to finance an investment programme by issuing bonds. The potential investors in the bonds will assess the riskiness of the investment

---

[21] A wage profile shows the real wage of the worker at each different age. It generally slopes upwards (on account of early career promotions), peaks at some age in the 40s or early 50s, and then declines gently until retirement age, as the worker switches to a less onerous and lower-paid job towards the end of his career.

and price the bonds accordingly. If the company's managers undertake an investment programme that is actually riskier than the one announced, this will enhance the value of the shares, since the higher expected returns from the investment programme, if it is successful, will accrue to shareholders and this will be incorporated into the share price, while the additional risk of the investment programme failing will lead to the market value of the bonds declining.

Jensen and Meckling argue that the use of *implicit* or *inside debt* (in the form of, say, unfunded liabilities in the pension scheme) is a cheap way of reducing the agency cost that other debt holders need to incur to ensure that the managers do not reallocate value to shareholders in this way. The managers will be interested in protecting the company from insolvency. They will therefore wish to avoid risks that disadvantage bondholders or which have serious employment implications for themselves (e.g., being fired). Unfunded pension liabilities therefore encourage managerial decisions that aim to keep the company in business, and this is in the long-term interests of the company's shareholders as well. Unfunded pension liabilities can reduce the cost of monitoring managers and, in turn, workers.

For all this to work, however, the rewards to managers and workers must also be incentive compatible, i.e., future earnings of managers and workers must be positively correlated with future profits and hence returns on the firm's equity. If this is the case, then managers and workers have an incentive to balance the interests of bondholders and shareholders, and all the interests of the different parties to the company are aligned.

Bargaining Ploy

Ippolito (1985b) argues that unfunded pension liabilities allow companies to improve their bargaining position with trade unions, which might be tempted to make excessive wage demands that could jeopardise the solvency of the company. An unfunded pension scheme renders workers as bondholders ('hostages') of the firm, thereby giving them a stake in its continued operation and success.

Risk Sharing

Arnott and Gersovitz (1980) argue that small risk-averse firms may use unfunded pension liabilities in order to share risk with risk-averse workers.

Underfunded Pension Schemes and Pension Fund Insurance

The government-backed Pension Benefit Guaranty Corporation (PBGC) (established by ERISA (Employee Retirement Income Security Act), 1974) insures US corporate pension schemes against the insolvency of the corporate sponsor. The Pension Protection Fund (established in 2005) performs the same role in the UK. Corporate pension policy can be influenced by the existence of such insurance schemes.

Bulow (1982) examines the value of pensions in a company with and without pension fund insurance from the PBGC.

Define:

A = accrued (vested and unvested) benefits
V = vested benefits
F = funded benefits = assets in pension fund
T = termination (discontinuance) benefits
G = guaranteed benefits by PBGC ($<V$)
$PBGCL$ = PBGC liability
FL = firm liability above F
S = market value of firm's equity

Prior to the existence of the PBGC, the value of the worker's claim in the event of termination was:

$$T = \min(F, V) \tag{3.12}$$

The firm had the right to terminate the scheme and have no additional liability even if $V > F$. However, the firm has an implicit liability to its employees of $(V - F)$ and if it does not wish the workers to walk away from the firm, it will have to promise to pay the workers this sum in higher wages.

ERISA changed the position of the firm in a significant way. The firm's net liability is now:

$$FL = \min(A - F, \max\{0, \min[G - F, 0.3S]\}) \tag{3.13}$$

If the pension scheme terminates with funded benefits exceeding accrued benefits ($F > A$), the firm actually has a surplus in the plan. If funded benefits exceed guaranteed benefits but are below accrued benefits ($G < F < A$), the firm faces no additional liability. If funded benefits are below guaranteed benefits, the firm is liable up to 30% of its equity value and the PBGC pays out the difference.

The PBGC liability is therefore:

$$PBGCL = \max(0, G - F - 0.3S) \qquad (3.14)$$

and the value of the termination benefits to the employees is:

$$T = PBGCL + FL + F = \min(A, \max\{G, F\}) \qquad (3.15)$$

Sharpe (1976), Harrison and Sharpe (1983) and Ippolito (1986) show that a company in financial distress has an incentive to underfund its pension scheme and follow a risky investment strategy (one which invests in equities rather than bonds), in the knowledge that the government will take on the pension liabilities in the event of its insolvency. In other words, the optimal policy maximises the difference between the value of the insurance and its cost, i.e., (3.13) is minimised and (3.14) is maximised.

Bodie (1996) shows that the shortfall risk facing the PBGC depends on the financial strength of the company sponsoring the plan, the level of underfunding of insured benefits, and the degree of mismatch between the market risks of insured benefits and plan assets.

3.6.3   Performance-Related Fund Management Fees

Starks (1987) (see also Bhattacharya and Pfleiderer, 1985; Gervais *et al.*, 2005) considers performance-related fund management fees as a vehicle for dealing with the agency costs in the agency relationship between a fund manager and the owner of the fund (in our case, the trustees of a pension fund). An appropriate incentive contract must be one that minimises the chance of conflict between the principal and agent. This will involve a fee structure with a risk-sharing rule that allocates the investment performance risk between the trustee and fund manager.

Starks considers two types of performance-related fee. One is a *bonus performance* (BP) *fee*:

$$F_{BP} = \begin{cases} F_0 & \text{if } r \leq r_B \\ F_0 + k(r - r_B) & \text{if } r > r_B \end{cases} \qquad (3.16)$$

where r is the realised return on the fund generated by the fund manager, r_B is the benchmark return specified in the contract, F_0 is the flat-rate fee that the fund manager receives irrespective of his performance, and k is the proportion of the outperformance of the benchmark received by the fund manager as a performance-related fee.

The second is a *symmetric performance* (SP) *fee*:

$$F_{SP} = F_0 + k(r - r_B) \tag{3.17}$$

where the flat-rate fee is cut if the fund manager underperforms the benchmark.

Starks shows that the BP fee is not incentive compatible as it induces the fund manager to take on a higher level of risk than desired by the trustees. The higher-risk portfolio will have a higher expected return, but also more volatility. If the return turns out to be higher than the benchmark, the fund manager receives a proportion k of this. But he is not penalised if the fund underperforms. The SP fee, on the other hand, is incentive compatible since it aligns the interests of the fund manager with those of the trustees. The fund manager will assume no greater risk than desired by the trustees, since any out- or underperformance of the benchmark is shared symmetrically.

However, active fund managers have to devote resources to identify the investments that outperform the benchmark. The SP fee structure induces the fund manager to devote a lower level of resources than desired by the trustees. The lower is k, the lower will be the optimal level of resources applied by the fund manager. If the level of resources devoted by the fund manager cannot be observed accurately by the trustees, an agency problem will still exist. The BP fee structure will lead to an even lower level of resources being applied. This is because the fund manager faces no downside risk and so does not need to expend resources on protecting his downside. An even larger agency problem exists in this case.

So the SP fee structure is superior to the BP fee structure but does not solve all agency problems.

3.6.4   Shareholder Activism and Corporate Governance

Fund managers need to ensure that the companies in which they invest act in the best interests of shareholders. In this case, the shoe is on the other foot. Now it is the fund managers who have to provide the appropriate incentives to company directors, including the directors of the company for which they are managing the pension fund. Monks (1997) shows how the attitudes of pension fund managers have changed from the strategy of selling the shares in companies whose managements they were unhappy with, to one where they exercise their rights to *shareholder activism*.

At the same time, companies have improved their corporate governance procedures. *Corporate governance* is the system by which companies are directed and controlled. In 1992 in the UK, the Cadbury Committee on corporate governance (chaired by Sir Adrian Cadbury) proposed a code of best practice for companies that included the appointment of independent non-executive directors to represent the interests of shareholders by guarding against undue concentrations of power in the boardroom, and by ensuring the proper disclosure of relevant information. In 1995, the Greenbury Committee on executive pay (chaired by Sir Richard Greenbury) published a code of conduct on the way directors' remuneration (including pension benefits) should be set and then disclosed in company accounts. The benefit is measured as the value of the accrued pension rights earned over the year. Further, the definition of final pensionable salary excludes performance bonuses. In January 1998, the Hempel Committee on corporate governance (chaired by Sir Ronald Hempel) recommended that the Stock Exchange incorporate a super code on corporate governance in its Listing Rules. The super code endorses the Cadbury and Greenbury codes, proposes that the roles of chairman and chief executive should be separate where this is possible, recommends that up to one-third of company boards should comprise independent directors, requires all executive directors to submit themselves for re-election at least every 3 years, urges institutional investors to vote in AGMs 'according to their best judgment' but opposes mandatory voting on the grounds that the result would be 'unthinking votes in favour of the board unwilling or unable to take an active interest in the company', and proposes the improved monitoring of corporate behaviour. The aim is to have a corporate governance framework that was more flexible and less prescriptive (involving less box ticking) than the previous system. The code would apply to all companies regardless of size. In June 1998, the Stock Exchange issued the super code and requires listed companies to disclose their compliance with it.

These measures and similar ones in other countries have done much to deal with key agency problems in companies. However, many other agency problems remain. The most prominent in recent years involves corporate disclosure in the light of the Enron and Worldcom scandals in the USA. This led to the 2002 Sarbanes-Oxley Act on financial and accounting disclosure.

3.6.5   Moral Hazard, Adverse Selection and Disability Pensions

Company pension schemes often allow for early retirement on the grounds of disability. In many schemes, the pension received is more than actuarially fair, i.e., the pension is larger than it would be if it were based purely on the individual's age and length of service. However, a moral hazard problem arises when 'disability' constitutes private information, as discussed by Diamond and Mirrlees (1978, 1985). How can the pension scheme be sure the worker is genuinely disabled?

To deal with the problem, an incentive-compatible benefit rule must set the pension benefit at a level that makes healthy workers indifferent between remaining in work and claiming that they are disabled. This means that to avoid the moral hazard problem, the disability pension must be less than the normal pension.

Another issue concerning private (asymmetric) information is *adverse selection*. Adverse selection is another problem common in insurance: those who are most likely to claim are the keenest to take out insurance. Individuals whose private information tells them that they are likely to become long-term ill or disabled at some time in the future are the most likely to seek jobs offering pension schemes with the most generous disability benefits. The solution, as discussed by Whinston (1983) and Hoy (1989), is, as in the case of moral hazard, a set of incentive-compatible benefit rules that involve the careful screening of job applicants and *ex post* separation of different risk classes.

3.7 CONCLUSIONS

Historically, companies offered pensions to their workers as an act of altruism, a reward for long and loyal service. Later, pensions came to be recognised as a form of deferred pay. In perfect capital and labour markets, workers will be indifferent as to whether their compensation comes in the form of wages or pensions, since they can use the capital markets to achieve their preferred mix (e.g., they can borrow against future pensions if the pension component is high relative to the wage component). In the real world, this indifference will not hold. There are a number of reasons for this: imperfect capital markets, risk, tax breaks, firm-specific human capital, and selection or sorting effects. These factors can remove or reinforce the desirability of pensions as part of the compensation package.

Pensions can also be viewed as contingent claims, providing both incentives to encourage the worker to greater effort and insurance to cover a range of risks, such as investment risk. These risks can be shared between the company and the worker. But the reward and risk-sharing elements of the pension plan will only be effective if the pension rights do not vest immediately. This allows training costs to be recovered, for example. At the other end of the age range, it also requires mandatory retirement, once the worker's marginal product falls below the reservation wage.

Views differ as to whether pension liabilities are implicit or explicit liabilities of the company. Some interpret pensions as part of a long-term implicit contract between the employer and the worker, intended to cover the worker's employment in the company until he retires. Some interpret pensions as part of an explicit contract, which by definition must be short-term in nature. Pensions in the first case are valued on a projected benefits basis; pensions in the second case are valued on an accrued benefits basis. Workers who quit their jobs before retirement lose part of their pension wealth in the first case, but not in the second.

There are a number of agency relationships in pension schemes and pension funds, and these involve costs. Examples include insider-trustees who act in the interests of the company, rather than the pension scheme's beneficiaries, and fund managers who might take risks with the fund's assets in order to maximise their income. Some economists argue that pension fund investment is a straightforward process of investing exclusively in riskless bonds to maximise the breaks.

QUESTIONS

1. Describe the history of occupational pension provision in developed countries.
2. Explain EET.
3. Explain the altruistic view of pensions.
4. Explain the deferred pay view of pensions.
5. Why are pensions neutral in a world of perfect capital markets?
6. What is vesting?
7. Explain the compensating wage principle.
8. Define economic pension liabilities.
9. Why does pensions neutrality break down when capital markets are imperfect?
10. How does risk affect the worker's attitude towards pensions?
11. How do firms recover training costs?
12. In an optimal employment contract, when is it optimal to undercompensate the worker and when is it optimal to overcompensate the worker (relative to the worker's marginal product)?
13. What are selection and sorting effects?
14. Explain the contingent claims view of pensions.

15. Explain the difference between the implicit and explicit views of corporate pension liabilities.
16. Explain the difference between the projected benefits and the accrued benefits methods of valuing pension liabilities.
17. Explain the difference between service cost and financing cost.
18. What is the pension capital loss from quitting and why does it arise?
19. Why are there mandatory retirement clauses in employment contracts?
20. Explain the time inconsistency problem using a pensions example to illustrate.
21. When do companies have an incentive to fully fund their pension funds and invest the pension fund in bonds?
22. Why do principal–agent problems exist?
23. What are the main types of agency cost?
24. Give some examples of the kind of agency relationships that exist in pension schemes and pension funds.
25. What is an incentive-compatible contract?
26. What is *ex-post* settling up?
27. What is the agency hypothesis concerning insider-trustees?
28. Why do companies sometimes underfund their pension schemes?
29. What are bonding costs? Explain how they can be used in pension schemes.
30. What problems face a pension fund insurance agency?
31. How can performance-related fund management fees deal with the agency costs facing a pension fund?
32. Explain the role of shareholder activism in effective corporate governance.
33. Explain the moral hazard and adverse selection issues surrounding disability pensions.

REFERENCES

Arnott, R. and Gersovitz, M. (1980) Corporate financial structure and the funding of private pension plans, *Journal of Public Economics*, **13**, 231–247.

Azariadis, C. (1975) Implicit contracts and underemployment equilibria, *Journal of Political Economy*, **83**, 1183–1202.

Besley, T. and Pratt, A. (2003) Pension Fund Governance and the Choice between Defined Benefit and Defined Contribution Plans, Discussion Paper 3955, Centre for Economic Policy Research, June.

Bhattacharya, S. and Pfleiderer, P. (1985) Delegated portfolio management, *Journal of Economic Theory*, **36**, 1–25.

Black, F. (1980) The tax consequences of long run pension policy, *Financial Analysts Journal*, **36**, 1–28.

Blake, D. (1998) Pension schemes as options on pension fund assets: implications for pension fund management, *Insurance: Mathematics & Economics*, **23**, 263–286.

Blinder, A. (1981) *Private Pensions and Public Pensions: Theory & Fact*, W.S. Woytinsky Lecture No. 5, Institute of Public Policy Studies, University of Michigan.

Bodie, Z. (1996) What the Pension Benefit Guaranty Corporation can learn from the Federal Savings and Loans Insurance Corporation, *Journal of Financial Services Research*, **10**, 83–100.

Bodie, Z., Light, J., Mørck, R. and Taggart, R. (1985) Corporate pension policy: an empirical investigation, *Financial Analysts Journal*, **41**, 10–16.

Brealey, R. and Myers, S. (1991) *Principles of Corporate Finance*, McGraw-Hill, New York.

Bulow, J. (1982) What are corporate pension liabilities? *Quarterly Journal of Economics*, **97**, 435–452.

Cocco, J. and Volpin, P. (2005) The Corporate Governance of Defined Benefit Pension Plans: Evidence from the UK, Discussion Paper 4932, Centre for Economic Policy Research, February.

Cooper, R. and Ross, T. (2002) Pensions: theories of underfunding, *Labor Economics*, **8**, 667–689.

Diamond, P. and Mirrlees, J. (1978) A model of social insurance with variable retirement, *Journal of Public Economics*, **10**, 295–336.

Diamond, P. and Mirrlees, J. (1985) Insurance aspects of pensions, in Wise, D. (ed.), *Pensions, Labor and Individual Choice*, University of Chicago Press, Chicago.

Fabel, O. (1994) *The Economics of Pensions and Variable Retirement Schemes*, John Wiley & Sons, Chichester.

Fama, E. (1980) Agency problems and the theory of the firm, *Journal of Political Economy*, **88**, 288–307.

Gervais, S., Lynch, A. and Musto, D. (2005) Delegated monitoring of fund managers: an economic rationale, *Review of Financial Studies*, **18**, 1139–1169.

Harrison, J. and Sharpe, W. (1983) Optimal funding and asset allocation rules for defined benefit pension plans, in Bodie, Z. and Shoven, J. (eds), *Financial Aspects of the United States Pension System*, University of Chicago Press, Chicago.

Hoy, M. (1989) The value of screening mechanisms under alternative insurance possibilities, *Journal of Public Economics*, **39**, 177–206.

Ippolito, R. (1985a) The implicit pension contract and true economic pension liabilities, *American Economic Review*, **75**, 1031.

Ippolito, R. (1985b) Economic function of underfunded pension plans, *Journal of Law and Economics*, **28**, 611–651.

Ippolito, R. (1986) *Pensions, Economics and Public Policy*, Dow Jones-Irwin, Homewood IL.

Ippolito, R. (1997) *Pension Plans and Employee Performance: Evidence, Analysis and Policy*, University of Chicago Press, Chicago.

Jensen, M.C. (1998) Self-Interest, altruism, incentives and agency theory, in Jensen, M.C. (ed.), *Foundations of Organizational Strategy*, Harvard University Press, Cambridge, MA.

Jensen, M.C. and Meckling, W. (1976) Theory of the firm: managerial behavior, agency costs and ownership structure, *Journal of Financial Economics*, **3**, 305–360.

Lazear, E. (1979) Why is there mandatory retirement?, *Journal of Political Economy*, **87**, 1261–1284.

Lazear, E. (1983) Pensions as severance pay, in Bodie, Z. and Shoven, J. (eds), *Financial Aspects of the United States Pension System*, University of Chicago Press, Chicago.

Lazear, E. (1985) Incentive effects of pensions, in Wise, D. (ed.), *Pensions, Labor and Individual Choice*, University of Chicago Press, Chicago.

Logue, D. (1979) A theory of pensions, chapter 3 in *Legislative Influence on Corporate Pension Plans*, American Enterprise Institute, Washington, DC.

McCarthy, D. and Neuberger, A. (2003) *Pensions Policy: Evidence on Aspects of Savings Behaviour and Capital Markets*, Centre for Economic Policy Research, London.

McGill, D., Brown, K., Haley, J. and Schieber, S. (2005) *Fundamentals of Private Pensions*, Oxford University Press, Oxford.

Merton, R. (1985) Implicit labor contracts viewed as options: a discussion of 'insurance aspects of pensions', in Wise, D. (ed.), *Pensions, Labor and Individual Choice*, University of Chicago Press, Chicago.

Monks, R. (1997) Corporate governance and pension plans, in Gordon, M., Mitchell, O. and Twinney, M. (eds), *Positioning Pensions for the Twenty-First Century*, University of Pennsylvania Press, Philadelphia, 139–158.

Montgomery, E., Shaw, K. and Benedict, M. (1992) Pensions and wages, *International Economic Review*, **33**, 111–128.

Munnell, A. (1982) *The Economics of Private Pensions*, Brookings Institution, Washington, DC.

Myers, S. and Majluf, N. (1984) Corporate financing and investment decisions when firms have information that investors do not have, *Journal of Financial Economics*, **13**, 187–221.

Petersen, M. (1992) Pension reversions and wealth transfers, *Quarterly Journal of Economics*, **107**, 1033–1056.

Pontiff, J., Shleifer, A. and Weisbach, M. (1990) Reversions of excess pensions assets on takeovers, *Rand Journal*, **21**, 600–613.

Rauh, J. (2006) Investment and financing constraints: evidence from the funding of corporate pension plans, *Journal of Finance*, **61**, 33–71.

Sharpe, W. (1976) Corporate pension funding policy, *Journal of Financial Economics*, **3**, 183–193.

Squires, L.W. (1912) *Old Age Dependency in the United States*, Macmillan, New York.

Starks, L. (1987) Performance incentive fees: an agency theoretic approach. *Journal of Financial and Quantitative Analysis*, **22**, 17–32.

Tepper, I. (1981) Taxation and corporate pension policy, *Journal of Finance*, **36**, 1–13.

Tepper, I. and Affleck, A. (1974) Pension plan liabilities and corporate financial strategies, *Journal of Finance*, **29**, 1549–1564.

Treynor, J. (1977) The principles of corporate pension policy, *Journal of Finance*, **32**, 627–638.

Webb, D. (2004) Sponsoring Company Finance and Investment and Defined Benefit Pension Scheme Deficits, Discussion Paper 487, Financial Markets Group, London School of Economics.

Whinston, M. (1983) Moral hazard, adverse selection, and the optimal provision of social insurance, *Journal of Public Economics*, **22**, 49–71.

Wise, D. (ed.) (1985) *Pensions, Labor and Individual Choice*, University of Chicago Press, Chicago.

4

Pensions in the Diamond–Samuelson Overlapping Generations Model with Certain Lifetimes

The *overlapping generations (OLG) model* is the cornerstone of modern macroeconomics. Macroeconomics deals with the aggregate behaviour of individuals, companies and governments. The OLG model is a dynamic economic model that generalises the lifecycle model. It begins with a representative individual from each generation and then aggregates across all individuals alive concurrently.

The behaviour of individuals, companies and governments in the OLG model is assumed to influence the dynamic behaviour of the economy over time. The key control variables are the savings and labour supply decisions of individuals. The key policy variable is the tax rate set by the government. The key parameters of the model are the marginal propensity to save, the marginal rate of time preference, the degree of risk aversion of individuals, the depreciation rate of capital, and the growth rate in population. The key state variable is the aggregate physical capital stock, which is the outcome of the accumulation of previous savings and labour supply decisions, and these depend on the model's parameters and the value of the policy variables chosen. The level of the capital stock is also important for determining the value of other variables that the model generates, such as the wage rate and the rate of interest.

Box 4.1 Dynamic Models

A dynamic model or system defines an intertemporal relationship between three sets of variables: control variables, policy variables and state variables. A *control variable* is one whose value is chosen (or controlled) by the agent whose behaviour the model is seeking to explain over time. A *policy variable* is one whose value is chosen by a party external to the agent (such as the government) and which influences the behaviour of the agent over time. A *state variable* measures the state of (i.e., is determined by) the model or system at a particular time. The model will also contain parameters: these are variables whose values have been set to fixed constants in the model. The state variables will reflect the time path of the control and policy variables for a given set of parameters.

We first derive the OLG model and then examine pensions in the OLG model, first with exogenous labour supply and retirement and then with endogenous labour supply and retirement.[1]

4.1   THE TWO-PERIOD DIAMOND–SAMUELSON OLG MODEL

The original OLG model was developed by Samuelson (1958) and Diamond (1965). Individuals are allocated to finitely lived generations (with certain lifetimes) according to their date of birth, and at any one time more than one generation will be alive. Each generation will trade with both the generation ahead of it and the generation behind it at different stages in its lifecycle.

The model can be used to study the aggregate consequences of lifecycle savings by individuals. The capital stock is the outcome of individuals saving during their working lives in order to finance their consumption during retirement. We assume that capital is the only asset that savings can be held in. The net capital stock increases over time as a result of bequests (whether intended or unintended) to the next generation.

The simplest OLG model is the two-period model of youth and old age. At any point in time, there will be two generations or cohorts alive, young and old (see Table 4.1). We wish to characterise the nature of the equilibrium that results from the two generations trading with each other. We assume that the individuals within each generation have the objective of maximising their lifetime utility and that firms exist to maximise profits. We also assume that all individuals within each generation are identical.

---

[1] Exogenous means determined outside the model, endogenous means determined within the model.

Table 4.1 Two-period overlapping generations

Generation	Time Period					
	0	1	2	3	4	5
−1	Old					
0	Young	Old				
1		Young	Old			
2			Young	Old		
3				Young	Old	
4					Young	Old

4.1.1 Individuals

Individuals are assumed to work in the first period ('youth') and be retired in the second period ('old age'). However, they want to consume in both periods and so must save when young in order to acquire capital which they consume (dissave) when old. Suppose further that the population grows at the constant rate n between generations.

At time t, a typical young individual has discounted (time-separable[2]) lifetime utility:

$$\Lambda_t^Y \left(C_t^Y, C_{t+1}^O \right) = U \left(C_t^Y \right) + \left(\frac{1}{1+\rho} \right) U \left(C_{t+1}^O \right) \tag{4.1}$$

where 'Y' stands for 'youth' and 'O' stands for 'old age'; this is also known as a *direct utility function*. The parameter ρ measures the rate of time preference of the individual. The higher is ρ, the more impatient the individual is and the more highly valued is consumption in youth compared with consumption in old age; such an individual is a natural spender. By contrast, individuals with a low value of ρ have a great deal of patience and so will be willing to postpone consumption; such an individual is a natural saver. The utility function satisfies the conditions that marginal utility is positive ($U'(x) = \partial U/\partial x > 0$) but decreasing ($U''(x) = \partial^2 U/\partial x^2 < 0$) in consumption; see Figure 2.1.

---

[2] This means that the utility in each period depends only on that period's consumption and not on the consumption from other periods (which would be the case if there was habit persistence, for example). This implies that lifetime utility is the (discounted) sum of each period's utility.

When young, the individual supplies one unit of labour (i.e., is assumed to be in full-time employment for his whole career) and receives a wage W_t which is either consumed (C_t^Y) or saved (S_t). The savings will be used entirely to finance retirement consumption. When old, the individual does not work, but draws down the savings together with interest (r_{t+1}) on the savings to finance consumption in retirement. To begin with, we will assume that wages and interest rates are exogenous.

The individual therefore faces two budget constraints, one in youth and one in old age:

$$C_t^Y + S_t = W_t \tag{4.2}$$

$$C_{t+1}^O = (1 + r_{t+1})S_t \tag{4.3}$$

The single lifetime budget constraint is found by substituting (4.3) into (4.2):

$$W_t = C_t^Y + \frac{C_{t+1}^O}{1 + r_{t+1}} \tag{4.4}$$

The young individual chooses C_t^Y and C_{t+1}^O to maximise (4.1) subject to (4.4). The Lagrangean function for this problem is:

$$\underset{\{C_t^Y, C_{t+1}^O\}}{Max} \ \Psi_t^Y = U\left(C_t^Y\right) + \left(\frac{1}{1+\rho}\right) U\left(C_{t+1}^O\right)$$
$$+ \lambda_t \left(W_t - C_t^Y - \frac{C_{t+1}^O}{1 + r_{t+1}} \right) \tag{4.5}$$

where λ_t is the Lagrange multiplier. The first-order conditions (FOCs) for a maximum are:

$$U'\left(C_t^Y\right) - \lambda_t = 0 \tag{4.6}$$

$$\left(\frac{1}{1+\rho}\right) U'\left(C_{t+1}^O\right) - \lambda_t \left(\frac{1}{1+r_{t+1}}\right) = 0 \tag{4.7}$$

where $U'\left(C_t^Y\right)$ and $U'\left(C_{t+1}^O\right)$ are the *marginal utilities* of consumption in youth and old age, respectively.

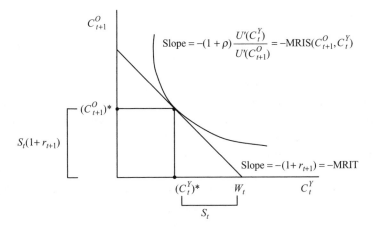

Figure 4.1 Optimal consumption and savings in the overlapping generations model

These FOCs can be combined to give the *consumption Euler equation*:[3]

$$(1 + \rho) \frac{U'\left(C_t^Y\right)}{U'\left(C_{t+1}^O\right)} = 1 + r_{t+1} \tag{4.8}$$

where the left-hand side of (4.8) is known as the *marginal rate of intertemporal substitution* between consumption in old age and consumption in youth ($\text{MRIS}(C_{t+1}^O, C_t^Y)$) and the right-hand side is known as the *marginal rate of intertemporal transformation* (and measures the rate at which one unit of currency can be transferred into the future; in other words, it measures the return on savings).

The optimal consumption in the two periods can be determined implicitly using equations (4.4) and (4.8) and will depend on the two exogenous variables W_t and r_{t+1}. This is shown in Figure 4.1.

Only in the case of particular functional forms for the utility function can an explicit equation for optimal consumption be determined. The most commonly used functional form is the iso-elastic utility function:

$$U(C_t) = \begin{cases} \dfrac{C_t^{1-1/\sigma}}{1 - 1/\sigma}, & \sigma > 0, \sigma \neq 1 \\ \ln(C_t), & \sigma = 1 \end{cases} \tag{4.9}$$

---

[3] This determines how optimal consumption between consecutive periods is related.

We define:

$$\theta[C_t] = -\frac{U''(C_t)C_t}{U'(C_t)} \qquad (4.10)$$

as the (positive) *elasticity of marginal utility.*[4,5]

The inverse of $\theta[C_t]$ ($\sigma[C_t] = 1/\theta[C_t]$) is known as the *intertemporal substitution elasticity* (ISE). The ISE measures the willingness to smooth consumption over time. When ISE is low (i.e., below unity, which occurs when $U''(C_t)$ is high, i.e., when the utility function exhibits a lot of curvature, or when C_t is high), the willingness to engage in consumption smoothing over time is high. A 1% increase in wages today will lead to a less than 1% increase in consumption today, which allows some of the increase in wages to be consumed in future periods. When the utility function is highly curved, an increase in consumption results in a lower increase in utility than when the utility function is less curved, and this lowers the value of an increase in consumption today relative to an increase in consumption in the future. The same is true when current consumption, C_t, is high, since this means $U'(C_t)$ is low and a further

---

[4] The general form of the elasticity of marginal utility is:

$$-\frac{\frac{d(U'(C_t)/U'(C_{t+1}))}{U'(C_t)/U'(C_{t+1})}}{\frac{d(C_t/C_{t+1})}{C_t/C_{t+1}}}$$

The iso-elastic utility function is an example of a homothetic function. For such a function, $U'(C_{t+1})$ is unaffected by a change in C_t/C_{t+1} unless C_{t+1} also changes. Holding C_{t+1} constant, then $d\left(U'(C_t)/U'(C_{t+1})\right) = dU'(C_t)/U'(C_{t+1})$ and $d(C_t/C_{t+1}) = dC_t/C_{t+1}$, so that

$$-\frac{\frac{d(U'(C_t)/U'(C_{t+1}))}{U'(C_t)/U'(C_{t+1})}}{\frac{d(C_t/C_{t+1})}{C_t/C_{t+1}}} = -\frac{\frac{dU'(C_t)/U'(C_{t+1})}{U'(C_t)/U'(C_{t+1})}}{\frac{dC_t/C_{t+1}}{C_t/C_{t+1}}} = -\frac{\frac{dU'(C_t)}{U'(C_t)}}{\frac{dC_t}{C_t}} = -\frac{U''(C_t)C_t}{U'(C_t)} = \theta[C_t]$$

when $dC_t = 1$.

[5] Equation (4.10) is also the equation for the coefficient of relative risk aversion. The degree of risk aversion measures the desire to stabilise consumption (i.e., avoid both very low and very high levels of consumption) across different states of the economy in the same time period. Individuals with a high degree of risk aversion value stable consumption patterns. There are two sources of potential volatility in the model, namely volatility associated with the two exogenous variables W_t and r_{t+1}. Individuals with a high degree of risk aversion prefer jobs with a low volatility of wages (W_t) across the states of the economy and savings plans with a low volatility of returns (r_{t+1}). To illustrate, suppose there are three possible states of the economy in each time period: boom, normal and slump. Although the wages in all jobs will be higher when the economy is booming and lower in an economic slump, risk-averse individuals will choose jobs with a lower dispersion of wages across the different possible states of the economy, since they dislike very low consumption in a slump and are prepared to trade this off against very high consumption in a boom. The same argument applies to savings plans.

increase in current consumption is not highly valued. An individual with a low ISE does not welcome large swings in consumption over time.[6]

With an iso-elastic utility function, ISE is constant and equal to σ. The logarithmic utility function $(\ln(C_t))$ is a special case of an iso-elastic utility function. It has an ISE of unity and is therefore sometimes known as a unit-elastic utility function: a 1% increase in wages leads to a 1% increase in consumption in the current and in all future periods.

With the iso-elastic utility function, the Euler equation becomes:

$$(1 + \rho)\frac{\left(C_t^Y\right)^{-1/\sigma}}{\left(C_{t+1}^O\right)^{-1/\sigma}} = 1 + r_{t+1} \tag{4.11}$$

Substituting (4.11) into (4.4), we can solve for optimal consumption in the two periods:

$$\left(C_t^Y\right)^* = \Theta^Y(\rho, r_{t+1}, \sigma)W_t \tag{4.12}$$

$$\left(C_{t+1}^O\right)^* = \Theta^O(\rho, r_{t+1}, \sigma)W_t \tag{4.13}$$

where:

$$\Theta^Y(\rho, r_{t+1}, \sigma) = \left[1 - \frac{\Theta^O(\rho, r_{t+1}, \sigma)}{1 + r_{t+1}}\right] \tag{4.14}$$

$$\Theta^O(\rho, r_{t+1}, \sigma) = \left[\left(\frac{1+\rho}{1+r_{t+1}}\right)^\sigma + \frac{1}{1+r_{t+1}}\right]^{-1} \tag{4.15}$$

Equations (4.12) and (4.13) show that an increase in:

- W_t increases consumption in both periods.
- ρ increases consumption in the first period and reduces it in the second.
- r_{t+1} increases consumption in the second period, but has an ambiguous effect on consumption in the first period (depending on the sizes of the parameters, consumption could rise, fall or remain unchanged).

With the logarithmic utility function, the equations for optimal consumption in the two periods simplify considerably:

$$\left(C_t^Y\right)^* = \left(\frac{1+\rho}{2+\rho}\right)W_t \tag{4.16}$$

$$\left(C_{t+1}^O\right)^* = \left(\frac{1+r_{t+1}}{2+\rho}\right)W_t \tag{4.17}$$

---

[6] An individual with a low ISE will also have a high degree of risk aversion. Such an individual does not welcome volatile consumption either over time or over states of the economy in a single time period.

These two equations show that an increase in:

- W_t increases consumption in both periods.
- ρ increases consumption in the first period and reduces it in the second.
- r_{t+1} increases consumption in the second period, but has no effect on consumption in the first period.

We can use the savings function to explain the generally ambiguous response of consumption in the first period to r_{t+1}:

$$W_t - C_t^Y = S(W_t, r_{t+1}) \qquad (4.18)$$

The partial derivatives of the savings function have the following properties:[7]

$$S_W = \frac{\partial S}{\partial W_t} = \frac{\theta \left[C_t^Y\right]/C_t^Y}{\theta \left[C_{t+1}^O\right]/S_t + \theta \left[C_t^Y\right]/C_t^Y} \in (0,1) \qquad (4.19)$$

$$S_r = \frac{\partial S}{\partial r_{t+1}} = \frac{1 - \theta \left[C_{t+1}^O\right]}{(1 + r_{t+1})\left\{\theta \left[C_{t+1}^O\right]/S_t + \theta \left[C_t^Y\right]/C_t^Y\right\}} \begin{array}{c} < \\ = \\ > \end{array} 0 \quad (4.20)$$

Equation (4.19) shows that savings is a normal good:[8] an increase in wage income increases savings, but the effect is less than proportional. Further, as equations (4.12), (4.13), (4.16) and (4.17) confirm in the case of logarithmic utility functions, consumption in both periods is normal:

$$C_W^Y = \frac{\partial C_t^Y}{\partial W_t} = 1 - S_W > 0 \qquad (4.21)$$

$$C_W^O = \frac{\partial C_{t+1}^O}{\partial W_t} = (1 + r_{t+1})S_W > 0 \qquad (4.22)$$

Equation (4.20) shows that the response of savings to changes in the rate of interest (like the response of first-period consumption) is ambiguous. This is because the substitution and income effects of a change in the rate of interest work in opposite directions.

The *substitution effect* measures how individuals alter current consumption relative to future consumption in response to an increase in the rate of interest (which we can interpret as the price of time), holding income constant. An increase in the rate of interest increases (interest) income (for a given level of savings) and this increase in income has

---

[7] See Heijdra and van der Ploeg (2002, p. 591).

[8] With a normal good, consumption increases when income rises. This contrasts with an inferior good: when income increases, the consumption of an inferior good falls.

to be controlled for when measuring the substitution effect. The *income effect* measures how individuals alter current consumption relative to future consumption in response to an increase in the rate of interest, after controlling for the substitution effect. The *total effect* is the sum of the two effects.

A rise in r_{t+1} reduces the relative price of future consumption (see equation (4.4)), which induces the individual to substitute future for current consumption by increasing savings. Future consumption is now cheaper (in present value terms) than current consumption and so the substitution effect of an increase in r_{t+1} is always positive.

A rise in r_{t+1} induces individuals to increase consumption in both periods and reduce savings: the income effect on savings is generally negative.

Equation (4.20) shows that the net effect depends on: $\sigma[C_t] = 1/\theta[C_t]$.

$$S_r \gtreqless 0 \Leftrightarrow \theta[C^O_{t+1}] \lesseqgtr 1 \Leftrightarrow \sigma[C^O_{t+1}] \gtreqless 1 \tag{4.23}$$

If the ISE exceeds unity, the substitution effect dominates and savings depends positively on the interest rate. The opposite holds when the ISE is less than unity. When the ISE equals unity, as in the case of a logarithmic utility function, the substitution and income effects cancel out and the total effect is zero. Figure 4.2 illustrates the case of an increase in the rate of interest from r_{t+1} to r'_{t+1} when the ISE exceeds

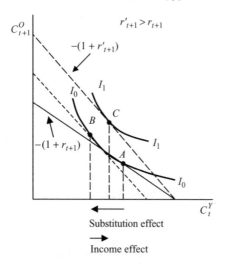

Figure 4.2 The total effect of an increase in the rate of interest: a positive substitution effect (*AB*) and a partially offsetting income affect (*BC*)

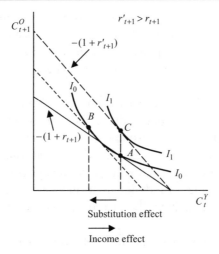

Figure 4.3   The total effect of an increase in the rate of interest: a positive substitution effect (*AB*) and a fully offsetting income affect (*BC*)

unity. Figure 4.3 illustrates the case of an increase in the rate of interest when the ISE equals unity.

4.1.2   Firms

Firms are assumed to produce output, Y_t, by hiring capital, K_t, from the current old generation, and labour, L_t, from the current young generation. Firms are assumed to operate in a *perfectly competitive market*.[9] The *production function*:[10]

$$Y_t = F(K_t, L_t) \qquad (4.24)$$

is assumed to be *linear homogeneous* (i.e., exhibit *constant returns to scale*[11]):

$$F(\alpha K_t, \alpha L_t) = \alpha F(K_t, L_t) \qquad (4.25)$$

Firms are assumed to choose K_t and L_t to maximise *profit* subject to (4.24):

$$\underset{\{K_t, L_t\}}{Max} \ \Omega_t = Y_t - (r_t + \delta) K_t - W_t L_t + \lambda_t (F(K_t, L_t) - Y_t) \qquad (4.26)$$

---

[9] This is a market in which there are no restrictions on entry to or exit from the market.

[10] This is a technological relationship showing the maximum output that can be produced with a given set of factors of production, such as capital and labour.

[11] This means, for example, that output is doubled if all inputs are doubled.

where λ_t is the Lagrange multiplier. Profit is defined as output minus the cost of the inputs and is equal to the first three terms on the right-hand side of equation (4.26). The FOCs for a maximum are:

$$r_t + \delta = F_K(K_t, L_t) \tag{4.27}$$

$$W_t = F_L(K_t, L_t) \tag{4.28}$$

where F_K and F_L are the *marginal products* of capital and labour,[12] and δ is the depreciation rate of capital ($0 < \delta < 1$). Equations (4.27) and (4.28) show that, at the profit-maximising optimum, factors of production are paid their marginal product: ($r_t + \delta$) is the rental rate on the current capital stock (and must be more than sufficient to cover depreciation) and W_t is the wage rate.

It is important to recognise that individual saving decisions depend on the future interest rate and hence the future capital stock and labour force:

$$r_{t+1} + \delta = F_K(K_{t+1}, L_{t+1}) \tag{4.29}$$

Because the production function is linear homogeneous, equation (4.24) can be written in per capita (or *intensive*) form:

$$y_t = F(k_t, 1) \equiv f(k_t) \tag{4.30}$$

where $y_t = Y_t/L_t$ is the output–labour ratio or *average product* of labour and $k_t = K_t/L_t$ is the capital–labour ratio.

Equations (4.28) and (4.29) become:

$$W_t = f(k_t) - k_t f'(k_t) \tag{4.31}$$

$$r_{t+1} + \delta = f'(k_{t+1}) \tag{4.32}$$

where equation (4.31) makes use of the following property which holds for linear homogeneous equations (known as *Euler's theorem*):

$$F = F_K K + F_L L \Leftrightarrow f = f'k + F_L \tag{4.33}$$

since $f' \equiv F_K$. One of the implications of equation (4.33) is that if factors of production are paid their marginal product, the output of the firm is allocated in full to the factors of production and the firm makes zero profits. In other words, pure profit is zero in a perfectly competitive market.

---

[12] These measure the additional output from adding an additional unit of capital or labour, respectively, to the production process, holding the other factor constant.

4.1.3 Market Equilibrium

The market equilibrium arises from aggregating over all the individuals and firms in the economy. The key variable determined in market equilibrium is the physical capital stock. The supply of capital comes from individuals as a result of their savings decisions. The demand for capital comes from firms.

The budget constraint for the economy in period t is:

$$Y_t + (1 - \delta)K_t = C_t + K_{t+1} \tag{4.34}$$

where C_t is the aggregate consumption of the young and the old in period t and Y_t is the aggregate output of all the firms in the economy.[13] This says that current output plus the undepreciated part of the capital stock can be used for current consumption or to provide next period's capital stock.

Equation (4.34) can be be rewritten:

$$\begin{aligned} Y_t &= C_t + K_{t+1} - (1 - \delta)K_t \\ &= C_t + \Delta K_{t+1} + \delta K_t \\ &= C_t + I_t \end{aligned} \tag{4.35}$$

where $\Delta K_{t+1} \equiv K_{t+1} - K_t$ and I_t is gross investment (i.e., investment before depreciation is taken into account).[14]

Aggregate consumption is the sum of consumption by the L_{t-1} young and L_t old:

$$C_t = L_{t-1}C_t^O + L_t C_t^Y \tag{4.36}$$

Since the old own the capital stock and since they do not wish to die with any assets (we assume they have no bequest motive), their consumption will equal the undepreciated part of the capital stock plus the rental payments received from the firms for use of the capital:

$$\begin{aligned} L_{t-1}C_t^O &= (r_t + \delta)K_t + (1 - \delta)K_t \\ &= (1 + r_t)K_t \end{aligned} \tag{4.37}$$

---

[13] As a result of the two assumptions of constant returns to scale and perfect competition, the FOCs (4.27) and (4.28) for the firm are the same as those for the economy as a whole, once all firms are aggregated together. This means that in effect we can treat the economy as having just a single perfectly competitive firm for all periods of the model. These assumptions therefore simplify the analysis considerably in respect of the firm-side of the model.

[14] Δ means a change in.

The aggregate consumption of the young is aggregate wage income less aggregate savings:

$$L_t C_t^Y = L_t W_t - L_t S_t \tag{4.38}$$

Substituting (4.37) and (4.38) into (4.36) gives:

$$C_t = (r_t + \delta)K_t + (1 - \delta)K_t + L_t W_t - L_t S_t$$
$$= Y_t + (1 - \delta)K_t - L_t S_t \tag{4.39}$$

recognising that factor incomes exhaust output ($Y_t = (r_t + \delta)K_t + L_t W_t$) in a perfectly competitive equilibrium (i.e., profits are zero).

The relationship between this period's aggregate savings and next period's capital stock is found by substituting (4.39) into (4.34):

$$L_t S_t = K_{t+1} \tag{4.40}$$

We assume the population grows at a constant rate n:

$$L_t = L_0 (1 + n)^t \tag{4.41}$$

The savings function (4.40) can be written in per capita form (using $S_t = S(W_t, r_{t+1})$) as:

$$S(W_t, r_{t+1}) = (1 + n)k_{t+1} \tag{4.42}$$

Capital market equilibrium is represented by a balance between the demand for capital by firms (($r_{t+1} + \delta) = f'(k_{t+1})$) and the supply of capital by individual savers ($S(W_t, r_{t+1}) = (1 + n)k_{t+1}$), conditional on the parameters of the model (e.g., r_{t+1}, L_t, n, δ, ρ, and σ).

4.1.4 Dynamics, Stability and the Steady State

Substituting for W_t and r_{t+1} (from (4.31) and (4.32)) in the capital supply equation (4.42) gives:

$$(1 + n)k_{t+1} = S[f(k_t) - k_t f'(k_t), f'(k_{t+1}) - \delta] \tag{4.43}$$

This is known as the *fundamental (non-linear) difference equation* relating the future capital stock per worker with the current capital stock per worker (where the capital stock is the state variable of the model).[15]

---

[15] A difference equation is a dynamic model explaining the dynamic behaviour of the state variable (in this case k_{t+1}) in discrete time (as a function of the control and policy variables, the previous history of the state variable, and for a given set of parameter values of the model). If, as in this case, the difference equation is fully specified with only a single previous value of the state variable (i.e., k_t), it is known as a first-order difference equation.

It can be used to study the dynamic path of the capital stock (which shows the state of the economy) and its stability. We can totally differentiate (4.43) to get:

$$\frac{dk_{t+1}}{dk_t} = \frac{-S_W k_t f''(k_t)}{1 + n - S_r f''(k_{t+1})} \tag{4.44}$$

where S_W and S_r are given in (4.19) and (4.20). Equation (4.44) shows how next period's capital stock changes in response to a change in the current capital stock. In other words, it gives the gradient of the dynamic path of the state variable.

Stability[16] requires any deviations from a steady state to be dampened not amplified, implying that:

$$\left| \frac{dk_{t+1}}{dk_t} \right| < 1 \tag{4.45}$$

We will illustrate the dynamics and stability properties of the system using the *unit-elastic Diamond–Samuelson OLG model*. The unit-elastic model employs a constant-returns-to-scale Cobb–Douglas production function:[17]

$$y_t = k_t^{1-\varepsilon_L} \tag{4.46}$$

where ε_L is the share of labour in national income, and a logarithmic utility function:

$$U(C_t) = \ln(C_t) \tag{4.47}$$

so that

$$\sigma[C_t] = 1/\theta[C_t] = 1 \tag{4.48}$$

The savings function is therefore (using (4.16) and (4.18)):

$$S_t = \frac{W_t}{2 + \rho} \tag{4.49}$$

and the wage rate is:

$$W_t = \varepsilon_L k_t^{1-\varepsilon_L} \tag{4.50}$$

---

[16] A dynamic model is stable if, when the model is shocked out of equilibrium, it returns to an equilibrium state in finite time.

[17] A constant-returns-to-scale Cobb–Douglas production function has the *extensive* form $Y_t = L_t^{\varepsilon_L} K_t^{1-\varepsilon_L}$ and the intensive form given in (4.46).

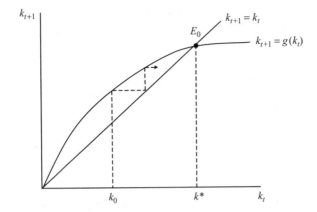

Figure 4.4 Phase diagram of the unit-elastic Diamond–Samuelson OLG model
Source: Heijdra and van der Ploeg (2002). Reproduced by permission of Oxford University Press

and (4.43) becomes (combining (4.49) and (4.50)):

$$k_{t+1} = g(k_t) \equiv \left(\frac{\varepsilon_L}{(1+n)(2+\rho)} \right) k_t^{1-\varepsilon_L} \qquad (4.51)$$

The *phase diagram* of the unit-elastic Diamond–Samuelson OLG model is shown in Figure 4.4. The phase diagram shows the dynamics of the state variable over consecutive periods. The equation $k_{t+1} = g(k_t)$ is known as the *phase line*.

The steady state equilibrium of the model ($k_{t+1} = k_t = k^*$) is given by:

$$k^* = g(k^*) \qquad (4.52)$$

This is unique and stable: from wherever the economy starts (e.g., k_0), it will eventually end up at k^*. Once the economy has reached E_0 in Figure 4.4, it will remain in a *steady state* unless it is disturbed. Thereafter the capital–labour ratio will remain constant over time, i.e., $k_{t+1} = k_t = k^*$. Such an economy is said to follow a *golden-age path* (Diamond, 1965).

4.1.5   Optimality and Efficiency

There might exist a steady state golden-age path for the Diamond–Samuelson OLG model, but is that path optimal and is it efficient?

The path is *optimal* if it is consistent with each individual maximising lifetime utility. Consider a representative individual in a steady state. The lifetime utility of this individual is given by:

$$\Lambda^Y = U(C^Y) + \left(\frac{1}{1+\rho}\right) U(C^O) \tag{4.53}$$

By dealing with a representative agent, we can easily scale up to the whole economy.

The economy-wide steady state budget constraint is found as follows. Substitute (4.36) into (4.34) to give:

$$Y_t + (1 - \delta)K_t - K_{t+1} = L_{t-1}C_t^O + L_t C_t^Y \tag{4.54}$$

Putting this in per capita form, incorporating the per capita technology constraint ($y_t = f(k_t)$) and imposing the steady state ($k_{t+1} = k_t = k$)[18] gives the economy-wide steady state budget constraint:

$$f(k) - (n + \delta)k = C^Y + \frac{C^O}{1+n} \tag{4.55}$$

Equation (4.55) shows that at any particular moment in time, the consumption of the young and old individuals in the economy cannot exceed output after allowing for the depreciation of existing capital and the new capital needed for the growing population.

Along the optimal golden-age path, the steady state budget constraint is satisfied, as are the following FOCs:

$$(1 + \rho)\frac{U'(C^Y)}{U'(C^O)} = 1 + n \tag{4.56}$$

$$f'(k) = n + \delta \tag{4.57}$$

These are the conditions for efficiency in the economy. Samuelson called them the *biological interest rate consumption golden rule* and the *production golden rule*. They can be compared with the conditions that arise in market equilibrium (see (4.8) and (4.32)):

$$(1 + \rho)\frac{U'(C_t^Y)}{U'(C_{t+1}^0)} = 1 + r_{t+1} \tag{4.58}$$

$$f'(k_{t+1}) = r_{t+1} + \delta \tag{4.59}$$

The two sets of conditions will be the same if the market interest rate equals the population growth rate:

$$r = f'(k) - \delta = n \tag{4.60}$$

---

[18] This implies that the capital stock, like the labour supply, grows at the rate n.

In general, this condition will not hold, so the market economy is not guaranteed to allocate resources efficiently over time. If the steady state interest rate is below the population growth rate ($r < n$), the economy will become *dynamically inefficient*: there will be an overaccumulation of capital (excess savings), and consumption in youth will be too low to maximise the lifetime utility of the representative agent. The capital stock will become so large that its productivity is lowered by the need to devote resources both to maintaining it and to give newborn workers the same level of capital stock as existing workers. Such a situation is not *Pareto-optimal*:[19] every generation could be made better off by reducing the capital stock and increasing consumption.

In the case of the unit-elastic model, the steady state interest rate is found by substituting the steady state capital–labour ratio from (4.51) into (4.59):

$$r = \left(\frac{(1 - \varepsilon_L)(1 + n)(2 + \rho)}{\varepsilon_L} \right) - \delta \qquad (4.61)$$

Blanchard and Fischer (1989, p. 147) used the following calibration, based on two equal periods of life of 30 years. The share of labour in national income is $\varepsilon_L = 0.75$. Population grows at 1% p.a., so $n = 1.01^{30} - 1 = 0.348$. Capital depreciates at 5% p.a., so $\delta = 1 - 0.95^{30} = 0.785$. If individuals are fairly impatient and have a pure discount rate of 3% p.a., then $\rho = 1.03^{30} - 1 = 1.427$. Using (4.61), $r = 0.754$, which is much bigger than n. If, on the other hand, individuals are fairly patient and have a pure discount rate of 1% p.a., $\rho = 1.01^{30} - 1 = 0.348$ and $r = 0.269$, which is below n. The rate of time preference would have to be above 1.4% p.a. for *dynamic efficiency* (i.e., $r > n$) to hold.

4.2 PENSIONS IN THE DIAMOND–SAMUELSON OLG MODEL WITH EXOGENOUS LABOUR SUPPLY AND RETIREMENT

The Diamond–Samuelson OLG model can be used to study the impact of pension schemes. In addition to assuming that lifetimes are fixed, we will also assume that the labour supply and retirement decisions are exogenous.

---

[19] A Pareto-optimal allocation of resources is one for which no reallocation of resources will make one individual better off without making someone else worse off.

4.2.1 State Pension Scheme

We will consider first a state pension scheme. Suppose the government introduces a state pension (or social security) scheme that is paid for by lump-sum taxes (T_t) and transfers (P_t) between the young and old generations. The budget constraints of an individual in its two life periods are:

$$C_t^Y + S_t = W_t - T_t \qquad (4.62)$$

$$C_{t+1}^O = (1 + r_{t+1})S_t + P_{t+1} \qquad (4.63)$$

The lifetime budget constraint for this individual is:

$$W_t - T_t + \frac{P_{t+1}}{1 + r_{t+1}} = C_t^Y + \frac{C_{t+1}^O}{1 + r_{t+1}} \qquad (4.64)$$

Lifetime wealth consists of after-tax wages when young and the present value of the pension to be received when old.

There are two types of pension system, a fully-funded system and an unfunded (pay-as-you-go, or PAYG) system.

Fully-Funded State Pension Scheme

In a fully-funded scheme, the government invests the contributions of the young and pays out these with interest as a pension when that generation retires. The pension is therefore determined as follows:

$$P_{t+1} = (1 + r_{t+1})T_t \qquad (4.65)$$

One of the key properties of a fully-funded system is its *neutrality*: an economy with a fully-funded system is identical to an economy without a pension system. This is shown as follows. Substituting (4.65) into (4.64) gives:

$$W_t = C_t^Y + \frac{C_{t+1}^O}{1 + r_{t+1}} \qquad (4.66)$$

which shows that the tax and pension elements of the scheme vanish from the individual's lifetime budget constraint and hence do not influence the individual's optimal lifecycle consumption plan. That is, C_t^Y and C_{t+1}^O are precisely what they would be in an economy without a pension system. We first came across this neutrality result in Section 3.2 when discussing Blinder (1981).

This means that the sum of savings and tax is determined by:

$$S_t + T_t = S(W_t, r_{t+1}) \qquad (4.67)$$

Whatever level of lump-sum tax set by the government, the individual's personal savings will be adjusted to satisfy (4.67). If the government sets a high level of tax, which indicates a high pension in retirement, private savings for future retirement will be offsettingly low and vice versa.

What happens to the taxes collected? A key requirement of the neutrality result is that the government uses the tax receipts productively by lending them to firms to pay for productive capital, in precisely the same way that individual personal savings are used. The economy-wide capital stock is:

$$K_t = K_t^H + K_t^G \qquad (4.68)$$

where K_t^H is the capital stock owned by individuals and $K_t^G = L_{t-1}T_{t-1}$ is the capital stock owned by the government.

Factor prices are unchanged:

$$W_t = f(k_t) - k_t f'(k_t) \qquad (4.69)$$

$$r_{t+1} + \delta = f'(k_{t+1}) \qquad (4.70)$$

The economy-wide budget constraint is unchanged:

$$Y_t + (1 - \delta)K_t = C_t + K_{t+1} \qquad (4.71)$$

Finally, the formula for total consumption is unchanged:

$$C_t = Y_t + (1 - \delta)K_t - L_t(S_t + T_t) \qquad (4.72)$$

This is shown as follows. Aggregate consumption is the sum of consumption by the old and consumption by the young (using (4.33)):

$$
\begin{aligned}
C_t &= L_{t-1}C_t^O + L_t C_t^Y \\
&= \left\{ (r_t + \delta)\, K_t^H + (1 - \delta)\, K_t^H + L_{t-1}P_t \right\} + \left\{ L_t\, (W_t - S_t - T_t) \right\} \\
&= Y_t + (1 - \delta)\, K_t^H - (r_t + \delta)\, K_t^G + L_{t-1}P_t - L_t\, (S_t + T_t) \\
&= Y_t + (1 - \delta)\, K_t - L_t\, (S_t + T_t) + \left[L_{t-1}P_t - (1 + r_t)\, K_t^G \right] \\
&= Y_t + (1 - \delta)\, K_t - L_t\, (S_t + T_t) \qquad (4.73)
\end{aligned}
$$

since:

$$L_{t-1}P_t - (1 + r_t)K_t^G = L_{t-1}[P_t - (1 + r_t)T_{t-1}] = 0 \qquad (4.74)$$

So an economy with a fully-funded state pension system, where the government invests the taxes in the productive capital stock, has an identical outcome as an economy with no pension system. This result is fairly intuitive. Since individuals know that the government is only carrying out the savings that they would be doing anyway (and earning the same rate of interest), these individuals will only be concerned about the total level of savings $(S_t + T_t)$ and not its composition.

This neutrality result only goes through, however, if the level of taxation does not exceed the level of savings that individuals would make in the absence of a state pension system. This requires:

$$T_t < (1 + n)k_{t+1} \tag{4.75}$$

If the inequality in (4.75) is reversed, there is forced oversaving and the neutrality result disappears (see Section 3.2).

Unfunded State Pension Scheme

In an unfunded PAYG system, the pensions of the old are paid by taxes *in the same period*.

Since in period t, there are L_{t-1} pensioners each receiving pensions of P_t, and L_t young workers each paying in taxes of T_t, the PAYG system balance is given by:

$$L_{t-1}P_t = L_t T_t \tag{4.76}$$

which implies:

$$P_t = \frac{L_t}{L_{t-1}}T_t \tag{4.77}$$
$$= (1 + n)T_t$$

which demonstrates that the rate of return on the PAYG pension system is equal to n, the population growth rate.

Suppose that the contribution rate for the system is held constant over time $(T_{t+1} = T_t = T)$, so that $P_t = (1 + n)T$.

Now the lifetime budget constraint for the individual is (using (4.64)):

$$\hat{W}_t \equiv W_t - \left(\frac{r_{t+1} - n}{1 + r_{t+1}}\right)T = C_t^Y + \frac{C_{t+1}^O}{1 + r_{t+1}} \tag{4.78}$$

The equation shows the *Aaron* (1966) *condition*, the condition under which a PAYG pension system is superior to a funded one. If $n > r_{t+1}$, lifetime wealth will be higher with a PAYG scheme than a funded one

($\hat{W}_t > W$). The contribution (T) will be viewed as a subsidy by a young individual: the individual is getting a return (n) on his investment in the PAYG scheme that exceeds the return (r_{t+1}) he would get if he saved for his pension privately. The opposite holds if $n < r_{t+1}$: now the contribution will be viewed as a tax.

The individual maximises lifetime utility:

$$\Lambda_t^Y = U(C_t^Y) + \left(\frac{1}{1+\rho}\right) U(C_{t+1}^O) \tag{4.79}$$

subject to (4.78). The consumption Euler equation takes the familiar general form:

$$(1+\rho)\frac{U'(C_t^Y)}{U'(C_{t+1}^O)} = 1 + r_{t+1} \tag{4.80}$$

In the unit-elastic model (where utility is logarithmic and the production function is constant-returns-to-scale Cobb–Douglas), the optimal consumption plan is:

$$(C_t^Y)^* = \left(\frac{1+\rho}{2+\rho}\right) \hat{W}_t \tag{4.81}$$

$$(C_{t+1}^O)^* = \left(\frac{1+r_{t+1}}{2+\rho}\right) \hat{W}_t \tag{4.82}$$

and the savings function is:

$$\begin{aligned}
S_t &= W_t - T - C_t^Y \\
&= W_t - T - \left(\frac{1+\rho}{2+\rho}\right)\left[W_t - \left(\frac{r_{t+1}-n}{1+r_{t+1}}\right)T\right] \\
&= \left(\frac{1}{2+\rho}\right) W_t - \left[1 - \left(\frac{1+\rho}{2+\rho}\right)\left(\frac{r_{t+1}-n}{1+r_{t+1}}\right)\right] T \\
&= S(W_t, r_{t+1}, T)
\end{aligned} \tag{4.83}$$

We can show that:

$$\begin{aligned}
&S_W \in (0,1) \\
&S_r > 0 \\
&S_T \in (-1,0) \text{ if } r_{t+1} > n \\
&S_T < -1 \text{ if } r_{t+1} < n
\end{aligned} \tag{4.84}$$

The key difference between a PAYG and a funded system is that the former does not lead to capital accumulation (there is simply a transfer between the young and the old in the same time period), whereas the latter does.

In a PAYG system, only private savings influence the capital stock, so the capital market equilibrium condition is:

$$L_t S_t = K_{t+1} \tag{4.85}$$

This is demonstrated as follows. Consumption by the old is:

$$L_{t-1} C_t^O = (r_t + \delta) K_t + (1 - \delta) K_t + L_{t-1} P_t \tag{4.86}$$

while consumption of the young is:

$$L_t C_t^Y = L_t (W_t - S_t - T_t) \tag{4.87}$$

so that aggregate consumption is (using (4.33)):

$$\begin{aligned}
C_t &= (r_t + \delta) K_t + (1 - \delta) K_t + L_{t-1} P_t + L_t (W_t - S_t - T_t) \\
&= Y_t + (1 - \delta) K_t + [L_{t-1} P_t - L_t T_t] - L_t S_t \\
&= Y_t + (1 - \delta) K_t - L_t S_t
\end{aligned} \tag{4.88}$$

since $[L_{t-1} P_t - L_t T_t] = 0$. Substituting (4.88) into the budget constraint for the economy:

$$Y_t + (1 - \delta) K_t = C_t + K_{t+1} \tag{4.89}$$

gives (4.85).

Substituting (4.83) into (4.85) gives:

$$S(W_t, r_{t+1}, T) = (1 + n) k_{t+1} \tag{4.90}$$

which shows how future capital is linked to current savings with a PAYG system.

With a Cobb–Douglas production function ($y_t = k_t^{1-\varepsilon_L}$), the factor price equations become:

$$W_t = W(k_t) = \varepsilon_L k_t^{1-\varepsilon_L} \tag{4.91}$$

$$r_{t+1} = r(k_{t+1}) = (1 - \varepsilon_L) k_{t+1}^{-\varepsilon_L} - \delta \tag{4.92}$$

Substituting these into (4.90), gives the fundamental difference equation describing the path of the economy with a PAYG system:

$$k_{t+1} = g(k_t, T) \tag{4.93}$$

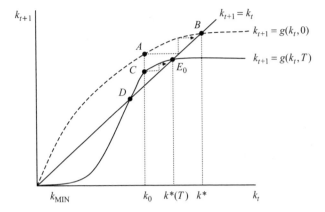

Figure 4.5 PAYG pensions in the unit-elastic model
Source: Heijdra and van der Ploeg (2002). Reproduced by permission of Oxford University Press

The partial derivatives are:

$$g_k \equiv \frac{\partial g}{\partial k_t} = \frac{S_W W'(k_t)}{1 + n - S_r r'(k_{t+1})} > 0 \qquad (4.94)$$

$$g_T \equiv \frac{\partial g}{\partial T} = \frac{S_T}{1 + n - S_r r'(k_{t+1})} < 0 \qquad (4.95)$$

where S_W and S_r come from (4.90).

Equation (4.93) is shown in Figure 4.5. It has an elongated S-shape. This can be seen by writing out the difference equation in full:

$$(1+n)k_{t+1} = \frac{W(k_t) - T}{2 + \rho} - \left(\frac{1+\rho}{2+\rho}\right)\left(\frac{(1+n)T}{1+r(k_{t+1})}\right) \qquad (4.96)$$

As $k_{t+1} \to 0$, the second term on the right-hand side of (4.96) vanishes, since $r_{t+1}(k_{t+1}) \to +\infty$. Therefore $W(k_{MIN}) = T$. The PAYG system is not feasible when $k_t < k_{MIN}$, since the wage rate is too low ($W(k_t) < T$).

Differentiating the difference equation gives:

$$\frac{dk_{t+1}}{dk_t} = \frac{W'(k_t)}{(1+n)[2 + \rho + (1 + \rho)T \psi(k_{t+1})]} \geq 0 \qquad (4.97)$$

where:

$$\psi(k_{t+1}) = \frac{-r'(k_{t+1})}{[1 + r(k_{t+1})]^2} \qquad (4.98)$$

Equation (4.98) satisfies the following:

$$\begin{cases} \psi(k_{t+1}) \to \infty \text{ as } k_{t+1} \to 0 \\ \psi(k_{t+1}) \to 0 \text{ as } k_{t+1} \to \infty \end{cases} \quad (4.99)$$

Also $W'(k_t) \to 0$ as $k_t \to \infty$ and $W'(k_{MIN}) > 0$.

Taking all these factors into account implies that $g(k_t, T)$:

- is horizontal at $k_t = k_{MIN}$;
- is upward sloping for $k_t > k_{MIN}$;
- becomes horizontal as k_t becomes very large.

It therefore follows that $g(k_t, T)$ intersects the steady state line $k_{t+1} = k_t$ twice.

The dashed line in Figure 4.5 is the unit-elastic model without a PAYG system and the economy converges to point B. For example, if the initial capital–labour ratio is k_0, the economy will move from A to the steady state at B.

Suppose a PAYG system is introduced in period $t = 0$, when the initial capital–labour ratio is k_0. The old generation receives a pension of $P = (1 + n)T$ even though they have contributed nothing to the pension system. This is known as a *windfall gain* and the old spend it entirely on increased consumption (since they have no bequest motive):

$$C_0^O = (1 + n)[(1 + r(k_0))k_0 + T)] \quad (4.100)$$

Since the interest rate is predetermined (as a consequence of k_0 being predetermined), it follows that:

$$\frac{dC_0^O}{dT} = 1 + n > 0 \quad (4.101)$$

The old generation are therefore unambiguously better off.

The effect on the young generation is ambiguous. First, they must pay taxes T in the current period, but receive a pension of $(1 + n)T$ when they retire. The net effect of the two transactions is to change lifetime income by:

$$\frac{\partial \hat{W}_0}{\partial T} = -\left(\frac{r(k_1) - n}{1 + r(k_1)}\right) \underset{>}{\overset{<}{=}} 0 \quad (4.102)$$

depending on whether $r(k_1)$ is greater or less than the population growth rate n. Second, what happens to k_1 itself and therefore $r(k_1)$ depends on the savings of the young in period $t = 0$.

However, (4.90), (4.93) and (4.95) indicate that the overall effect of introducing a PAYG system (at time $t = 0$) is to reduce savings by the young and hence next period's capital stock ($dS/dT = (1 + n)dk_1/dT = (1 + n)g_T < 0$). In Figure 4.5, this is represented by AC. In the period immediately following the introduction of the PAYG system, the capital stock falls from A to C and thereafter converges to the final steady state of E_0. The capital stock always remains below the level without a PAYG system, both in the transition and in the steady state.

The long-run effect on the capital–labour ratio is found by imposing the steady state ($k_{t+1} = k_t$) on (4.93):

$$\frac{dk}{dT} = \frac{g_T}{1 - g_k} < 0 \qquad (4.103)$$

where $g_k \in (0, 1)$ follows from the stability condition. The steady state wage is lower (since $W'(k_t) > 0$) and the interest rate is higher (since $r'(k_t) < 0$).

The key point about a PAYG system, in contrast with a fully-funded system, is its *non-neutrality*: it leads to the crowding out of capital, a lower wage rate and a higher interest rate.

Although the first generation to receive the PAYG pension is better off, is the welfare of the steady state generation better off following the introduction of the PAYG system? To address this question, we need to work with the indirect utility function and the factor-price frontier.

The steady state *indirect utility function* is defined as:

$$\bar{\Lambda}^Y(W, r, T) = \underset{\{C^Y, C^O\}}{Max} \left\{ \Lambda^Y(C^Y, C^O) \, subject \, to \, \hat{W} = C^Y + \frac{C^O}{1 + r} \right\} \qquad (4.104)$$

where $\Lambda^Y(C^Y, C^O)$ is the steady state *direct utility function* (see (4.79)) and

$$\hat{W} \equiv W - \left(\frac{r - n}{1 + r}\right) T \qquad (4.105)$$

is lifetime income with a PAYG system.

The indirect utility function shows the maximum attainable utility, given income and the interest and tax rates; this contrasts with the direct utility function which shows the maximum attainable utility, given consumption in the two periods of life. The indirect utility function is found by substituting the values for optimal consumption into the direct utility function. The following identity holds:

$$\bar{\Lambda}^Y(W, r, T) \equiv \Lambda(C^Y(W, r, T)^*, C^O(W, r, T)^*) \tag{4.106}$$

where $C^Y(W, r, T)^*$ and $C^O(W, r, T)^*$ are the optimal consumption in youth and old age.

With logarithmic utility the indirect utility function:

$$\bar{\Lambda}^Y = \omega_0 + \left(\frac{2+\rho}{1+\rho}\right) \ln \hat{W} + \left(\frac{1}{1+\rho}\right) \ln(1+r) \tag{4.107}$$

where ω_0 is a constant.

The indirect utility function has the following properties:

$$\frac{\partial \bar{\Lambda}^Y}{\partial W} = \frac{\partial \Lambda^Y}{\partial C^Y} > 0 \tag{4.108}$$

$$\frac{\partial \bar{\Lambda}^Y}{\partial r} = \left(\frac{S}{1+r}\right) \frac{\partial \Lambda^Y}{\partial C^Y} > 0 \tag{4.109}$$

$$\frac{\partial \bar{\Lambda}^Y}{\partial T} = -\left(\frac{r-n}{1+r}\right) \frac{\partial \Lambda^Y}{\partial C^Y} \stackrel{>}{<} 0 \tag{4.110}$$

These are proved as follows. If we take the direct utility function evaluated at steady state values:

$$\Lambda^Y(C^Y, C^O) = U(C^Y) + \left(\frac{1}{1+\rho}\right) U(C^O) \tag{4.111}$$

partially differentiate it and utilise the consumption Euler equation (at steady state values):

$$(1+\rho) \frac{U'(C^Y)}{U'(C^O)} = 1 + r \tag{4.112}$$

we get:

$$\frac{\partial \bar{\Lambda}^Y}{\partial W} = \frac{\partial \Lambda^Y}{\partial C^Y} \left[\frac{\partial C^Y}{\partial W} + \left(\frac{1}{1+r}\right) \frac{\partial C^O}{\partial W}\right] = \frac{\partial \Lambda^Y}{\partial C^Y} \tag{4.113}$$

since from the lifetime budget constraint:

$$\hat{W} = C^Y + \frac{C^O}{1+r} \tag{4.114}$$

the term in square brackets is equal to unity.

In the same way:

$$
\begin{aligned}
\frac{\partial \bar{\Lambda}^Y}{\partial r} &= \frac{\partial \Lambda^Y}{\partial C^Y}\left[\frac{\partial C^Y}{\partial r} + \left(\frac{1}{1+r}\right)\frac{\partial C^O}{\partial r}\right] \\
&= \frac{\partial \Lambda^Y}{\partial C^Y}\left[\frac{C^O - (1+n)T}{(1+r)^2}\right] \\
&= \frac{\partial \Lambda^Y}{\partial C^Y}\left[\frac{(1+r)S}{(1+r)^2}\right]
\end{aligned}
\tag{4.115}
$$

Similarly:

$$
\begin{aligned}
\frac{\partial \bar{\Lambda}^Y}{\partial T} &= \frac{\partial \Lambda^Y}{\partial C^Y}\left[\frac{\partial C^Y}{\partial T} + \left(\frac{1}{1+r}\right)\frac{\partial C^O}{\partial T}\right] \\
&= -\left(\frac{r-n}{1+r}\right)\frac{\partial \Lambda^Y}{\partial C^Y}
\end{aligned}
\tag{4.116}
$$

where the second line follows from (4.105).

Equations (4.108) and (4.109) show that steady state welfare responds positively to factor prices. However, factor prices respond in opposite directions to tax changes in the long run:

$$
\frac{dW}{dT} = W'(k)\frac{dk}{dT} < 0
\tag{4.117}
$$

$$
\frac{dr}{dT} = r'(k)\frac{dk}{dT} > 0
\tag{4.118}
$$

Equation (4.118) shows that the introduction of a PAYG system crowds out private capital and so raises the interest rate. Equation (4.117) shows that the lower capital per worker reduces the marginal product of labour and hence the wage rate.

But the changes in W and r are not independent of each other, since they both depend on the capital–labour ratio:

$$
W = f(k) - kf'(k)
\tag{4.119}
$$

$$
r + \delta = f'(k)
\tag{4.120}
$$

so that

$$
\begin{aligned}
W &= f(k) - k(r + \delta) \\
&= \phi(r)
\end{aligned}
\tag{4.121}
$$

which defines the *factor–price frontier*. This shows the necessary relationship between W and r for the equilibrium conditions (4.119) and (4.120) to hold.

This implies that:

$$\frac{dW}{dr} = \phi'(r) = -k \tag{4.122}$$

$$\frac{d^2W}{dr^2} = \phi''(r) = -\frac{dk}{dr} = -\frac{1}{f''(k)} \tag{4.123}$$

The factor–price frontier for a Cobb–Douglas production function is:

$$W = \varepsilon_L \left(\frac{1 - \varepsilon_L}{r + \delta} \right)^{(1-\varepsilon_L)/\varepsilon_L} \tag{4.124}$$

which is convex to the origin in $w - r$ space.

We now have the tools to assess the welfare effects of the introduction of a PAYG system. Differentiating the indirect utility function with respect to T:

$$
\begin{aligned}
\frac{d\bar{\Lambda}^Y}{dT} &= \frac{\partial \bar{\Lambda}^Y}{\partial W}\frac{dW}{dT} + \frac{\partial \bar{\Lambda}^Y}{\partial r}\frac{dr}{dT} + \frac{\partial \bar{\Lambda}^Y}{\partial T} \\
&= \frac{\partial \Lambda^Y}{\partial C^Y}\left[\frac{dW}{dT} + \left(\frac{S}{1+r}\right)\frac{dr}{dT} - \left(\frac{r-n}{1+r}\right)\right] \\
&= -\frac{\partial \Lambda^Y}{\partial C^Y}\left(\frac{r-n}{1+r}\right)\left[1 + k\frac{dr}{dT}\right] \propto \operatorname{sgn}(n-r)
\end{aligned}
\tag{4.125}
$$

using (4.104), (4.105), (4.108)–(4.110) and $S = (1 + n)k$. The term in square brackets shows the two effects on welfare of the introduction of a PAYG system. The first is the direct effect of T on lifetime income and the second is the indirect effect of T on the interest rate. Both effects work in the same direction, which will be positive if $n > r$ and negative if $n < r$.

Suppose the economy is initially dynamically inefficient with too much capital (i.e., $n > r$). The introduction of a PAYG system will increase welfare (a result first proved by Aaron, 1966). This is because there is oversaving by the young generation which drives down the interest rate. The introduction of a PAYG system partially substitutes private saving for 'saving' for a PAYG pension. The return on the latter (which equals the biological interest rate, n) exceeds the former (r). Although the reduction in the capital stock lowers the wage, this is more than offset by the increase in the interest rate in a dynamically inefficient economy. However, if the economy happens to be in golden-rule equilibrium ($n = r$), the introduction of a PAYG system has no effect on steady state welfare.

4.2.2   The Equivalence of PAYG and Government Debt

Auerbach and Kotlikoff (1987) showed that a PAYG system is equivalent to a type of government debt policy, namely debt-financed fiscal policy. The PAYG system leads to an additional asset, government bonds, being introduced alongside capital.

To see this, we need to introduce the *government budget constraint*:

$$\Delta B_{t+1} \equiv B_{t+1} - B_t = r B_t + L_{t-1} P_t - L_t T_t \tag{4.126}$$

where B_t is the size of the national debt (i.e., stock of government bonds) at the beginning of period t, B_{t+1} is the size of the national debt at the end of period t, and $r B_t$ is the debt service charge in period t (interest on government bonds). Pensions to the old generation are paid for by taxes from the young generation and additional borrowing, ΔB_{t+1}.

Since the interest on government bonds is the same as the interest on capital, individuals will be indifferent to the composition of savings across the two assets.

Individuals maximise lifetime utility:

$$\Lambda_t^Y \left(C_t^Y, C_{t+1}^O \right) = U \left(C_t^Y \right) + \left(\frac{1}{1+\rho} \right) U \left(C_{t+1}^O \right) \tag{4.127}$$

subject to the lifetime budget constraint:

$$\hat{W}_t \equiv W_t - T_t + \frac{P_{t+1}}{1 + r_{t+1}} = C_t^Y + \frac{C_{t+1}^O}{1 + r_{t+1}} \tag{4.128}$$

The optimal savings function is:

$$S_t = S(\hat{W}_t, r_{t+1}) \tag{4.129}$$

Savings can be used to hold the capital stock or government bonds, so the capital market equilibrium condition is:

$$L_t S_t = B_{t+1} + K_{t+1} \tag{4.130}$$

This is demonstrated as follows. Consumption by the old is:

$$L_{t-1} C_t^O = (r_t + \delta) K_t + (1 - \delta) K_t + (1 + r_t) B_t + L_{t-1} P_t \tag{4.131}$$

while consumption by the young is:

$$L_t C_t^Y = L_t (W_t - S_t - T_t) \tag{4.132}$$

so that aggregate consumption is (using (4.33)):

$$
\begin{aligned}
C_t &= (r_t + \delta)K_t + (1 - \delta)K_t + (1 + r_t)B_t + L_{t-1}P_t + L_t(W_t - S_t - T_t) \\
&= Y_t + (1 - \delta)K_t + [(1 + r_t)B_t + L_{t-1}P_t - L_t T_t] - L_t S_t \\
&= Y_t + (1 - \delta)K_t + B_{t+1} - L_t S_t
\end{aligned}
$$

$$(4.133)$$

since $[L_{t-1}P_t - L_t T_t] = 0$ and assuming new bonds are issued to cover the debt service charge. Substituting (4.133) into the budget constraint for the economy:

$$
Y_t + (1 - \delta)\, K_t = C_t + K_{t+1} \tag{4.134}
$$

and rearranging gives (4.130).

The equivalence proposition of Auerbach and Kotlikoff is as follows. For a given economy with a particular level of government debt, there is a corresponding economy without government debt, but with a set of age-specific lump-sum taxes and transfers that generates the same equilibrium in terms of time paths for (young and old) consumption and the capital stock $\left\{C_t^Y, C_t^O, k_t\right\}_{t=0}^{\infty}$.

To demonstrate this equivalence, we need the following set of equations:

$$
C_t^O = (1 + r(k_t))(1 + n)(k_t + b_t) + P_t \tag{4.135}
$$

the consumption equation for an old individual

$$
U'(C_t^Y) = \left(\frac{1 + r(k_{t+1})}{1 + \rho}\right) U'(C_{t+1}^O) \tag{4.136}
$$

the consumption Euler equation for a young individual

$$
W(k_t) - T_t - C_t^Y = S_t = (1 + n)(k_{t+1} + b_{t+1}) \tag{4.137}
$$

the budget constraint of a young individual

$$
(1 + n)b_{t+1} = (1 + r(k_t))b_t + \frac{P_t}{1 + n} - T_t \tag{4.138}
$$

the per capita government budget constraint, where $b_t = B_t/L_t$ is the per capita national debt, k_0 and b_0 are given, and

$$
W(k_t) = f(k_t) - k_t f'(k_t) \tag{4.139}
$$
$$
r(k_t) = f'(k_t) - \delta \tag{4.140}
$$

the factor pricing equations.

Government policy impacts the model in two ways. First, the government transfers resources in the form of debt service and pensions to the old:

$$\Gamma_t^{GO} = (1 + r(k_t))(1 + n)b_t + P_t \qquad (4.141)$$

Second, the government receives resources in the form of bond purchases and taxes from the young:

$$\Gamma_t^{YG} = (1 + n)b_{t+1} + T_t \qquad (4.142)$$

The net transfer of resources to the government is:

$$L_t\Gamma_t^{YG} - L_{t-1}\Gamma_t^{GO} = 0 \qquad (4.143)$$

which follows from equation (4.138). Since we assume that government consumption is zero, the government merely takes from the young and transfers it all to the old. Once Γ_t^{YG} is set, we know:

$$\Gamma_t^{GO} = (1 + n)\Gamma_t^{YG} \qquad (4.144)$$

To show the equivalence result, we need to show that the individual components of the government budget constraint (b_{t+1}, b_t, P_t, T_t) are irrelevant to the determination of the optimal paths of (young and old) consumption and the capital stock.

Consider two specific government policies with the following sets of components for the government budget constraint:

- The first is associated with a tax-financed PAYG pension system with no government debt: $b_t' = 0$, $T_t' = T$ and $P_t' = (1 + n)T$.
- The second is associated with a debt-financed fiscal policy in which there are only taxes on the young and no pension system: $b_t'' = T/(1 + r_t)$, $T_t'' = T - (1 + n)b_{t+1}''$ and $P_t'' = 0$.

Both these policies will lead to the same time paths for (young and old) consumption and the capital stock $\{C_t^Y, C_t^O, k_t\}_{t=0}^{\infty}$ because the time paths for the resource transfers from the young to the government and from the government to the old $\{\Gamma_t^{YG}, \Gamma_t^{GO}\}_{t=0}^{\infty}$ are the same under both policies.

This can be seen by substituting the above conditions into (4.142) and (4.141). For the first policy we have:

$$(\Gamma_t^{YG})' = (1 + n)b_{t+1}' + T_t' = T \qquad (4.145)$$

$$(\Gamma_t^{GO})' = (1 + r(k_t))(1 + n)b_t' + P_t' = (1 + n)T \qquad (4.146)$$

For the second policy, we have:

$$\left(\Gamma_t^{YG}\right)'' = (1+n)b''_{t+1} + T''_t = (1+n)b''_{t+1} + T - (1+n)b''_{t+1} = T$$
(4.147)

$$\left(\Gamma_t^{GO}\right)'' = (1+r_t)(1+n)b''_t + P''_t = (1+r_t)(1+n)\frac{T}{(1+r_t)}$$

$$= (1+n)T$$
(4.148)

As a result, equations (4.135)–(4.138) will be the same for both policies, so a debt-financed fiscal policy with age-related taxes and transfers is identical to a PAYG pension system.

4.2.3 Transitional and Welfare Effects

The analysis above examined the welfare effects of a PAYG system on the steady state generations and showed the conditions under which these generations would be better off: the steady state economy had to be dynamically inefficient ($n > r$).

We now consider the transitional costs of moving from the initial growth path to the golden-rule path. Different generations are affected differently.

At the time of the introduction of the PAYG system, the old generation is unambiguously better off. The amount they gain in the last period of their life is (see (4.101)):

$$U'\left(C_0^O\right)\frac{dC_0^O}{dT} = U'\left(C_0^O\right)(1+n) > 0$$
(4.149)

and they have contributed nothing for this gain.

The transition generation will, like the subsequent steady state generations, also gain if the economy is dynamically inefficient. This is because when the population is growing sufficiently rapidly ($n > r$), it is easy for each generation to pay the pensions of the previous generation. The transitional young generation (the one that suddenly has to pay the taxes that are paid out to the old generation as a state pension) knows that the generations following it will be large enough to easily honour the promise of paying a pension to it. Every generation is better off and no generation is worse off, so the introduction of a PAYG pension system is Pareto-improving (and therefore socially desirable) in a dynamically inefficient economy.

However, Abel *et al.* (1989) showed that developed economies are unlikely to be dynamically inefficient. When economies are dynamically efficient ($r > n$), equation (4.125) shows that the steady state generations (and the transitional young generation) will be worse off with the introduction of a PAYG system, even though the transitional old generation will be better off (see (4.149)).

Since one generation is better off and all other generations are worse off, the introduction of the PAYG system is no longer Pareto-improving, but is it socially desirable? This depends on the form of the *social welfare function* that the economy, through its political and social institutions, adopts. The social welfare function weights the lifetime utilities of different generations:

$$SW_t = w \left(\Lambda_{t-1}^Y, \Lambda_t^Y, \ldots, \Lambda_\infty^Y \right) \tag{4.150}$$

Some political/social systems might value the welfare of the elderly more highly than that of the young; others might value the welfare of the current living generations more highly than those of future generations as yet unborn, and so on.

Suppose policy A yields a higher value for (4.150) than policy B, then policy A is socially preferred to policy B ($SW_t^A > SW_t^B$), even though some generations might be worse off under A than B.

4.2.4   From PAYG to a Funded Pension Scheme

Suppose there exists a PAYG pension system in a dynamically efficient economy. Although the first generation receiving this pension was better off, all other generations are worse off. Is it possible to move to a funded pension system in such an economy in a way that is Pareto-improving?

It is an important question, since we know that when $r > n$, the steady state generations gain from the removal of a PAYG system (see (4.125), which shows that $d\bar{\Lambda}^Y/dT < 0$, so that as T falls, $\bar{\Lambda}^Y$ will increase). However, the (transition) generation, that is young at the time of the switch, loses out. It has to pay twice for its pension. It has paid taxes to pay for the PAYG pensions of the old generation in expectation of receiving a PAYG pension when it gets old, a pension that will no longer be paid. It also has to start contributing to its own funded pension scheme. So if nothing else happens, the transitional generation is unambiguously worse off by the introduction of the funded system.

But is it possible for the future steady state generations who will be better off to compensate the transition generation? Can enough of the welfare gains of the steady state generations be transferred to the transition generation to compensate it for the welfare loss it will experience from the policy switch? In other words, can a mechanism be found to make the policy switch Pareto-improving? These questions were asked by Breyer (1989). One common policy for switching welfare gains and losses between generations is bond policy, which can break the link between the taxes on the young $(L_t T_t)$ and the pension payments to the old in the same generation $(L_{t-1} P_t)$. Breyer found that, so long as labour supply is exogenous, no such bond path could be found to improve the welfare of the transition generation without making at least one future generation worse off. In other words, there was no Pareto-improving way of moving to a funded pension system when labour supply is exogenous.

4.3   PAYG PENSIONS IN THE DIAMOND–SAMUELSON OLG MODEL WITH ENDOGENOUS LABOUR SUPPLY AND RETIREMENT

As we have seen, a PAYG system influences the savings of the young generation. It also influences the timing of retirement, a point first recognised by Feldstein (1974). To account for this, we need to make the labour supply decision of the young generation endogenous: individuals can decide how much to work. The model up to now has assumed that the labour supply was fixed. We also make the contribution to the PAYG system proportional to income, in contrast with the fixed lump-sum contribution amount that has been levied so far. Finally, we assume that the pension is actuarially and intragenerationally fair: someone who works harder than someone else gets a correspondingly higher pension, in contrast with the fixed lump-sum pension awarded to all those who have retired. These assumptions are clearly more realistic than the previous ones, but as a consequence of them, it is possible that the PAYG system distorts the optimal labour supply decisions of the young generation. We assume that the optimisation decision of the firm remains the same as in Section 4.2.

4.3.1   Individuals

The lifetime utility of a young individual i born at time t is:

$$\Lambda_t^{Y,i} = \Lambda^Y \left(C_t^{Y,i}, C_{t+1}^{O,i}, 1 - N_t^i \right) \qquad (4.151)$$

where N_t^i is labour supply and $(1 - N_t^i)$ is leisure, and full employment is given by $N_t^i = 1$.

Individual i's budget constraints in the two periods of his life are:

$$C_t^{Y,i} + S_t^i = W_t N_t^i - T_t^i \qquad (4.152)$$

$$C_{t+1}^{O,i} = (1 + r_{t+1}) S_t^i + P_{t+1}^i \qquad (4.153)$$

where:

$$T_t^i = \tau_L W_t N_t^i \qquad (4.154)$$

$$P_{t+1}^i = \left(\tau_L W_{t+1} \sum_{j=1}^{L_{t+1}} N_{t+1}^j \right) \left(\frac{N_t^i}{\sum_{j=1}^{L_t} N_t^j} \right) \qquad (4.155)$$

and where $\tau_L \in (0, 1)$ is the proportional income tax rate. Equation (4.154) shows that the contribution rate to the PAYG system is proportional to the labour income earned by individual i. Equation (4.155) shows the pension received by individual i. It is equal to individual i's relative labour supply share (second term in brackets) of the total tax revenue collected from the next generation (first term in brackets).

The lifetime budget constraint for individual i is:

$$W_t N_t^i - \tau_L \left(1 - \frac{W_{t+1} \sum_{j=1}^{L_{t+1}} N_{t+1}^j}{W_t (1 + r_{t+1}) \sum_{j=1}^{L_t} N_t^j} \right) W_t N_t^i = C_t^{Y,i} + \frac{C_{t+1}^{O,i}}{1 + r_{t+1}} \qquad (4.156)$$

It depends on both the wages earned by the next generation and the labour the next generation supplies in aggregate. This is because, in a PAYG system, the pension is paid by the next generation, and so depends on the size of that generation and the effort it puts in during its working life.

The FOCs for consumption in both periods and for labour supply (from maximising (4.151) subject to (4.156)) are:

$$\frac{\partial \Lambda^Y}{\partial C_{t+1}^{O,i}} = \left(\frac{1}{1 + r_{t+1}} \right) \left(\frac{\partial \Lambda^Y}{\partial C_t^{Y,i}} \right) \qquad (4.157)$$

$$\left(-\frac{\partial \Lambda^Y}{\partial N_t^i} \right) = \frac{\partial \Lambda^Y}{\partial (1 - N_t^i)} = (1 - \tau_{L,t}^E) W_t \left(\frac{\partial \Lambda^Y}{\partial C_t^{Y,i}} \right) \qquad (4.158)$$

$$\tau_{L,t}^E \equiv \tau_L \left[1 - \left(\frac{W_{t+1}}{W_t} \right) \left(\frac{\sum_{j=1}^{L_{t+1}} N_{t+1}^j}{\sum_{j=1}^{L_t} N_t^j} \right) \left(\frac{1}{1 + r_{t+1}} \right) \right] \qquad (4.159)$$

Equation (4.157) is the consumption Euler equation linking optimal consumption in both periods. Equation (4.158) shows that labour supply is determined so that the marginal rate of substitution between consumption and labour (and between consumption and leisure) during youth is equal to the after-tax wage rate. In other words, individuals choose to work up until the point where the marginal cost of an extra hour of work (the reduced utility from an hour of leisure foregone) is equal to the marginal benefit of an extra hour worked (the product of the after-tax wage and the utility from the additional consumption financed from spending these extra wages).

Equation (4.159) shows that it is the effective tax rate $\tau_{L,t}^E$, rather than the official tax rate τ_L, that determines labour supply (Breyer and Straub, 1993). To simplify matters, suppose that all individuals are identical or homogeneous (so that $N_t^i = N_t$ and we can drop the index i) and that the population grows at a constant rate n (so that $L_{t+1} = L_t(1+n)$). In this case, equation (4.159) becomes:

$$\tau_{L,t}^E \equiv \tau_L \left[1 - \left(\frac{W_{t+1}}{W_t} \right) \left(\frac{(1+n)N_{t+1}}{N_t} \right) \left(\frac{1}{1+r_{t+1}} \right) \right] \quad (4.160)$$

If labour supply is constant over time ($N_{t+1} = N_t$) and the Aaron condition holds (the growth rate of the population and wages exceeds the rate of interest), then $\tau_{L,t}^E < 0$, i.e., the PAYG system acts like an employment subsidy rather than a tax, a point also first recognised by Breyer and Straub (1993).

Optimal consumption in both periods and labour supply for the representative individual are:

$$\left(C_t^Y \right)^* = C^Y \left(W_t^N, r_{t+1} \right) \quad (4.161)$$

$$\left(C_{t+1}^O \right)^* = C^O \left(W_t^N, r_{t+1} \right) \quad (4.162)$$

$$\left(N_t \right)^* = N \left(W_t^N, r_{t+1} \right) \quad (4.163)$$

where:

$$W_t^N = W_t \left(1 - \tau_{L,t}^E \right) \quad (4.164)$$

is the net (after effective tax) wage rate.

The effect of a change in the official tax rate on the individual's labour supply decision is (in elasticity form):

$$\frac{\tau_L}{N_t} \frac{\partial N_t}{\partial \tau_L} = -\varepsilon_{W^N}^N \left(\frac{\tau_{L,t}^E}{1 - \tau_{L,t}^E} \right) \quad (4.165)$$

where:

$$\varepsilon_{W^N}^N = \frac{W^N}{N} \frac{\delta N}{\delta W^N} \tag{4.166}$$

is the (net wage rate) elasticity of labour supply.

The effect of the contribution rate on the supply of labour depends on whether:

- The Aaron condition is satisfied ($\tau_{L,t}^E < 0$) or not ($\tau_{L,t}^E > 0$).
- The substitution effect in labour supply dominates the income effect ($\varepsilon_{W^N}^N > 0$) or vice versa ($\varepsilon_{W^N}^N < 0$).

If the labour supply curve is upward sloping ($\varepsilon_{W^N}^N > 0$) and the Aaron condition holds ($\tau_{L,t}^E < 0$), an increase in the official tax rate decreases labour supply.

4.3.2 Market Equilibrium

We now aggregate across individuals to derive economy-wide relationships. The first point to note is that when labour supply is endogenous, the total number of workers in the economy (L_t) does not necessarily coincide with the amount of effective labour used in production ($L_t N_t$). However, by redefining the capital–labour ratio as $k_t \equiv K_t/(L_t N_t)$, the original factor pricing equations still hold:

$$W(k_t) = f(k_t) - k_t f'(k_t) \tag{4.167}$$

$$r(k_t) = f'(k_t) - \delta \tag{4.168}$$

Future capital depends on aggregate current savings:

$$(1+n)N_{t+1}k_{t+1} = S_t \tag{4.169}$$

The general expressions for the labour supply and savings equations are:

$$N_t = N\left(W_t\left(1 - \tau_{L,t}^E\right), r_{t+1}\right) \tag{4.170}$$

$$S_t \equiv \frac{C^O\left(W_t\left(1 - \tau_{L,t}^E\right), r_{t+1}\right) - (1+n)\,\tau_L\,W_{t+1}N_{t+1}}{1 + r_{t+1}} \tag{4.171}$$

Substituting (4.170) and (4.171) into (4.169) gives:

$$(1+n)\,N\left(W_{t+1}\left(1 - \tau_{L,t+1}^E\right), r_{t+2}\right) k_{t+1}$$
$$= \frac{C^O\left(W_t\left(1 - \tau_{L,t}^E\right), r_{t+1}\right) - (1+n)\,\tau_L\,W_{t+1}N_{t+1}}{1 + r_{t+1}} \tag{4.172}$$

This is the fundamental difference equation determining the capital stock over time. In general, this equation does not have a unique solution, because from (4.160) $\tau_{L,t+1}^E$ depends on N_{t+2}, which from (4.170) depends on k_{t+2} (since $r_{t+2} = r(k_{t+2})$), k_{t+1} (since $W_{t+1} = W(k_{t+1})$) and $\tau_{L,t+2}^E$, and so on. The current capital–labour ratio depends on all future values of the capital–labour ratio and for different future values of the capital–labour ratio, there will be different current values. Equation (4.172) therefore generates multiple solutions.

We do get a unique solution in the unit-elastic model, however, as we show shortly. We first examine the steady state consequences of an endogenous labour supply.

4.3.3   The Steady State

First we look at the welfare consequences for PAYG pensions, using the indirect utility function:

$$\bar{\Lambda}^Y(W, r, \tau_L) = \underset{\{C^Y, C^O, N\}}{Max}\left\{\Lambda^Y\left(C^Y, C^O, 1 - N\right) \text{ subject to } \right.$$

$$\left. \hat{W}N = C^Y + \frac{C^O}{1+r}\right\} \tag{4.173}$$

where $\Lambda^Y(C^Y, C^O, 1 - N)$ is the direct utility function and

$$\hat{W}N = W\left[1 - \tau_L\left(\frac{r-n}{1+r}\right)\right]N \tag{4.174}$$

is net (after-tax) lifetime income with a PAYG system, proportional contributions and endogenous labour.

The indirect utility function has the following properties:

$$\frac{\partial \bar{\Lambda}^Y}{\partial W} = \frac{\partial \Lambda^Y}{\partial C^Y}\left[1 - \tau_L\left(\frac{r-n}{1+r}\right)\right]N > 0 \tag{4.175}$$

$$\frac{\partial \bar{\Lambda}^Y}{\partial r} = \left(\frac{S}{1+r}\right)\frac{\partial \Lambda^Y}{\partial C^Y} > 0 \tag{4.176}$$

$$\frac{\partial \bar{\Lambda}^Y}{\partial \tau_L} = -WN\left(\frac{r-n}{1+r}\right)\frac{\partial \Lambda^Y}{\partial C^Y} \gtrless 0 \tag{4.177}$$

The effect of a marginal change in the official tax rate on steady state welfare is:

$$\frac{d\bar{\Lambda}^Y}{d\tau_L} = \frac{\partial\bar{\Lambda}^Y}{\partial W}\frac{dW}{d\tau_L} + \frac{\partial\bar{\Lambda}^Y}{\partial r}\frac{dr}{d\tau_L} + \frac{\partial\bar{\Lambda}^Y}{\partial\tau_L}$$

$$= \frac{\partial\Lambda^Y}{\partial C^Y}\left\{\left[1 - \tau_L\left(\frac{r-n}{1+r}\right)\right]N\frac{dW}{d\tau_L} + \left(\frac{S}{1+r}\right)\frac{dr}{d\tau_L}\right.$$

$$\left. - \left(\frac{r-n}{1+r}\right)WN\right\}$$

$$= -\left(\frac{r-n}{1+r}\right)N\frac{\partial\Lambda^Y}{\partial C^Y}\left[W + (1-\tau_L)k\frac{dr}{d\tau_L}\right] \tag{4.178}$$

using equations (4.175)–(4.177), and the relationships:

$$\frac{dW}{dr} = \phi'(r) = -k \tag{4.179}$$

and

$$S_t = (1+n)N_{t+1}k_{t+1} \tag{4.180}$$

There are two important features of equation (4.178). First, if the economy is initially in the golden-rule equilibrium ($r = n$), then there is no welfare effect on steady state generations from marginal changes in the official tax rate. The effective tax rate is zero in this case:

$$\tau_L^E = \tau_L\left(\frac{r-n}{1+r}\right) = 0 \tag{4.181}$$

and there is no distortion to the optimal labour supply.

Second, if the economy is not in golden-rule equilibrium ($r \neq n$), the sign of the welfare effect is the same as the sign of the final term in square brackets in equation (4.178), which shows that the PAYG system influences welfare via changes to lifetime resources (first term) and through changes to the capital–labour ratio (second term). In general, however, the sign of $dr/d\tau_L$ and hence that of $d\bar{\Lambda}^Y/d\tau_L$ are ambiguous.

In the case of the unit-elastic model, we get a clearcut result:

$$\Lambda_t^Y = \ln C_t^Y + \lambda_N\ln(1-N_t) + \left(\frac{1}{1+\rho}\right)\ln C_t^O \tag{4.182}$$

where ρ is the rate of time preference and λ_N measures the intensity of the labour supply effect. By maximising (4.182) subject to:

$$W_t N_t^i - \tau_L \left(1 - \frac{W_{t+1} \sum_{j=1}^{L_{t+1}} N_{t+1}^j}{W_t \left(1 + r_{t+1}\right) \sum_{j=1}^{L_t} N_t^j}\right) W_t N_t^i = C_t^{Y,i} + \frac{C_{t+1}^{O,i}}{1 + r_{t+1}}$$

(4.183)

we get:

$$\left(C_t^Y\right)^* = \left(\frac{1+\rho}{2 + \rho + \lambda_N \left(1+\rho\right)}\right) W_t^N$$

(4.184)

$$\left(C_{t+1}^O\right)^* = \left(\frac{1 + r_{t+1}}{2 + \rho + \lambda_N \left(1+\rho\right)}\right) W_t^N$$

(4.185)

$$\left(N_t\right)^* = \left(\frac{2+\rho}{2 + \rho + \lambda_N \left(1+\rho\right)}\right)$$

(4.186)

where:

$$W_t^N = W_t \left(1 - \tau_{L,t}^E\right)$$

(4.187)

is the effective after-tax wage rate.

In the unit-elastic model, consumption both when young and old is a normal good (i.e., increases with the after-tax wage). Further, labour supply is constant over time ($N_{t+1} = N_t = N$), since the income and substitution effects cancel each other out. The effective after-tax wage becomes:

$$W_t^N \equiv W_t \left(1 - \tau_{L,t}^E\right) \equiv W_t \left[1 - \tau_L \left(1 - \left(\frac{W_{t+1}}{W_t}\right) \left(\frac{1+n}{1 + r_{t+1}}\right)\right)\right]$$

(4.188)

This responds negatively to increases in both the tax rate and the rate of interest. As a consequence, equation (4.184) indicates that consumption in youth depends negatively on the rate of interest. Equation (4.185) indicates that consumption during old age depends positively on the rate of interest and positively on the tax rate if the Aaron condition holds ($\tau_{L,t}^E < 0$). Equation (4.186) shows that when $\lambda_N = 0$, the labour supply is exogenous and equal to unity.

The fundamental difference equation (4.93) can be written in explicit form in the unit-elastic model:

$$(1+n)k_{t+1} = \frac{(1 - \tau_L)W_t(k_t)}{2 + \rho} - \left(\frac{1+\rho}{2+\rho}\right) \left(\frac{\tau_L(1+n)W_{t+1}(k_{t+1})}{1 + r_{t+1}(k_{t+1})}\right)$$

(4.189)

which is a first-order difference equation in the capital–labour ratio of the form $k_{t+1} = g(k_t, \tau_L)$. This generates a unique solution for the time path of the capital–labour ratio. The indeterminacy problem of the general model (4.94) disappears because the labour supply elasticity is zero in the unit-elastic model (i.e., the optimally chosen labour supply is constant).

The long-run impact of the PAYG system on the capital–labour ratio is found by evaluating the partial derivatives of $k_{t+1} = g(k_t, \tau_L)$ at the steady state values:

$$g_k \equiv \frac{\partial k_{t+1}}{\partial k_t} = \frac{(1 - \tau_L) W'}{(1 + n)(2 + \rho)\left[1 + \tau_L \left(\frac{1+\rho}{2+\rho}\right) \frac{(1+r)W' - Wr'}{(1+r)^2}\right]} > 0$$

(4.190)

$$g_{\tau_L} \equiv \frac{\partial k_{t+1}}{\partial \tau_L} = \frac{[1 + r + (1 + n)(1 + \rho)]W}{(1 + r)(1 + n)(2 + \rho)\left[1 + \tau_L \left(\frac{1+\rho}{2+\rho}\right) \frac{(1+r)W' - Wr'}{(1+r)^2}\right]} < 0$$

(4.191)

where:

$$W' = \frac{dW(k)}{dk} > 0$$

(4.192)

$$r' = \frac{dr(k)}{dk} < 0$$

(4.193)

Stability requires $g_k \in (0, 1)$. As a consequence:

$$\frac{dk}{d\tau_L} = g_{\tau_L} \equiv \frac{g_{\tau_L}}{1 - g_k} < 0$$

(4.194)

which shows that the long-run impact of a PAYG system on the capital–labour ratio is negative.

4.3.4 Welfare Effects

In both models examined so far (the model with exogenous labour supply and lump-sum taxes and the model with endogenous labour supply and proportionate taxes), the existence of a PAYG system crowds out the capital–labour ratio (see (4.103) and (4.194)) and leads to a reduction in welfare for a dynamically efficient economy (see (4.125) and (4.178)).

However, there is a key difference in the two models: the imposition of lump-sum contributions (T) to the PAYG system does not cause a distortion in the labour supply decision, whereas proportionate contributions

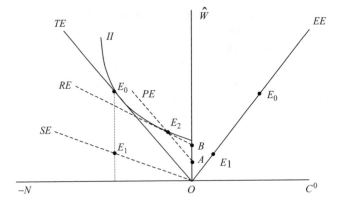

Figure 4.6 Deadweight loss of taxation
Source: Heijdra and van der Ploeg (2002). Reproduced by permission of Oxford University Press

(τ_L) do. A distortionary tax creates a *deadweight loss* (DWL) to the economy equal to the difference between the income needed by a young individual to compensate him for the loss of utility caused by the tax and the revenue raised by the tax.

Figure 4.6 shows the DWL of the pension contribution for a steady-state generation in the unit-elastic model in a dynamically efficient economy ($r > n$) and constant factor prices (Belan and Pestieau, 1999). To derive this we need to solve the model in two stages.

In the first stage, steady state lifetime income is defined as:

$$\hat{W} \equiv W \left(1 - \tau_L \left(\frac{r - n}{1 + r} \right) \right) N = W \left(1 - \tau_L^E \right) N \qquad (4.195)$$

and a young individual maximises steady state lifetime utility:

$$\Lambda^Y = \ln C^Y + \left(\frac{1}{1 + \rho} \right) \ln C^O \qquad (4.196)$$

subject to:

$$\hat{W} = C^Y + \frac{C^O}{1 + r} \qquad (4.197)$$

Optimal steady state consumption is given by:

$$\left(C^Y \right)^* = \left(\frac{1 + \rho}{2 + \rho} \right) \hat{W} \qquad (4.198)$$

$$\left(C^O \right)^* = \left(\frac{1 + r}{2 + \rho} \right) \hat{W} \qquad (4.199)$$

The right-hand panel of Figure 4.6 shows how old-age consumption is linked to lifetime income along *EE*.

Substituting (4.198) and (4.199) into the utility function (4.182) and budget constraint (4.183) gives:

$$\Lambda^Y = \left(\frac{2+\rho}{1+\rho}\right) \ln \hat{W} + \lambda_N \ln (1 - N) + \ln \left[\left(\frac{1+\rho}{2+\rho}\right) \left(\frac{1+r}{2+\rho}\right)^{1/(1+\rho)} \right]$$

(4.200)

and

$$\hat{W} \equiv W \left(1 - \tau_L \left(\frac{r - n}{1 + r}\right)\right) N = W \left(1 - \tau_L^E\right) N$$

(4.201)

In the second stage, the individual chooses the labour supply to maximise (4.200) subject to (4.201):

$$N = \left(\frac{2 + \rho}{2 + \rho + \lambda_N (1 + \rho)}\right)$$

(4.202)

The left-hand panel of Figure 4.6 shows the second stage. *TE* shows the pre-tax budget constraint, i.e., when $\tau_L^E = 0$ (note that *minus N* is measured along the horizontal axis). The initial equilibrium is at E_0 along indifference curve *II*. The same initial equilibrium for old-age consumption is shown at E_0 in the right-hand panel.

If now a positive effective tax is imposed ($\tau_L^E > 0$), the budget constraint in the left-hand panel rotates to the left to *SE*. In the unit-elastic model, the income and substitution effects cancel each other out, so that labour supply does not change (see equation (4.202)). The new equilibrium is therefore at E_1 in both panels.

The substitution effect of the tax change is found by moving the new budget constraint upwards (see *RE*) until it is tangential to the original indifference curve at E_2. The substitution effect is the shift from E_0 to E_2 and the income effect is the shift from E_2 to E_1. Thus, *OB* measures the income compensation (denoted Z_0) the young individual would need to achieve the pre-tax utility level. The equation of this line is:

$$\hat{W} = Z_0 + W (-N) \left(1 - \tau_L^E\right)$$

(4.203)

The tax revenue collected is found by drawing a line *PE* parallel to the original budget constraint *TE* through E_2. The equation of this line is:

$$\hat{W} = Z_0 - T + W (-N)$$

(4.204)

where T is the vertical distance AB. By evaluating these two equations at E_2 (i.e., equating them), we find that

$$T = \tau_L^E WN \qquad (4.205)$$

so that AB measures the tax revenue collected from the individual.

So DWL of the tax is OA, the difference between the income needed to compensate the individual for the loss of utility caused by the distortionary tax (OB) and the tax revenue raised (AB). In other words, the costs of the proportional tax-financed PAYG system are greater than the benefits and the difference is called a DWL.

4.3.5   From PAYG to a Funded Pension Scheme

In the case of the model with exogenous labour supply and retirement, the transition from a PAYG to a funded pension system was not Pareto-improving since resources could not be found to compensate the old generation at the time of the reform without making future generations worse off (Section 4.2.4).

However, in the case where the labour supply is endogenous and contributions to the PAYG system are proportional to income, the PAYG system is distortionary. In this case, as pointed out by Homburg (1990), Breyer and Straub (1993) and Belan and Pestieau (1999), a gradual shift to a funded system can be achieved in a Pareto-improving manner so long as non-distortionary lump-sum taxes can be used during the transition phase. Resources are released by moving from a distortionary to a non-distortionary system (the DWL is recovered), and these can be used to compensate the losing generation (the transitional generation that has to pay twice for its pension, once in the form of taxes to the PAYG system for a pension it will no longer receive and once in the form of contributions to the new funded system).

4.4   CONCLUSIONS

The overlapping generations model, in which each generation deals with both the generation ahead of it and the generation behind it, is a powerful vehicle for analysing pension systems. The key state variable in the Diamond–Samuelson OLG model is the physical capital stock, and it represents the dynamic path of the economy as a whole.

When labour supply and retirement are exogenous in the Diamond–Samuelson model and when a state pension system is introduced that is fully funded, there will be no change to the dynamic path of the economy, so long as the fund invests in the capital stock and so generates the same rate of return as on private savings. If, instead, an unfunded PAYG state pension system is introduced, the outcome will be non-neutral. The unfunded scheme will be superior to the funded scheme if the Aaron condition holds, i.e., the growth rate in the population (which equals the rate of return on the unfunded scheme) exceeds the rate of return on the capital stock (which equals the rate of return on a funded scheme). These conditions, however, imply that the economy is dynamically inefficient: there is too much capital in the economy and welfare would be increased if the capital stock was reduced and consumption increased. In practice, developed economies are not dynamically inefficient, so that funded schemes are, in principle, superior to unfunded schemes. However, with an exogenous labour supply, it is impossible to move from an unfunded to a funded pension scheme without making the transition generation (which has to pay both for its own funded pension and for the PAYG pension of the previous generation) worse off.

When labour supply and retirement are endogenous, and respond to the taxes, it is possible to move gradually from an unfunded to a funded scheme in a Pareto-improving manner, so long as non-distortionary lump-sum taxes are used during the transition phase.

QUESTIONS

1. Explain the two-period overlapping generations model.
2. Explain the structure of dynamic models.
3. Explain the significance of the capital stock in the Diamond–Samuelson OLG model.
4. What is a time-separable lifetime utility function?
5. Define the lifetime budget constraint in the two-period OLG model.
6. Explain the consumption Euler equation.
7. What is the marginal rate of intertemporal substitution?
8. What is the marginal rate of intertemporal transformation?
9. Define and interpret an intertemporal substitution elasticity.
10. Explain the substitution and income effects of a change in the rate of interest on consumption in youth.
11. Explain how the intertemporal substitution elasticity affects the total effect of a change in the rate of interest on consumption in youth.

12. What is a linear homogeneous production function?
13. What is Euler's theorem?
14. Explain the fundamental difference equation in the Diamond–Samuelson OLG model.
15. Explain the unit-elastic Diamond–Samuelson OLG model and examine its dynamics and stability properties.
16. What is the biological interest rate?
17. Examine optimality and efficiency in the Diamond–Samuelson OLG model.
18. What is the golden-rule equilibrium?
19. What is the consumption golden rule?
20. What is the production golden rule?
21. Define an economy that is dynamically inefficent. How does such an economy arise?
22. Explain how a fully-funded state pension scheme can be neutral in the Diamond–Samuelson OLG model with exogenous labour supply and retirement.
23. What is the Aaron condition?
24. Explain what happens to savings, the capital stock, wages and the interest rate when an unfunded state pension scheme is introduced in the Diamond–Samuelson OLG model with exogenous labour supply and retirement.
25. Explain the difference between a direct and indirect utility function.
26. Explain what happens to the welfare of different generations in a dynamically inefficient economy when a PAYG pension system is introduced.
27. Explain how a PAYG pension system is formally equivalent to a debt-financed fiscal policy.
28. Explain what happens to the welfare of different generations in a dynamically efficient economy when a PAYG pension system is introduced. How does a social welfare function resolve this problem?
29. In the Diamond–Samuelson OLG model with exogenous labour supply and retirement and with dynamic efficiency, can a move from a PAYG pension scheme to a funded pension scheme be Pareto-improving? Explain.
30. In the Diamond–Samuelson OLG model with endogenous labour supply and retirement and with dynamic efficiency, can a move from a PAYG pension scheme to a funded pension scheme be Pareto-improving? Explain.

REFERENCES

There are a number of textbooks explaining the OLG model. The best (and the one closely followed here) is:

Heijdra, B. and van der Ploeg, F. (2002) *Foundations of Modern Macroeconomics*, Oxford University Press, Oxford (ch. 17: Intergenerational Economics II).

See also:

Blanchard, O. and Fischer, S. (1989) *Lectures on Macroeconomics*, MIT Press, Cambridge, MA (ch. 2: Consumption and Investment: Basic Infinite Horizon Models, ch. 3: The Overlapping Generations Model).
McCandless, G. and Wallace, N. (1991) *Introduction to Dynamic Macroeconomic Theory: An Overlapping Generations Approach*, Harvard University Press, Cambridge, MA.
Romer, D. (2000) *Advanced Macroeconomics*, McGraw-Hill, New York (ch 2: Infinite Horizon and Overlapping Generation Models).

Other References

Aaron, H. (1966) The social insurance paradox, *Canadian Journal of Economics and Political Science*, **32**, 371–374.
Abel, A., Mankiw, N., Summers, L. and Zeckhauser, R. (1989) Assessing dynamic efficiency: theory and evidence, *Review of Economic Studies*, **56**, 1–19.
Auerbach, A. and Kotlikoff, L. (1987) *Dynamic Fiscal Policy*, Cambridge University Press, Cambridge.
Belan, P. and Pestieau, P. (1999) Privatising social security: a critical assessment, *Geneva Papers on Risk and Insurance Theory*, **24**, 114–130.
Blinder, A. (1981) *Private Pensions and Public Pensions: Theory & Fact*, W.S. Woytinsky Lecture No. 5, Institute of Public Policy Studies, University of Michigan.
Breyer, F. (1989) On the intergenerational Pareto efficiency of pay as you go financed pension systems, *Journal of Institutional and Theoretical Economics*, **145**, 643–658.
Breyer, F. and Straub, M. (1993) Welfare effects of unfunded pension systems when labour supply is endogenous, *Journal of Public Economics*, **50**, 77–91.
Diamond, P. (1965) National debt in a neoclassical growth model, *American Economic Review*, **55**, 1126–1150.
Feldstein, M. (1974) Social security, induced retirement, and aggregate capital accumulation, *Journal of Political Economy*, **82**, 905–926.
Homburg, S. (1990) The efficiency of unfunded pension systems, *Journal of Institutional and Theoretical Economics*, **146**, 640–647.
Samuelson, P. (1958) An exact consumption–loan model of interest with or without the social contrivance of money, *Journal of Political Economy*, **66**, 467–482.

5

Pensions in the Blanchard–Yaari Overlapping Generations Model with Uncertain Lifetimes

The Diamond–Samuelson OLG model assumes that individuals will live for exactly two periods, a period of youth and a period of old age. It ignores lifetime uncertainty. Yaari (1965) introduced the notion of lifetime uncertainty in a model of lifetime saving. Later, Blanchard (1985) used Yaari's framework to build a continuous-time OLG model with new generations being born continuously.[1] The Blanchard–Yaari OLG model is therefore more realistic than the Diamond–Samuelson OLG model. It can be used to examine the effects of introducing a pay-as-you-go pension scheme when labour supply is endogenous and there is mandatory retirement.

5.1 THE BLANCHARD–YAARI OLG MODEL WITH UNCERTAIN LIFETIMES

5.1.1 Yaari's Contribution

Yaari pointed out two problems that need to be addressed when lifetimes are uncertain. First, since the time of death D is random then so is an individual's lifetime utility: individuals have to maximise their *expected* utility (this is known as the *expected utility hypothesis*). Second, the constraint that the individual's wealth at the time of death cannot be negative is also now stochastic. If $A(t)$ is the value of real assets at time t, then $A(D)$ is stochastic and we must ensure that $A(D) \geq 0$ holds with certainty.

Suppose that we denote the density function of D as $f(D)$ and that no one lives beyond $\bar{D}$. Then D lies in the interval $[0, \bar{D}]$ with probability 1:

$$\int_0^{\bar{D}} f(D)dD = 1, \quad f(D) \geq 0 \tag{5.1}$$

---

[1] The version of the model used here is based on Heijdra and van der Ploeg (2002, ch. 16: Intergenerational Economics I).

Suppose that the individual's lifetime utility is given by:

$$\Lambda(D) = \int_0^{\bar{D}} U(C(s))e^{-\rho s}ds \tag{5.2}$$

where $U(C(s))$ is the instantaneous utility of consumption at time s and ρ is the pure rate of time preference: labour is supplied inelastically and so does not appear in the utility function.

Expected lifetime utility is given by:

$$\begin{aligned}
E\Lambda(D) &= \int_0^{\bar{D}} f(D)\Lambda(D)dD \\
&= \int_0^{\bar{D}} \left[\int_s^{\bar{D}} f(D)dD \right] U(C(s))e^{-\rho s}ds \\
&= \int_0^{\bar{D}} [1 - F(s)]U(C(s))e^{-\rho s}ds
\end{aligned} \tag{5.3}$$

where:

$$[1 - F(s)] = \int_s^{\bar{D}} f(D)dD \tag{5.4}$$

is the probability that the individual will still be alive at time s.

The individual's wealth dynamics are given by:

$$\dot{A}(s) = r(s)A(s) + W(s) - C(s) \tag{5.5}$$

where:

$$\dot{A}(s) = \frac{dA(s)}{ds} \tag{5.6}$$

is the instantaneous change in real assets, $r(s)$ is the interest rate and $W(s)$ is wage income, all at time s. We will assume that both $r(s)$ and $W(s)$ are known and that the only source of uncertainty is the length of lifetime.

The terminal wealth constraint, $\Pr\{A(D) \geq 0\} = 1$, requires the following conditions to hold:

$$\begin{cases} \dot{A}(s) = W(s) - C(s) \geq 0 \text{ if } A(s) = 0 \\ A(\bar{D}) = 0 \end{cases} \tag{5.7}$$

The individual maximises expected lifetime utility (5.3), subject to (5.5), (5.7) and an initial wealth level $A(0)$. The first-order conditions

(FOCs) are:

$$[1 - F(s)]U'(C(s)) = \lambda(s) \qquad (5.8)$$

$$\frac{\dot{\lambda}(s)}{\lambda(s)} = \rho - r(s) \qquad (5.9)$$

where $\lambda(s)$ is the *co-state variable*[2] associated with the wealth constraint (5.5) and measures the expected marginal utility of wealth (and $\dot{\lambda}(s) = d\lambda(s)/ds$). Equation (5.8) is the standard first-order condition equating the expected marginal utility of current consumption to the expected marginal utility of wealth (i.e., future consumption). Equation (5.9), which shows the optimal dynamics of the co-state variable, indicates that the expected marginal utility of wealth increases over time if the rate of time preference (which measures the intensity of the desire for current consumption relative to future consumption) exceeds the interest rate (and vice versa). This makes sense: the greater the rate of time preference, the greater will be current consumption and the less wealth accumulation there will be, and this raises the expected marginal utility of wealth.

If we differentiate (5.8) with respect to s, we get:

$$-f(s)U'(C(s)) + [1 - F(s)]U''(C(s))\dot{C}(s) = \dot{\lambda}(s) \qquad (5.10)$$

where:

$$f(s) = \frac{dF(s)}{ds} \qquad (5.11)$$

$$\dot{C}(s) = \frac{dC(s)}{ds} \qquad (5.12)$$

If we divide (5.10) by (5.8) and substitute out $\dot{\lambda}(s)/\lambda(s)$ using (5.9), we get the individual's *consumption Euler equation* in the presence of lifetime uncertainty:

$$\frac{\dot{C}(s)}{C(s)} = \sigma(C(s))[r(s) - \rho - \beta(s)] \qquad (5.13)$$

where:

$$\sigma(C(s)) = -\frac{U'(C(s))}{C(s)U''(C(s))} > 0 \qquad (5.14)$$

---

[2] This is the equivalent of the Lagrange multiplier in a discrete time model.

is the *intertemporal substitution elasticity* (ISE) and

$$\beta(s) = \frac{f(s)}{[1 - F(s)]} \qquad (5.15)$$

is the probability of dying at time s (also called the *force of mortality*, *mortality drag* or the *hazard rate*).

Equation (5.13) shows that the hazard rate appears with a negative sign in the consumption Euler equation, thereby reducing the optimal growth rate in consumption over time. This is the *first result* from Yaari's model: the uncertainty attached to survival results in the individual discounting the utility derived from future consumption more heavily. The subjective discount rate is $\rho + \beta(s)$ rather than ρ, the subjective discount rate in the presence of a certain lifetime. Equation (5.13) shows that the optimal growth rate in consumption will be low when the ISE is low or when the interest gap $(r(s) - \rho - \beta(s))$ is low: $r(s)$ measures the marginal benefit from delaying consumption in terms of the extra interest earned, while $\rho + \beta(s)$ shows the marginal cost.

Yaari pointed out that the uncertainty attached to life can be hedged by purchasing a *life annuity* from an insurance company. A life annuity pays a fixed annual amount to the buyer, so long as the buyer is alive; payments stop when the buyer dies.

In Yaari's model, the annuity is tradeable and can be bought and sold. The rate of return on the annuity $r^A(s)$ must exceed the riskless interest rate $r(s)$ given the uncertainties attached to the annuity. If the individual sells the annuity, he receives a life-insured loan. He pays a higher rate of interest than the market rate for this, but does not need to return the principal when he dies.

The rate of return on the annuity $r^A(s)$ is determined by the principle of actuarial fairness. Assume one unit of an annuity is purchased at time s and held until $s + ds$. Interest of $r^A(s)$ is paid if the purchaser survives until $s + ds$ (which occurs with probability $1 - F(s + ds)$), while no interest is paid if the purchaser dies between s and $s + ds$.

Actuarial fairness implies that:

$$\lim_{ds \to 0} (1 + r^A(s)ds) \left[\frac{1 - F(s + ds)}{1 - F(s)} \right] = \lim_{ds \to 0} (1 + r(s)ds) \qquad (5.16)$$

The left-hand side is the (expected) return on the annuity and, in the absence of arbitrage, this must equal the return on the alternative investment, namely an investment earning the market rate of interest. The term on the left in square brackets is less than unity and accounts for the fact that the purchaser might die between s and $s + ds$.

Equation (5.16) can be rewritten:

$$r^A(s) = \lim_{ds \to 0} \left[\frac{1 - F(s)}{1 - F(s+ds)} \right] r(s) + \lim_{ds \to 0} \left[\frac{(F(s+ds) - F(s))/ds}{1 - F(s+ds)} \right]$$

$$= r(s) + \beta(s) \tag{5.17}$$

so that the return on the annuity exceeds the risk-free rate by the force of mortality at time (and age) s. When an individual annuitant dies, this creates a *mortality profit* to the annuity provider (i.e., life office), which passes this on to those annuitants still alive. The profit at time (and age) s is equal to the hazard rate, $\beta(s)$.

Since $\beta(s) \to \infty$ as $s \to \bar{D}$, this also implies that $r^A(s) \to \infty$ as $s \to \bar{D}$. The closer the individual gets to the maximum possible age $\bar{D}$, the higher will be the probability of dying and the higher the required return on the annuity.

Yaari showed that it was optimal for the individual, in the absence of a bequest motive, to hold all their financial assets in annuities, i.e., to fully insure against loss of life. This is because the reduction in utility if the individual runs out of assets before death is so great and because annuities yield the highest return of all assets available (which is all the individual cares about in the absence of a bequest motive). The individual's wealth dynamics therefore become:

$$\dot{A}(s) = r^A(s)A(s) + W(s) - C(s) \tag{5.18}$$

Now the restriction on wealth (5.7) is automatically satisfied, since the individual never runs out of assets and leaves no assets when he dies.

The individual's lifetime solvency condition is:

$$A(0) + \int_0^{\bar{D}} e^{-\int_0^s r^A(u)du}(W(s) - C(s))ds = 0 \tag{5.19}$$

This states that the present value of lifetime consumption (using continuous discounting) cannot exceed the initial value of financial assets plus the present value of lifetime labour income (i.e., *human capital*).

The individual maximises expected lifetime utility (5.3), subject to the solvency condition (5.19). The FOC for this problem (i.e., when all wealth is annuitised) is given by the consumption Euler equation:

$$\frac{\dot{C}(s)}{C(s)} = \sigma(C(s)) \left[r^A(s) - \rho - \beta(s) \right]$$

$$= \sigma(C(s)) [r(s) - \rho] \tag{5.20}$$

using (5.17). This shows Yaari's *second result*: the Euler equation with the lifetime fully insured (first line of (5.20)) is the same as the Euler equation with no lifetime uncertainty (second line of (5.20)).

5.1.2 Blanchard's Contribution

Blanchard (1985) used these results as the basis of his continuous-time overlapping generations model. He assumed the probability of death was exponential:

$$f(D) = \begin{cases} \beta e^{-\beta D} & \text{for } D \geq 0 \\ 0 & \text{for } D < 0 \end{cases} \tag{5.21}$$

implying that:

$$[1 - F(s)] = \int_s^\infty f(D)dD = \frac{f(s)}{\beta} \tag{5.22}$$

$$\beta(s) = \frac{f(s)}{[1 - F(s)]} = \beta \tag{5.23}$$

In Blanchard's model, the hazard rate is constant and independent of the individual's age, implying that the expected remaining lifetime of an individual is $1/\beta$ however old they are (Blanchard's model has sometimes been called a *model of perpetual youth*). Yaari, in contrast, had assumed more realistically that the hazard rate was age-dependent. The advantage of Blanchard's simplifying assumption is that it is easy to aggregate across individuals in order to derive aggregate relationships.

5.1.3 Individuals

Assume an individual born at time v is still alive at time t and has a logarithmic utility function (which has ISE = 1). Their expected remaining lifetime utility is given by:

$$E\Lambda(v, t) = \int_t^\infty [1 - F(s - t)] \ln C(v, s) e^{-\rho(s-t)} ds$$

$$= \int_t^\infty \ln C(v, s) e^{-(\rho+\beta)(s-t)} ds \tag{5.24}$$

where $C(v, s)$ is planned consumption at time s for an individual born at time v. As in Yaari's model, labour is supplied inelastically.

The individual's wealth dynamics are given by:

$$\dot{A}(v, s) = [r(s) + \beta] A(v, s) + W(s) - T(s) - C(v, s) \qquad (5.25)$$

where $T(s)$ is lump-sum taxes levied by the government. The individual's wealth is held entirely in annuities bought from a life company. While alive the individual receives $[r(s) + \beta] A(v, s)$ from the life company, but at the time of death all remaining assets $A(v, D)$ revert to the life company.

The solvency condition for the individual becomes:

$$\lim_{s \to \infty} e^{-R^A(t,s)} A(v, s) = 0 \qquad (5.26)$$

where:

$$R^A(t, s) = \int_t^s [r(u) + \beta] \, du \qquad (5.27)$$

is the compound factor between t and s.

By combining (5.25) and (5.26) we derive the individual's lifetime budget constraint:

$$A(v, t) + \bar{W}(t) = \int_t^\infty C(v, s) e^{-R^A(t,s)} ds \qquad (5.28)$$

where $\bar{W}(t)$ is human capital, defined as the present value of after-tax labour income, discounted using the annuity factor:

$$\bar{W}(t) = \int_t^\infty [W(s) - T(s)] e^{-R^A(t,s)} ds \qquad (5.29)$$

Equation (5.28) is Blanchard's version of Yaari's lifetime budget constraint (5.19) and states that (discounted) lifetime consumption cannot exceed the value of the individual's human and financial capital.

The individual maximises expected lifetime utility (5.24) subject to the lifetime budget constraint (5.28). The FOCs are (5.28) and

$$\left(\frac{1}{C(v, s)}\right) e^{-(\rho+\beta)(s-t)} = \lambda(t) e^{-R^A(t,s)} \quad \forall s \in [t, \infty) \qquad (5.30)$$

where $1/C(v, s)$ is the marginal utility of time s consumption when utility is logarithmic, and $\lambda(t)$ is the co-state variable for the lifetime budget constraint (5.28) and measures the marginal expected utility of lifetime wealth. By differentiating (5.30) with respect to s, we derive the individual's consumption Euler equation:

$$\frac{\dot{C}(v, s)}{C(v, s)} = r(s) - \rho \qquad (5.31)$$

which takes into account that $\sigma(C(s)) = 1$ in the case of logarithmic utility.

Equation (5.30) shows that consumption is chosen at each time to equate the appropriately discounted marginal utilities of consumption and lifetime wealth. For $s = t$, we have:

$$C(v, t) = \frac{1}{\lambda(t)} \qquad (5.32)$$

By incorporating (5.32) and (5.28) into (5.30):

$$\int_t^\infty C(v, t)e^{-(\rho+\beta)(s-t)}ds = \int_t^\infty C(v, s)e^{-R^A(t,s)}ds \qquad (5.33)$$

we can show that optimal consumption is proportional to total wealth. Integrating both sides gives (using (5.28)):

$$\left(\frac{C(v, t)}{\rho + \beta}\right)\left[-e^{-(\rho+\beta)(s-t)}\right]_t^\infty = A(v, t) + \bar{W}(t) \qquad (5.34)$$

which implies that:

$$C(v, t) = (\rho + \beta)\left[A(v, t) + \bar{W}(t)\right] \qquad (5.35)$$

Optimal consumption when $s = t$ is proportional to total wealth. The marginal propensity to consume out of total wealth is equal to the *effective rate of time preference* when lifetimes are uncertain, $\rho + \beta$.

5.1.4 Aggregate Consumption

Aggregate consumption is found by aggregating over all cohorts of the population alive. The Blanchard model assumes that a new generation of size $H(s, s) = \beta H(s)$ is born at every instant of time, where $H(s)$ is the total population at time s. Because there are no bequests in the model, each newborn generation starts with zero financial wealth: $A(s, s) = 0$. Also, at each instant of time, a proportion of the population dies with probability β, i.e., $\beta H(s)$ in total. At each instant, births and deaths exactly match and so the total population is constant over time and to simplify matters we normalise the population on unity (i.e., $H(s) = 1$). A cohort born at time v will be of size $\beta e^{\beta(v-t)}$ at time $t > v$, since $\beta(1 - e^{\beta(v-t)})$ members of the cohort will have died in the interval $[v, t]$. Buiter (1988) subsequently generalised the model to include differential birth and death rates, thereby allowing for population growth and decline.

Since we know the size of each generation at time t, we can aggregate over all generations to derive aggregate consumption at time t (using equation (5.35)):

$$
\begin{aligned}
C(t) &= \beta \int_{-\infty}^{t} e^{\beta(v-t)} C(v, t) \, dv \\
&= \beta \int_{-\infty}^{t} e^{\beta(v-t)} (\rho + \beta) \left[A(v, t) + \bar{W}(t) \right] dv \qquad (5.36) \\
&= (\rho + \beta) \left[\beta \int_{-\infty}^{t} e^{\beta(v-t)} A(v, t) \, dv + \beta \int_{-\infty}^{t} e^{\beta(v-t)} \bar{W}(t) \, dv \right] \\
&= (\rho + \beta) \left[A(t) + \bar{W}(t) \right]
\end{aligned}
$$

where $A(t)$ and $\bar{W}(t)$ are now aggregate financial and human capital, respectively. This aggregation, in which the aggregate consumption function has precisely the same form as the individual consumption function, is only possible because of the assumption that each individual faces the same hazard rate at each instant however old they are and this leads to a marginal propensity to consume out of total wealth that is generation independent.

Aggregate financial assets are given by:

$$
A(t) = \beta \int_{-\infty}^{t} e^{\beta(v-t)} A(v, t) \, dv \qquad (5.37)
$$

The dynamics of financial asset accumulation are given by (using Leibnitz's rule):

$$
\dot{A}(t) = \beta A(t, t) - \beta A(t) + \beta \int_{-\infty}^{t} e^{\beta(v-t)} \dot{A}(v, t) \, dv \qquad (5.38)
$$

where the first term shows the assets of newborns ($A(t, t) = 0$), the second is the assets of those who died, and the third is the change in the value of the assets of existing individuals.

Box 5.1   Leibnitz's Rule for Differentiating under the Integral Sign

Suppose:

$$f(x) = \int_{l(x)}^{u(x)} g(x, y)\, dy$$

for $x \in [a, b]$ and $y \in [l, u]$.
Then:

$$\frac{df(x)}{dx} = \int_{l(x)}^{u(x)} \frac{\delta g(x, y)}{\delta x}\, dy + g(x, u(x)) \frac{du(x)}{dx} - g(x, l(x)) \frac{dl(x)}{dx}$$

Substituting (5.25) into (5.38) gives the aggregate wealth accumulation equation for the economy:

$$
\begin{aligned}
\dot{A}(t) &= -\beta A(t) + \beta \int_{-\infty}^{t} e^{\beta(v-t)} \Big[[r(t) + \beta]\, A(v, t) + W(t) \\
&\qquad\qquad\qquad\qquad -T(t) - C(v, t) \Big] dv \\
&= -\beta A(t) + [r(t) + \beta]\, A(t) + W(t) - T(t) - C(t) \\
&= r(t)A(t) + W(t) - T(t) - C(t)
\end{aligned}
\tag{5.39}
$$

Equation (5.25) shows that for the individual, financial wealth still grows at the actuarial rate of interest $r(t) + \beta$, while for the economy as a whole, equation (5.39) shows that aggregate financial wealth grows at the economy-wide rate of interest, $r(t)$. This is because $\beta A(t)$ does not count as part of aggregate wealth accumulation, but represents a transfer from those who die to those who remain alive.

The dynamics of aggregate consumption are found by differentiating the first line of equation (5.36) with respect to t:

$$\dot{C}(t) = \beta C(t, t) - \beta C(t) + \beta \int_{-\infty}^{t} e^{\beta(v-t)} \dot{C}(v, t)\, dv \tag{5.40}$$

This can be used to derive the aggregate consumption Euler equation in Blanchard's model:

$$
\begin{aligned}
\frac{\dot{C}(t)}{C(t)} &= r(t) - \rho - \beta\,(\rho + \beta)\frac{A(t)}{C(t)} \\
&= \frac{\dot{C}(v, t)}{C(v, t)} - \beta\frac{C(t) - C(t, t)}{C(t)}
\end{aligned}
\tag{5.41}
$$

which is derived by substituting the following expressions into (5.40) and then using the first row of (5.36) to substitute out the integral term:

- Newborns consume a proportion of their human wealth at birth (see equation (5.35)):

$$C(t, t) = (\rho + \beta)\bar{W}(t)$$

- Aggregate consumption is proportional to total wealth (see equation (5.36)):

$$C(t) = (\rho + \beta)\left[A(t) + \bar{W}(t)\right]$$

- Individual consumption growth satisfies $\forall s \in [t, \infty)$ (see equation (5.31)):

$$\dot{C}(v, s) = (r(s) - \rho)C(v, s)$$

Equation (5.41) shows that the aggregate consumption Euler equation is equal to the individual consumption Euler equation plus an adjustment that accounts for the turnover of generations. Older and richer generations have a higher level of consumption than younger generations, but all generations have the same growth rate in optimal consumption because they face the same interest rate. Aggregate consumption growth is below individual consumption growth because the new generations that replace existing generations have no wealth and so their consumption $C(t, t)$ is below average consumption $C(t)$ in equation (5.41).

5.1.5 Firms

Firms produce identical goods in a perfectly competitive economy subject to a linearly homogeneous production function:

$$Y(t) = F(K(t), L(t)) \tag{5.42}$$

The market value of a representative firm will equal the present value of its future profit stream:

$$V(t) = \int_t^\infty [Y(s) - W(s)L(s) - I(s)] e^{-R(t,s)} ds \tag{5.43}$$

where $I(s)$ is gross investment and

$$R(t, s) = \int_t^s r(u)\, du \tag{5.44}$$

which in turn will equal the replacement value of its capital stock:

$$V(t) = K(t) \tag{5.45}$$

The firm selects labour and capital to maximise (5.43) subject to (5.42) and the constraint on capital accumulation:

$$\dot{K}(t) = I(t) - \delta K(t) \tag{5.46}$$

where δ is the rate of depreciation on capital.

The FOCs for a maximum are where factors are paid their marginal products:

$$r(t) + \delta = F_K(K(t), L(t)) \tag{5.47}$$

$$W(t) = F_L(K(t), L(t)) \tag{5.48}$$

where F_K and F_L are the marginal products of capital and labour.

5.1.6   Government and Market Equilibrium

The government's budget identity is:

$$\dot{B}(t) = r(t)B(t) + G(t) - T(t) \tag{5.49}$$

This shows that the government spends $G(t)$ on goods and services and raises $T(t)$ in lump-sum taxes from individuals; debt interest on current debt $B(t)$ is $r(t)B(t)$.

The government's long-term solvency condition is:

$$\lim_{s \to \infty} e^{-R^A(t,s)} B(s) = 0 \tag{5.50}$$

that is, government debt cannot in the long run grow at a faster rate than the rate of interest.

Using equations (5.50) and (5.49), we derive the government's budget constraint:

$$B(t) = \int_t^\infty [T(s) - G(s)] e^{-R(t,s)} ds \tag{5.51}$$

Current debt must be paid off with future *primary surpluses* (i.e., the government must in future collect more in net taxes than it pays out in goods and services).

In the Blanchard model, goods and factor markets clear instantaneously. Goods market equilibrium requires the supply of goods to equal aggregate demand (which is the sum of private and public consumption plus investment):

$$Y(t) = C(t) + I(t) + G(t) \tag{5.52}$$

Financial market equilibrium requires that assets are fully allocated to capital or government bonds:

$$A(t) = K(t) + B(t) \tag{5.53}$$

In the labour market, wage flexibility ensures that the demand for labour equals the aggregate supply by individuals:

$$L(t) = 1 \tag{5.54}$$

The Blanchard–Yaari model is summarised by the following set of differential equations[3] and equilibrium conditions:

$$\dot{C}(t) = [r(t) - \rho] C(t) - \beta (\rho + \beta) [K(t) + B(t)] \tag{5.55}$$

$$\dot{K}(t) = F(K(t), L(t)) - C(t) - G(t) - \delta K(t) \tag{5.56}$$

$$\dot{B}(t) = r(t)B(t) + G(t) - T(t) \tag{5.57}$$

$$r(t) + \delta = F_K(K(t), L(t)) \tag{5.58}$$

$$W(t) = F_L(K(t), L(t)) \tag{5.59}$$

$$L(t) = 1 \tag{5.60}$$

5.1.7   The Phase Diagram

The *phase diagram*[4] for the model in $C(t) - K(t)$ space is drawn in Figure 5.1 under the simplifying assumptions that $B(t) = G(t) = T(t) = 0$.

The $\dot{K}(t) = 0$ locus corresponds to the combination of points in $C(t) - K(t)$ space for which the capital stock (see equation (5.56)) is in equilibrium and net investment is zero over time. When $K(t) = 0$, $Y(t) = 0$ and hence $C(t) = 0$, so the locus passes through the origin (A_1). It will also be vertical at that point since $F_K(K(t), L(t)) \to \infty$ as

---

[3] A differential equation is a dynamic model explaining the dynamic behaviour of a variable in continuous time (as a function of the control and policy variables, the previous history of the state variable(s), and for a given set of parameter values of the model).

[4] The phase diagram for a dynamic model shows the equilibrium loci of the model's control and state variables (in this case aggregate consumption and the capital stock, respectively) together with the dynamic forces that operate when the system is not in equilibrium.

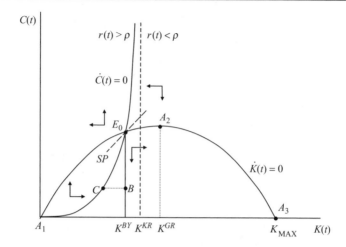

Figure 5.1 Phase diagram of the Blanchard–Yaari OLG model
Source: Heijdra and van der Ploeg (2002). Reproduced by permission of Oxford University Press

$K(t) \to 0$. *Golden-rule* (GR) *consumption* (i.e., when consumption is maximised) occurs where the $\dot{K}(t) = 0$ locus reaches a maximum (A_2):

$$\left. \frac{dC(t)}{dK(t)} \right|_{\dot{K}(t)=0} = 0 \quad \Rightarrow \quad F_K \left(K^{GR}, 1 \right) = \delta \tag{5.61}$$

The maximum attainable capital stock occurs when total output is used for replacement investment and consumption is zero (A_3):

$$\frac{F \left(K_{MAX}, 1 \right)}{K_{MAX}} = \delta \tag{5.62}$$

For points above the $\dot{K}(t) = 0$ locus, consumption is too high, given the capital stock, which means that net investment is negative and so the capital stock will fall; this is shown by the left-pointing horizontal arrows. The opposite dynamics hold for points below the $\dot{K}(t) = 0$ locus; this is shown by the right-pointing horizontal arrows.

The $\dot{C}(t) = 0$ locus corresponds to the combination of points in $C(t) - K(t)$ space for which aggregate consumption is constant over time (see equation (5.55)). It is upward sloping through the origin, so long as $\beta > 0$ and $(r(t) - \rho) > 0$, as can be seen from the first row of equation (5.41) with $A(t) = K(t)$, since $B(t) = 0$:

$$C(t) = \frac{\beta (\rho + \beta)}{r(t) - \rho} K(t) \tag{5.63}$$

As $K(t)$ increases, $r(t)$ will decline and the $\dot{C}(t) = 0$ locus becomes vertical at the level of the capital stock for which the rate of interest equals the rate of time preference:

$$\frac{dC(t)}{dK(t)}\bigg|_{\dot{K}(t)=0} = \infty \quad \Rightarrow \quad r^{KR} = F_K\left(K^{KR}, 1\right) - \delta = \rho \qquad (5.64)$$

This level of capital stock is known as the *Keynes–Ramsey capital stock* (K^{KR}) and equation (5.64) is known as the *modified golden rule*.

Since $F_K(K^{KR}, 1) = \rho + \delta > \delta = F_K(K^{GR}, 1)$ and there are diminishing returns to capital ($F_{KK} < 0$), it follows that $K^{KR} < K^{GR}$. For points to the right of the vertical dashed line in Figure 5.1, capital is relatively abundant and the interest rate is below the rate of time preference. For points to the left of the vertical dashed line in Figure 5.1, capital is relatively scarce and the interest rate is above the rate of time preference.

The dynamics above and below the $\dot{C}(t) = 0$ locus depend on the balance between intergenerational–redistributional and capital scarcity effects. Consider points along the vertical line at K^{BY}. At E_0, we have $\dot{C}(t) = 0$. Point B has the same capital stock as at E_0, and hence the same rate of interest. From the second row of equation (5.41), individual consumption growth will be the same at both points ($\dot{C}(v, t)/C(v, t) = r(t) - \rho$), including that for newborn generations. However, $C(t)$ is lower at B than at E_0, and therefore the proportionate difference between average consumption and the consumption of the newborn, $(C(t) - C(t, t))/C(t)$, will be higher. This implies that the change in aggregate consumption will be lower (using the second row of equation (5.41)):

$$\dot{C}(t)|_B = \left(\left[\dot{C}(v, t)C(t)/C(v, t)\right] - \beta\left[C(t) - C(t, t)\right]\right) < \dot{C}(t)|_{E_0} = 0 \qquad (5.65)$$

The capital stock has to fall to point C in Figure 5.1 to restore $\dot{C}(t) = 0$. The smaller capital stock has two reinforcing effects. First, it raises individual consumption growth by increasing the rate of interest (see the first row of equation (5.41)). Second, it reduces the gap between average wealth (the wealth of the generation that dies) and the wealth of the newborn generation, which helps to increase aggregate consumption growth. So capital scarcity leads to an increase in consumption growth. For points below the $\dot{C}(t) = 0$ locus, the intergenerational–redistributional effect (5.65) dominates the capital scarcity effect and consumption falls over time; this is shown by the downward pointing arrows. The opposite set of dynamics holds for points above the $\dot{C}(t) = 0$ locus; this is shown by the upward pointing arrows.

Steady state equilibrium occurs at E_0 in Figure 5.1 at the intersection of the $\dot{K}(t) = 0$ and $\dot{C}(t) = 0$ loci. The equilibrium is unique and *saddle-point*[5] *stable*. The *saddle path*[6] is given by the locus *SP*. It shows the only two equilibrating paths that the economy can take if it does not start at equilibrium. These lie in the segments of the figure marked ⌐→ or ⌐↓. If the economy starts at any other point, it will move further away from equilibrium over time. Note that, as a result of lifetime uncertainty, the steady state levels of the capital stock and aggregate consumption are below the golden-rule levels (compare E_0 and A_2). This is true despite the fact that the optimal growth rate in consumption is the same whether lifetimes are certain or uncertain, so long as all wealth is annuitised (Yaari's second result).

5.2 PAYG PENSIONS IN THE BLANCHARD-YAARI OLG MODEL WITH ENDOGENOUS LABOUR SUPPLY AND MANDATORY RETIREMENT

Suppose the economy starts in steady state equilibrium E_0 without government debt, government spending or taxes ($\dot{B}(t) = B(t) = G(t) = T(t) = 0$) and the government introduces a programme of mandatory retirement and a PAYG pension scheme for those over this new retirement age, paying $P(t)$ which is financed by lump-sum taxes, $T(t)$, on those in work. The government's budget constraint now becomes:

$$\dot{B}(t) = P(t) - T(t) = 0 \qquad (5.66)$$

Suppose individuals must retire κ years after being born. Then the asset accumulation equation (5.25) becomes:

$$\dot{A}(v, s) = [r(s) + \beta] A(v, s) + W(s) - T(s) - C(v, s) \text{ if } (s - v) \leq \kappa$$
$$\dot{A}(v, s) = [r(s) + \beta] A(v, s) + P(s) - C(v, s) \text{ if } (s - v) > \kappa$$
$$\qquad (5.67)$$

---

[5] A saddle point (like the saddle on a horse) has the property of involving a maximum in one direction (in the case of Figure 5.1 the north west–south east direction) and a minimum in the perpendicular direction (north east–south west direction).

[6] The saddle path shows the set of routes the system can take to reach an equilibrium if it starts out of equilibrium.

Human capital (5.29) becomes generation specific:

$$\bar{W}(v,t) = \begin{cases} \int_t^{v+\kappa} [W(s) - T(s)]\, e^{-R^A(t,s)} ds & \text{if } t < v + \kappa \\ \int_t^{\infty} P(s) e^{-R^A(t,s)} ds & \text{if } t \geq v + \kappa \end{cases} \qquad (5.68)$$

and equations (5.34), (5.35) and the second and third lines of (5.36) are modified accordingly. In equation (5.68), we treat the PAYG pensions as deferred wages (financed by previous taxation) and include it as part of human capital.

The effect of this policy is essentially one of redistribution between different generations, and the intensity of the effect will depend on the generosity of the PAYG pension in relation to wages.

Suppose $P(t) = W(t)$, then it is clear from equation (5.29) that the human capital of those generations who suddenly find themselves in retirement will be unchanged, while the imposition of taxes on the younger generations will reduce their human capital. Assuming logarithmic utility, equation (5.35) shows that the consumption pattern of the retired will be unchanged, while the consumption of the younger generations will fall. Aggregate consumption will therefore fall. An inspection of equations (5.55) and (5.56) shows that both the $\dot{C}(t) = 0$ and the $\dot{K}(t) = 0$ loci shift down: in both cases, consumption is lower for the same capital stock. This is shown in Figure 5.2. Because the capital stock is slow to adjust, the economy jumps from the original equilibrium at E_0 (at the intersection of the original $(\dot{C}(t) = 0)_0$ and $(\dot{K}(t) = 0)_0$ loci) to A on

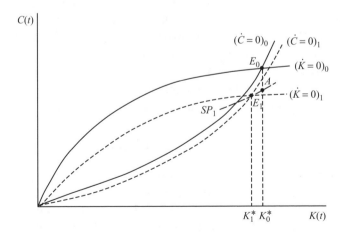

Figure 5.2 Mandatory retirement and a PAYG pension scheme in the Blanchard–Yaari OLG model

the new saddle path SP_1. It then slowly adjusts to the new equilibrium at E_1 (at the intersection of the new $(\dot{C}(t) = 0)_1$ and $(\dot{K}(t) = 0)_1$ loci).

In this case, aggregate consumption and the physical capital stock are lower than before. However, had the $\dot{C}(t) = 0$ locus shifted down by more than the $\dot{K}(t) = 0$ locus, the new equilibrium would have involved a higher capital stock.

In either case, consumption is unambiguously lower. Having fallen from E_0 to A immediately upon the introduction of the PAYG scheme, consumption falls even further from A to E_1, but this now takes place gradually over time. The explanation for this is that as more and more retired workers die out, an increasing proportion of aggregate consumption is accounted for by the younger generations with lower human capital. In addition, existing working generations discount current and future tax liabilities at the annuity rate $(r(t) + \beta)$, rather than the market interest rate $(r(t))$. This implies that these workers do not feel the full burden of the taxes and hence do not reduce their consumption by a sufficient amount. This leads to a crowding out of private investment at A (i.e., $\dot{K}(t) < 0$) and capital stock begins to fall. This reduces the marginal product of labour and raises the marginal product of capital, causing pre-tax wages to fall and the interest rate to rise. For both these reasons, human capital begins to fall even further as the economy moves from A to E_1.

A similar result in terms of lower aggregate consumption (although still with an ambiguous effect on capital stock) holds if the PAYG is less generous than this (i.e., if $P(t) < W(t)$), since the human capital of all generations is lower in this case. In this model, we get the same results even if the PAYG scheme is very generous (i.e., if $P(t) > W(t)$), since the imposition of mandatory retirement cuts total human capital and the transfer payments via the PAYG scheme from the young to the old will not increase aggregate consumption, since the marginal propensity to consume out of total wealth is the same for all generations.

5.3 CONCLUSIONS

The Blanchard–Yaari OLG model is more realistic than the Diamond–Samuelson OLG model because it allows for lifetime uncertainty. But it is also considerably more complex. It builds on two results from Yaari's original model. The first result is that individuals discount the future more heavily when there is uncertainty attached to the length of life. The second result is that it is optimal for individuals with no bequest motive to annuitise all their wealth and hence perfectly hedge the mortality risk that they face. If they do this, the growth rate of optimal consumption over the lifetime will be the same as in the case of no lifetime uncertainty. Blanchard modelled the uncertain lifetimes assuming a constant (age-independent) force of mortality. The resulting model is defined by a pair of differential equations explaining the dynamic behaviour of optimal aggregate consumption and the capital stock. The equilibrium of the model is unique and saddle-point stable.

The Blanchard–Yaari model can be used to examine the effect of introducing a PAYG pension scheme with mandatory retirement, financed by lump-sum taxes on the young. The imposition of lump-sum taxes and mandatory retirement reduces the human capital of the young and this leads to aggregate consumption falling, whatever the generosity of the pension scheme.

QUESTIONS

1. Explain the expected utility hypothesis.
2. What additional factors need to be taken into account when lifetimes are uncertain?
3. How does the consumption Euler equation change in the presence of lifetime uncertainty?
4. What is the force of mortality?
5. What is Yaari's first result?
6. What is a life annuity?
7. What is mortality profit?
8. Why is it optimal in the absence of a bequest motive to annuitise all wealth?
9. What is Yaari's second result?
10. Explain the model of perpetual youth.
11. How does each generation determine its optimal consumption in the Blanchard–Yaari model?
12. What is the effective rate of time preference in the Blanchard–Yaari model?
13. How is optimal aggregate consumption determined in the Blanchard–Yaari model?
14. Explain the shape of the $\dot{K}(t) = 0$ locus in the phase diagram of the Blanchard–Yaari model.
15. Explain the shape of the $\dot{C}(t) = 0$ locus in the phase diagram of the Blanchard–Yaari model.

16. Show how the equilibrium in the Blanchard–Yaari model is unique and saddle-point stable.
17. What happens in the Blanchard–Yaari model when the government introduces a programme of mandatory retirement and a PAYG pension scheme financed by lump-sum taxes on those in work?
18. How does the result in the previous question depend on the generosity of the pension system?

REFERENCES

Blanchard, O. (1985) Debts, deficits and finite horizons, *Journal of Political Economy*, **93**, 223–247.

Buiter, W. (1988) Death, productivity growth and debt neutrality, *Economic Journal*, **98**, 279–293.

Heijdra, B. and van der Ploeg, F. (2002) *Foundations of Modern Macroeconomics*, Oxford, University Press Oxford (ch. 16: Intergenerational Economics I).

Yaari, M. (1965) Uncertain lifetime, life insurance and the theory of the consumer, *Review of Economic Studies*, **32**, 137–150.

6
The Economics of Ageing and Generational Accounting

We examine two issues: the economics of ageing from a macroeconomic perspective and generational accounts (the difference between the present value of the taxes paid and the benefits received by a particular generation). We do this in the context of the Diamond–Samuelson overlapping generations (OLG) model as used in Heijdra and van der Ploeg (2002, ch. 17) and explained in detail in Chapter 4 (see also Bosworth and Burtless, 1998; Disney, 1996; Robinson and Srinivasan, 1997; Thompson, 1998; Weil, 1997).

6.1 THE MACROECONOMIC EFFECTS OF AGEING: DECLINING POPULATION GROWTH AND THE INCREASING DEPENDENCY RATIO

The *dependency ratio* is defined as the ratio of the number of pensioners to the number of workers in a society. In the standard Diamond–Samuelson OLG model, the growth rate of the population is assumed to be constant at n. At time t, the number of retired and working people are L_{t-1} and $L_t = (1 + n)L_{t-1}$, respectively, giving a dependency ratio of $1/(1 + n)$.

Table 6.1 shows that the dependency ratio in the world as a whole, and in developed countries in particular, is rising. The world's population is ageing rapidly as the proportion of old people increases relative to young people.

Population ageing is the result of either or both of two causes: a decrease in fertility and an increase in longevity. In developed societies, it requires 2.1 children per female to stabilise a population in the absence of immigration. If the fertility rate falls below this level, the population will start to age (i.e., the mean age of those alive will increase). If there is also an increase in longevity, the population will continue to increase, but will eventually begin to decline and the dependency ratio will increase rapidly.

Table 6.1   Age composition of the population (%)

	1950	1990	2025
World			
0–19	44.1	41.7	32.8
20–65	50.8	52.1	57.5
65+	5.1	6.2	9.7
OECD			
0–19	35.0	27.2	24.8
20–64	56.7	59.9	56.6
65+	8.3	12.8	18.6
USA			
0–19	33.9	28.9	26.8
20–65	57.9	58.9	56.0
65+	8.1	12.2	17.2

Source: Weil (1997). Reproduced by permission

There are two opposing views on whether longevity will continue to increase or not, and these two views clearly highlight the issue of *longevity risk*, the uncertainty attached to future life expectancy.

Oeppen and Vaupel (2002) show that longevity has been improving linearly since the 1840s at the rate of 3 months every year, and that there is no sign of this tailing off (see Figure 6.1). Other studies have shown that people who lived longer did not actually suffer many more years of ill-health. The 2002 English Longitudinal Study of Ageing (ELSA) found that the older old were amazingly healthy, both mentally and physically. For example, 30% of men in their 80s described their health as good or excellent. 72% of women and 84% of men aged 80–84 had no difficulty in walking at speeds of up to 1 mile an hour.

The explanations for the improvement in life expectancy are: better health in the womb and early childhood, less smoking, less exhausting and dangerous jobs, better education and the impact of medical advances. Deaths from coronary heart disease have fallen by 40% since 1980 in the USA. Aaron and Schwartz (2003) argue that advances in molecular biology could deliver 'truly revolutionary' improvements in longevity. However, there are big differences in the longevity experience of different social classes. ELSA found that members of the top social class live 5 years longer than those who live in the bottom social class. The well-off and well-educated experience the onset of

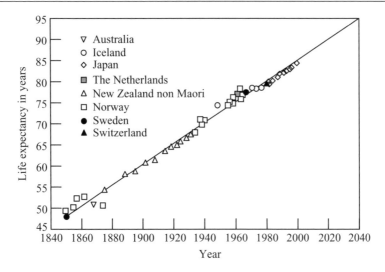

Figure 6.1   Linear improvements in life expectancy since the 1840s
Source: Oeppen and Vaupel (2002). Reprinted with permission from Broken limits of life expectancy by J. Oeppen and J.W. Vaupel. Copyright (2002) AAAS

mental and physical disabilities 15 years later than the poor and uneducated. This is partly due to smoking and poor diet, but also due to how much people feel they are in control of their lives and their feeling of self-worth.

The counter-view is made by Olshansky *et al.* (1990, 2001, 2005). They argue that life expectancy in the USA is set to fall within the next 50 years due to an 'obesity epidemic that will creep through all ages like a human tsunami'. The dramatic increase in obesity amongst younger generations would be a major factor in reducing life-expectancy levels. It is estimated that more than 30% of Americans (60m people) are obese. Obesity triples the risk of heart disease and produces a tenfold increase in the likelihood of developing diabetes. The negative impact on life expectancy occurs when obese Americans reach middle age. This will place a further burden on the US social security system by reducing the number of people who are able to work. However, it could eventually reduce the pension burden if people died before reaching retirement. By 2020, it is estimated that 20% of US healthcare expenditure will be devoted to dealing with the obesity problems facing 50–69-year-old US citizens. Olshansky *et al.* also argue that there must be an upper limit to life expectancy for biodemographic, biomechanical, biological reasons (the human body simply cannot last indefinitely).

Another serious issue is drug abuse by young people. Yet another serious risk (according to a 2005 World Health Organisation report) is the global spread of infectious diseases, in particular an influenza pandemic, caused by the spread of bird (avian) flu originating in SE Asia. The virus is currently difficult for humans to contract but could mutate if it is contracted by a person exposed to the human flu virus, which spreads easily amongst humans. Influenza pandemics (all thought to be derived from avian strains) occur three or four times a century, following the emergence of virus subtypes that spread easily amongst humans. In the twentieth century, the 1918–19 pandemic killed 50m people. There were less severe pandemics in 1957–58 and 1968–69. The killing of Hong Kong's 1.5m chicken population in 1997 is thought to have averted another pandemic at the end of the twentieth century.

The balance of evidence, however, appears to support the view that the increase in longevity seems to be a permanent effect. Martins *et al.* (2005), in a report from the Organisation for Economic Cooperation and Development, argue that: 'Currently there is no evidence of a deceleration in longevity'. The report states that female longevity has increased 'almost linearly' over the last 150 years, by 2.4 years per decade, and that conditional life expectancy at higher ages has recently accelerated (see Figure 6.2; see also the *Economist*, 2004). The OECD's simulations suggest that 'implementing piecemeal reforms is not the most efficient way to eliminate the policy-induced growth losses in the context of ageing'. Instead, 'Combining pension and labour market reforms is likely to

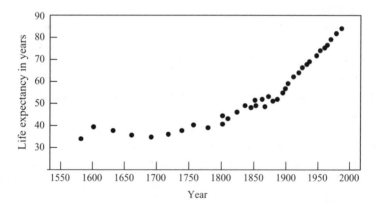

Figure 6.2   Female life expectancy since the 1550s
Source: Oeppen and Vaupel (2002). Reprinted with permission from Broken limits of life expectancy by J. Oeppen and J.W. Vaupel. Copyright (2002) AAAS

provide the best remedy to such losses and can, in some cases, offset the tendency of differential demographic developments to exacerbate income gaps among OECD countries'.[1]

Whether it is the Oeppen and Vaupel view or the Olshansky view that ultimately dominates, it seems that health and long-term care costs will be higher as the population ages (Folland *et al.* 2004; Phelps, 2003).

6.2   PENSIONS IN THE DIAMOND–SAMUELSON OLG MODEL WITH A VARIABLE POPULATION GROWTH RATE

The rising dependency ratio can be captured in the OLG model by introducing a variable population growth rate, n_t:

$$L_t = (1 + n_t)L_{t-1} \tag{6.1}$$

Assuming a constant contribution per person ($T_t = T$) into a PAYG scheme, the pension at t (P_t) will be:

$$P_t = (1 + n_t)T \tag{6.2}$$

The fundamental difference equation describing the path of the economy becomes (cf equation (4.90)):

$$S(W_t, r_{t+1}, n_{t+1}, T) = (1 + n_{t+1})k_{t+1} \tag{6.3}$$

where S is savings, W is gross (before tax) lifetime income, r is the interest rate and k is the capital–labour ratio.

Saving by the young depends negatively on the rate of population growth, n_{t+1}, since if n_{t+1} is high, the young will get a high pension when old ($P_{t+1} = (1 + n_{t+1})T$) and so do not need to save as much for their retirement when they are young. If a reduction in fertility is expected, on the other hand, this reduces the expected pension and hence lifetime income, and results in young individuals reducing both current and future consumption and increasing savings:

$$S_n \equiv \frac{\partial S}{\partial n_{t+1}} < 0 \tag{6.4}$$

The right-hand side of equation (6.3) shows that the fall in n_{t+1} will be associated with a rise in k_{t+1} for a given level of per capita saving on the left-hand side.

---

[1] Blake and Mayhew (2006) consider a range of pension and labour market reforms in the context of the demographic problems facing the UK state pension system.

If we substitute factor price equations of the form $W_t = W(k_t)$ and $r_{t+1} = r(k_{t+1})$ (such as equations (4.91) and (4.92)) into (6.3), we can derive the fundamental difference equation for the capital stock in implicit form (cf equation (4.93)):

$$k_{t+1} = g(k_t, n_{t+1}) \tag{6.5}$$

The partial derivatives are:

$$g_k \equiv \frac{\partial g}{\partial k_t} = \frac{S_W W'(k_t)}{1 + n_{t+1} - S_r r'(k_{t+1})} > 0 \tag{6.6}$$

$$g_n \equiv \frac{\partial g}{\partial n_{t+1}} = \frac{S_n - k_{t+1}}{1 + n_{t+1} - S_r r'(k_{t+1})} < 0 \tag{6.7}$$

where S_W and S_r are the relevant partial derivatives from equation (6.3).

A permanent reduction in the population growth rate from n_0 to n_1, say, generates a long-run increase in the capital stock, since:

$$\frac{dk}{dn} = \frac{g_n}{(1 - g_k)} < 0 \tag{6.8}$$

Figure 6.3 shows the transition path of the economy to the new steady state. Suppose the economy begins with initial capital of k_0. Prior to the reduction in population growth, the transition path for the economy would have followed the dotted line from A to E_0. The reduction in fertility has an impact effect of increasing savings, and the capital stock jumps to B and thereafter follows a new transition path to E_1. The

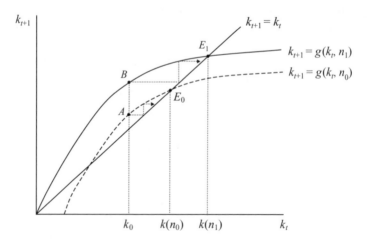

Figure 6.3   The effects of ageing
Source: Heijdra and van der Ploeg (2002). Reproduced by permission of Oxford University Press

long-run capital–labour ratio is higher because there are now relatively more old individuals who own lots of capital to provide an income in old age and relatively fewer young individuals of working age. A reduction in fertility, by increasing the capital–labour ratio, reduces the interest rate and increases wages (workers are scarcer than they were before and each of them has more capital).

The steady state welfare effect of a permanent reduction in fertility is found by differentiating the indirect utility function (see equation (4.104)):

$$\bar{\Lambda}^Y (W, r, T) = \underset{\{C^Y, C^O\}}{Max} \left\{ \Lambda^Y \left(C^Y, C^O \right) \text{ subject to } \hat{W} = C^Y + \frac{C^O}{1+r} \right\}$$

(6.9)

where $\Lambda^Y \left(C^Y, C^O \right)$ is the direct utility function and

$$\hat{W} \equiv W - \left(\frac{r-n}{1+r} \right) T$$

(6.10)

is lifetime income with a PAYG scheme.

Differentiating the indirect utility function with respect to n gives:

$$
\begin{aligned}
\frac{d\bar{\Lambda}^Y}{dn} &= \frac{\partial \bar{\Lambda}^Y}{\partial W} \frac{dW}{dn} + \frac{\partial \bar{\Lambda}^Y}{\partial r} \frac{dr}{dn} + \frac{\partial \bar{\Lambda}^Y}{\partial n} \\
&= \frac{\partial \Lambda^Y}{\partial C^Y} \left[\frac{dW}{dn} + \left(\frac{S}{1+r} \right) \frac{dr}{dn} + \frac{T}{1+r} \right] \\
&= \frac{\partial \Lambda^Y}{\partial C^Y} \left[-k \left(\frac{r-n}{1+r} \right) \frac{dr}{dn} + \frac{T}{1+r} \right] \gtrless 0
\end{aligned}
$$

(6.11)

where we have used:

$$\frac{\partial \bar{\Lambda}^Y}{\partial n} = \frac{T}{1+r} \frac{\partial \Lambda^Y}{\partial C^Y}$$

(6.12)

and where:

$$\frac{dr}{dn} = r' \frac{dk}{dn} > 0$$

(6.13)

When the economy is dynamically efficient ($r > n$), the first term in square brackets on the right-hand side of the last line of (6.11), which shows the long-run effect of fertility on the interest rate, is negative (using (6.13)): a fall in fertility therefore raises long-run welfare from this effect. The second term in square brackets measures the welfare effect from the return on the PAYG scheme, which falls as fertility falls thereby reducing welfare. The net effect on welfare from a change in fertility is therefore ambiguous. However, if the contribution to the PAYG scheme (T) is low and if the capital–labour ratio is relatively low (so that r is high relative to n), then a fall in fertility will raise welfare. On the other hand, if the PAYG scheme is very generous, so that T is high, then a fall in fertility will reduce welfare.

6.3 GENERATIONAL ACCOUNTING

The concept of *generational accounts* was introduced by Auerbach *et al.* (1991, 1994). A generational account is defined as the difference between the present value of the taxes paid and the benefits received by a particular generation. The sum of the generational accounts across all current and future generations must by definition be zero, so that a net benefit received by one generation must be paid for by another generation.

There is a strong relationship between the generational accounts and the government's budget constraint. This constraint states that 'the government's current net worth plus the present value of the government's net receipts from all current and future generations (the generational accounts) must be sufficient to pay for the present value of the government's current and future consumption' (Auerbach *et al.*, 1991, p. 58).

Buiter (1997) examined generational accounting in the OLG model with a constant population ($L_t = L_{t-1} = 1$). The *government's budget constraint* is:

$$B_{t+1} = (1 + r_t)B_t + G_t^O + G_t^Y - T_t^O - T_t^Y \tag{6.14}$$

where B_t is the stock of government bonds outstanding in period t, r_t is the interest paid on government bonds in period t, G_t^O and G_t^Y are the goods and services provided to the old and young generations free of charge in period t, and T_t^O and T_t^Y are the corresponding taxes collected (net of transfer payments).

Iterating equation (6.14) forward over T periods gives:

$$B_t = R_{t-1,T}^{-1} B_{t+T+1} + \sum_{s=0}^{T} R_{t-1,s}^{-1} \left(T_{t+s}^O + T_{t+s}^Y - G_{t+s}^O - G_{t+s}^Y \right) \tag{6.15}$$

where:

$$R_{t-1,s}^{-1} = \prod_{i=0}^{s} \left(\frac{1}{1 + r_{t+i}} \right) \tag{6.16}$$

is the discount factor.

The government's solvency condition is that government debt cannot grow at a faster rate than the rate of interest in the long run:

$$\lim_{T\to\infty} R_{t-1,T}^{-1} B_{t+T+1} = 0 \tag{6.17}$$

so that the government budget constraint is:

$$B_t = \sum_{s=0}^{\infty} R_{t-1,s}^{-1} \left(T_{t+s}^O + T_{t+s}^Y - G_{t+s}^O - G_{t+s}^Y \right) \tag{6.18}$$

This shows that if at any time there is positive outstanding government debt ($B_t > 0$), the government must at some future date run a *primary surplus* (collect more in net taxes than it pays out in goods and services) to remain solvent.

Individuals are assumed to earn an income during youth from which they consume, save and pay taxes net of transfers (e.g., child benefit); they also receive goods and services provided by the state during youth (e.g., education). Savings are assumed to be invested in either government bonds or physical capital. In old age, individuals receive their savings with interest and pay taxes net of transfers (e.g., state pensions); they also receive goods and services provided by the state during old age (e.g., health care).

In addition to consuming state-provided goods and services G_t^Y and G_{t+1}^O in youth and old age, the individual's budget constraint in each period of his life is:

$$C_t^Y + S_t = W_t - T_t^Y \tag{6.19}$$

$$C_{t+1}^O = (1 + r_{t+1}) S_t - T_{t+1}^O \tag{6.20}$$

where:

$$S_t = B_{t+1} + K_{t+1} \tag{6.21}$$

The lifetime budget constraint for this individual is found by combining equations (6.19) and (6.20):

$$W_t - T_{t,t} = C_t^Y + \frac{C_{t+1}^O}{1 + r_{t+1}} \tag{6.22}$$

where $T_{t,t}$ is the present value in period t (first subscript) of (lump-sum) taxes paid (net of transfers received) over the lifetime of a generation born in period t (second subscript):

$$T_{t,t} = T_t^Y + \frac{T_{t+1}^O}{1 + r_{t+1}} \tag{6.23}$$

Equation (6.23) can be used to rewrite the government budget constraint (6.18) as:

$$B_t + \sum_{s=0}^{\infty} R_{t-1,s}^{-1} \left(G_{t+s}^O + G_{t+s}^Y \right) = \sum_{s=t-1}^{\infty} T_{t-1,s} \qquad (6.24)$$

where the $T_{t-1,s}$ terms are defined as follows:

$$T_{t-1,t-1} \equiv \left(\frac{1}{1+r_t} \right) T_t^O \qquad (6.25)$$

for the current old generation

$$T_{t-1,t} \equiv \left(\frac{1}{1+r_t} \right) T_{t,t} = \left(\frac{1}{1+r_t} \right) \left[T_t^Y + \frac{T_{t+1}^O}{1+r_{t+1}} \right] \qquad (6.26)$$

for the current young generation

$$T_{t-1,s} \equiv R_{t-1,s-t}^{-1} T_{s,s} = R_{t-1,s-t}^{-1} \left[T_s^Y + \frac{T_{s+1}^O}{1+r_{s+1}} \right] \qquad (6.27)$$

for future generations, $s = t+1, t+2, \ldots$. Equation (6.24) states that the current value of the national debt plus the present value of government consumption must equal the present value of the taxes on current and future generations.

Table 6.2 Male generational accounts

Generation's age in 1991	Net payments ($\times$ \$1000)	Tax payments ($\times$ \$1000)	Transfer receipts ($\times$ \$1000)
0	78.9	99.3	20.4
10	125.0	155.3	30.3
20	187.1	229.6	42.5
30	205.5	258.5	53.0
40	180.1	250.0	69.9
50	97.2	193.8	96.6
60	−23.0	112.1	135.1
70	−80.7	56.3	137.0
80	−61.1	30.2	91.3
90	−3.5	8.8	12.3
Future	166.5		

Source: Auerbach *et al.* (1994, p. 80). Reproduced by permission

Table 6.2 shows the generational accounts for ten generations of US males in 1991 as presented in Auerbach *et al.* (1994, p. 80). The first column shows the age of each generation in 1991. The second column shows the generational accounts for each generation, and the third and fourth columns show the component parts, namely the present value of tax payments and transfer receipts. The table shows that 70-year-olds were the most favoured generation alive in 1991, each receiving $80,700 more in state benefits than they paid in taxes. The least favoured were 30-year-olds, who could expect to pay out $205,500 each more in taxes than they receive in benefits. So generous has been the net social security benefits to older US males that future generations will each have to make net payments of $166,500 (last row) to compensate. Similar results hold for the UK and other developed countries (Cardarelli *et al.*, 2000; Auerbach *et al.*, 1999).

6.4   CONCLUSIONS

Population ageing arises from a combination of decreasing fertility and increasing longevity. There are two contrasting views on whether longevity can continue to increase along the linear trend of 3 months per year that it has followed over the last 150 years. The Oeppen and Vaupel view is that this trend will indeed continue. The counter-view by Olshansky is that factors such as obesity and influenza pandemics, as well as limits to the effective life of the human frame, will place an upper limit on life expectancy.

The consequences for PAYG pensions of a rising dependency ratio can be analysed in the Diamond–Samuelson OLG model by introducing a variable population growth rate. A declining population growth rate increases saving by the young, since they will realise that PAYG pensions will be smaller in the future. This will increase both the capital stock and the capital–labour ratio. If the economy is dynamically efficient and the PAYG system is not very generous, it is possible to show that the welfare of future generations can actually increase in the face of falling fertility.

A generational account shows the difference between the present value of the taxes paid by a particular generation and the benefits it receives. If one generation receives a net benefit, this must be paid for by one or more future generations. The calculation of the generational accounts for the USA, UK and other developed countries shows that the generation born in the 1920s, and which benefited from the introduction of the social

security system in the 1930s, might turn out to be the most favoured
generation in history according to the generational accounts.

QUESTIONS

1. What is the dependency ratio?
2. What are the causes of population ageing?
3. What is longevity risk?
4. Compare the views of Oeppen and Vaupel on future trends in longevity with those of Olshansky.
5. Examine the consequences for the economy (in particular savings, the capital–labour ratio, wages and the interest rate) of a permanent reduction in the growth rate in population. What happens to welfare in these circumstances?
6. What are generational accounts?
7. What is the implication for government solvency of a positive national debt?
8. What is the pattern of the generational accounts of the current generations alive in developed countries?

REFERENCES

Aaron, H. and Schwartz, W. (eds) (2003) *Coping With Methuselah: The Impact of Molecular Biology on Medicine and Society*, Brookings Institution, Washington, DC.

Auerbach, A., Gokhale, J. and Kotlikoff, L. (1991) Generational accounts: a meaningful alternative to deficit accounting, in Bradford, D. (ed.), *Tax Policy and the Economy*, Vol. 5, MIT Press, Cambridge, MA, pp. 55–110.

Auerbach, A., Gokhale, J. and Kotlikoff, L. (1994) *Generational Accounting Around the World*, University of Chicago Press, Chicago.

Auerbach, A., Kotlikoff, L. and Leibfritz, W. (1999) Generational accounting: a meaningful way to evaluate fiscal policy, *Journal of Economic Perspectives*, **8**, 73–94.

Blake, D. and Mayhew, L. (2006) On the sustainability of the UK state pension system in the light of population ageing and declining fertility, *Economic Journal*, **116**, F286–F305.

Bosworth, B. and Burtless, G. (eds) (1998) *Aging Societies: The Global Dimension*, Brookings Institution Press, Washington, DC.

Buiter, W. (1997) Generational accounts, aggregate saving, and intergenerational distribution, *Economica*, **64**, 605–626.

Cardarelli, R., Sefton, J. and Kotlikoff, L. (2000) Generational accounting in the UK, *Economic Journal*, **110**, F547-F574.

Disney, R. (1996) A burden of dependency? Social security programs & intergenerational redistribution, ch. 2 in *Can We Afford to Grow Older? A Perspective on the Economics of Ageing*, MIT Press, Cambridge, MA.

Economist (2004) A Long, Long Life, 25 May.

Folland, S., Goodman, A. and Stano, M. (2004) *The Economics of Health and Health Care*, Prentice Hall, Englewood Cliffs, NJ.

Heijdra, B. and van der Ploeg, F. (2002) *Foundations of Modern Macroeconomics*, Oxford University Press, Oxford (ch. 17: Intergenerational Economics II).

Martins, J., Gonand, F., Antolin, P., de la Maisonneuve, C. and Yoo, K.-Y. (2005) The Impact of Ageing on Demand, Factor Markets and Growth, Economics Working Papers 420, Organisation for Economic Co-operation and Development, Paris.

Oeppen, J. and Vaupel, J.W. (2002) Broken limits of life expectancy, *Science*, **296**, (5570), 1029–1031.

Olshansky, S.J., Carnes, B.A. and Cassel, C. (1990) In search of Methuselah: estimating the upper limits to human longevity, *Science*, **250**, 634–640.

Olshansky, S.J., Carnes, B.A. and Désesquelles, A. (2001) Prospects for human longevity, *Science*, **291** (5508), 1491–1492.

Olshansky, S.J., Passaro, D., Hershow, R., Layden, J., Carnes, B.A., Brody, J., Hayflick, L., Butler, R.N., Allison, D.B. and Ludwig, D.S. (2005) A possible decline in life expectancy in the United States in the 21st century, *New England Journal of Medicine*, **352**, 1103–1110.

Phelps, C. (2003) *Health Economics*, Addison-Wesley, Boston.

Thompson, L. (1998) *Older and Wiser – The Economics of Public Pensions*, Urban Institute Press, Washington, DC.

Weil, D. (1997) The Economics of Population Ageing, in Rosenzweig, M. and Stark, O. (eds), *Handbook of Population and Family Economics*, North-Holland, Amsterdam.

7

Risk Sharing and Redistribution
in Pension Schemes

Welfare economics deals with the economic wellbeing of different members of society. This will depend on the initial distribution of resources (i.e., income and wealth) to, and any subsequent redistribution of resources between, different members of society, and on the ability of society to share risks between different members of society. Welfare economics therefore deals with issues of *equity* as opposed to issues of *efficiency*, and also with the consequences of different economic policies for equity and risk sharing. Welfare economics also deals with the consequences of *market failure*, i.e., when the market mechanism generates outcomes that are suboptimal and the state intervenes to improve the welfare of some (or all) groups of citizens.[1]

Different pension schemes have different redistributional capabilities. State pension schemes can (and generally do) redistribute income in retirement from rich members of society to poorer members of society. This is achieved through lower contributions (relative to income) and/or higher benefits (relative to contributions) for low-income people than high-income people. This is the deliberate and declared intention of most state pension schemes. It is not usually a declared policy of private pension schemes to redistribute income in a planned way, however. Nevertheless, private pension schemes are capable of deliberately and systematically redistributing income to different classes of member in ways that are not well understood to most scheme members.

Different types of pension scheme also involve different *ex ante* risks and have different ways of sharing those risks. They will therefore, depending on how the future evolves and how uncertainty is resolved, have different ways of *ex post* redistributing income and wealth between different classes of member. Any insurance policy (and a pension scheme

---

[1] We have sometimes examined welfare issues in previous chapters, but in this chapter we do this in a more systematic manner.

is an example of an insurance policy[2]) involves risk sharing prior to uncertainty resolution and a redistribution of resources from 'losers' to 'winners' after. With this type of redistribution of resources (unlike the one considered in the previous paragraph), it is not known *a priori* who will be benefiting from the redistribution.

What is the optimal level of risk sharing? Gordon and Varian (1988) argue that efficient risk sharing amongst individuals requires that each individual charges (and receives) the same *risk premium*[3] for an additional share of each risky prospect. When facing an aggregate risk, efficient risk sharing requires all individuals to experience the same change in their marginal utility of consumption. For example, if all individuals have logarithmic (i.e., unit-elastic) utility, then a 1% fall in national income will lead to all individuals reducing their consumption by 1% when there is efficient risk sharing. If some individuals are more *risk averse* than others, they might consider buying insurance from the *risk tolerant* who receive an insurance premium in exchange. If the risk tolerant are willing to accept this offer, the consumption of risk-averse members of society would fall by less than 1% when national income falls by 1% (but see below).

All individuals face risks during their lives, e.g., the risk of becoming unemployed during their working life. When someone becomes unemployed, their consumption falls and they do not save enough for their retirement. Welfare economics deals with risk-sharing devices that improve the welfare of society as a whole. A simple example of such a device is a social security system that taxes individuals in work in order to pay unemployment benefit to those who are unemployed and provides pensions to poor members of society when they get old. There are a number of factors to take into account when designing a risk-sharing system such as a social security system, two of the most important of which are moral hazard and adverse selection.

Moral hazard is the situation where someone becomes less careful once they are protected against some adverse event. For example, an individual might deliberately get fired from their job in order to draw unemployment benefit or they might deliberately save too little for their

---

[2] Bodie (1990) argues that the first role of a pension scheme is to provide retirement income insurance and to protect the member against economic insecurity in retirement.

[3] A risk premium is the compensation needed to induce an individual to take on an additional unit of risk.

retirement since they know the state will not allow them to live in poverty in old age. To discourage this from happening, the social security system might choose to rule out giving unemployment benefit to someone who deliberately lost their job or giving a pension to someone who failed to save at least a minimum amount for their retirement; or it might only offer reduced benefits in these circumstances. *Adverse selection* is the situation where only those most likely to claim unemployment benefit (say, because they happen to be incompetent workers and know this but cannot help it) or state pensions (say, because they know they are natural spenders not natural savers) want to participate in the social security system. To reduce the impact of this, the social security system has to be mandatory and so cover all workers and pensioners. Another mechanism for dealing with adverse selection that is used by private sector insurers is the careful screening of applicants prior to offering them policies.

Assuming the appropriate systems are in place to deal with moral hazard and adverse selection, a risk-sharing device can be welfare enhancing. But it is important to differentiate between the types of risk that can be shared in this way. The easiest risks to share are risks that are *idiosyncratic* or *specific* to the individual. Unemployment risk is an example of an idiosyncratic risk, since at any time some individuals will be unemployed while others are not. It is much harder in practice to share *aggregate* or *systematic* risks, since these risks are faced collectively by all members of society at the same time and cannot be traded. An example of this is an extreme economic recession or depression. If everyone is unemployed as a result of the depression (admittedly a very extreme case), a social security system cannot help to share risks, since everyone faces the same systematic risk at the same time. Private sector insurers are unlikely to be willing to assume an aggregate risk, despite, by definition, being more risk tolerant than their policy holders. They are therefore unlikely in practice to be willing to offer policies that insure against falls in national income.

All this has important implications both for individuals and firms and for society as a whole (both the current generation and future generations). We examine risks, risk sharing and redistribution, first in private pension schemes and then in state pension schemes. We also examine the role of the state in dealing with market failure in private sector pension provision. Finally we examine the viability of state pensions in the presence of a systematically ageing population and the transition costs of moving to funded pensions.

7.1   RISKS IN PRIVATE PENSION SCHEMES

A private pension scheme member faces the following risks (Bodie, 1990; Diamond, 1977, 1997):

- Replacement rate risk – the risk that the pension will be insufficient to maintain the same standard of living after retirement as before retirement as a result of inadequate contributions made during the accumulation stage.
- Investment risk – the risk that the retirement fund is inadequate as a result of poor investment performance.
- Interest rate risk – the risk that the pension annuity is low as a result of low interest rates at the time of retirement.
- Longevity risk – the risk that individuals will outlive their retirement savings.
- Inflation risk – the risk that inflation will reduce the purchasing power of retirement savings.
- Political risk – the risk of explicit changes by the government in the law that adversely affect the contributions to and/or benefits from a pension scheme, such as the removal of favourable tax breaks on contributions. There are three main sources of political risk:
  - Demographically induced political risk, e.g., the risk that the law will be changed to counter a demographic imbalance between, say, those paying for the tax breaks and those benefiting from them.
  - Economically induced political risk, e.g., the risk that some favourable tax break will be cut, because the government's budget deficit is too large.
  - Pure political risk, e.g., arising from a redistribution of benefits or changing tax breaks in favour of supporters of the political party in power, such as left-wing governments switching resources away from the rich to the poor.
- Portability risk – the risk that accrued pension benefits are not fully portable when the member changes jobs.
- Employer insolvency risk – the risk that the pension scheme has a deficit at the time the employer becomes insolvent.

Some of these risks can be insured against, while others cannot readily be insured against. We look first at personal pensions and then at occupational pensions.

7.2   RISK SHARING IN PERSONAL PENSION SCHEMES

Defined contribution (i.e., personal) pension schemes face all the risks listed in Section 7.1, except portability risk and employer insolvency risk.

The risk of an inadequate pension in retirement can be 'insured against' by making sufficient contributions into a personal pension scheme (PPS) when the member is young.

Investment risk directly affects members of DC schemes and the sponsors of DB schemes, unless the schemes are small insured schemes in which case the investment risk is faced by the insurance company managing the small scheme's assets. In the case of DC schemes, investment risk can be managed by investing in assets that are consistent with the risk tolerance of the DC scheme member: low risk tolerance suggests an investment in money market funds, medium risk tolerance suggests an investment in bonds, while high risk tolerance suggests an investment in equities.

Interest rate risk affects those people who need to buy life annuities from life insurance companies at retirement, such as members of DC schemes and the sponsors of mainly small insured DB schemes who purchase annuities for their retired members. The payouts on life annuities are made from the coupon payments on bonds purchased by the life insurance companies with the proceeds from selling the fund accumulated during the working life. If, at the time the annuity is purchased, interest rates are low, the cost of buying the bonds will be high and so the annuity that can be paid out will be correspondingly low. Interest rate risk can be hedged using derivative instruments such as futures and options, but this will be expensive. A cheaper alternative is to use staggered annuity purchases by staggering the timing of the purchases across the interest rate cycle, although this possibility is not really available to poor people who need as much money as possible when they retire.

The natural way to hedge longevity risk is to purchase a life annuity which guarantees to continue paying as long as the annuitant lives. In fact, an annuity is an essential feature of a pension plan. Yet in many countries (e.g., the USA, Germany, Italy, Japan and Australia) there is no requirement to purchase an annuity with the accumulated fund at retirement. Retirees can spend their money as fast as they like once they retire and therefore face the risk of running out of resources before they die. Most people underestimate how long they will live after they retire. O'Brien et al. (2005) found that UK men underestimate their life expectancy by 4.62 years and women underestimate their life expectancy by 5.95 years.

The annuities market is subject to the problem of adverse selection: individuals with higher than average life expectancy tend to be the keenest purchasers of annuities. Life insurance companies, aware of this, will price the annuities they sell accordingly. The average annuitant will find annuities poor value for money and avoid purchasing them if they are able to. The early evidence appeared to indicate that the cost loading for adverse selection was indeed high (Friedman and Warshawsky, 1990), but more recent evidence both for the USA and UK, the world's two most developed and competitive annuities markets, suggests the selection cost loading was not that excessive and that annuities represented good value for money (Mitchell *et al.* 1999; Finkelstein and Poterba, 2002). In countries without developed annuities markets, the family provides an alternative institutional framework for (at least partially) hedging longevity risk (Kotlikoff and Spivak, 1981).

Inflation risk can be hedged in DC schemes by buying indexed annuities, but this can be expensive. For example, with inflation expected to be 3% p.a., the initial payment with an indexed annuity will be 30% below that for a level annuity, it will take 11 years for the two payments to equal each other and 19 years for the total payments with the indexed annuity to exceed those from the level annuity. Most people, given the choice, choose the level annuity, but they are then exposed to inflation risk.

The susceptibility to political risk depends on the balance of political influence amongst different groups in the population. The key is to identify the *median voter*, the marginal (50th percentile) voter who decides the outcome of an election. If the median voter is a young person a long way from retirement, the election might put into power a political party that grants large tax breaks for private pension plans and pays for this by cutting state pension benefits for the elderly. If the median voter is elderly, the election might bring to power a government that increases pensions for the elderly by increasing taxes on the young. If the median voter is elderly, this is likely to be because the population is ageing and fertility is falling, and the dependency ratio is high. The young might begin to resent the burden that they face in supporting an ageing population and might decide to move to a country with a better demographic balance and hence lower taxes, increasing the prospect of intergenerational conflict amongst those who remain behind. Clearly, political risk is a risk that cannot be easily hedged.

One of the attractions of PPSs is the argument that they are not susceptible to demographically induced political risk (e.g., the risk that benefits will be cut because the dependency ratio has become too large). However, even without any change in legislation, increases in life expectancy reduce the amount of annual benefits they can provide, since the increased life expectancy is reflected in a lower annuity for a given lump sum.

PPSs have become susceptible to economically induced political risk. For example, in 1997, UK pension funds were required for the first time to pay tax on their receipts of UK dividends, and this reduced the typical annual returns on PPS investments by 3–4 basis points (Blake, 2004, table 2).

At present there have been no examples of pure political risk with PPSs in the UK. However, there have been periodic press reports that the Labour government that came to power in 1997 has considered taxing the 25% tax-free lump sum that PPS members can take out of their accumulated pension fund in exchange for a lower subsequent pension, an act that would impact most strongly on those individuals who are not the most natural supporters of the government. If implemented, this would have the effect of lowering the internal rate of return (IRR) on PPSs by 50 basis points (Blake, 2004, table 2).

7.3   RISK SHARING IN OCCUPATIONAL PENSION SCHEMES

Defined benefit pension schemes face all the risks listed in Section 7.1. As we shall now see, it is possible for these risks to be shared between the employer and employee, but it is conventional for most of the risks to be borne by the scheme sponsor. It is generally only portability risk that is borne exclusively by the scheme member. The sponsor can, in turn, hedge some of the risks he has assumed. For example, investment risk can be mitigated by investing in assets that match the growth characteristics of the liabilities: this is known as *asset–liability matching and management*. Since the liabilities in DB schemes generally grow in line with earnings, the most suitable assets will be those, such as equities, property and indexed bonds, most highly correlated with earnings growth over the long term.

A simple model of risk sharing in occupational pension schemes between employees and firms has been derived by McCarthy (2005). Employees are assumed to negotiate a total compensation package of wages and pensions that guarantees a minimum level of utility, taking into account the risks to which they are exposed, their attitude to risk, and their ability to insure or hedge these risks using financial and insurance markets. Firms are assumed to minimise the risk-adjusted total cost of employee compensation, subject to attracting sufficient numbers of employees to run their business.

To begin with, markets are assumed to be complete in the sense that employees and firms can hedge any risk they might face, including default by the other party. We then move to the case of incomplete markets and the causes of these. The nature of these causes will determine whether firms will be able to insure risks for their workers which third party insurers will not. The types of market incompleteness that are considered are untradeable risks, portfolio restrictions, transactions costs, taxation, externalities and selection effects.

7.3.1 Complete Markets

The worker is assumed to be employed by the firm for two periods. In the first period, the worker receives a certain wage W_0. In the second period, he receives a wage W_i if the state of the world in the second period is i (which occurs with probability p_i), where $i = 1, N$. It is not known what this wage will be in the first period. Given that markets are complete, we suppose that there exist N *basis* or *Arrow–Debreu securities*, one for each state of the world: the ith basis security pays 1 in state of the world i, at time 1, and 0 in every other state (see Arrow, 1964; Debreu, 1959). Suppose the time 0 price of the ith basis security is $q_i \in (0, 1)$.

At time 0, the worker has to decide how much of W_0 to consume (C_0) and how much to save in each of the basis securities (θ_i). He also has to plan his consumption in period 1, which will depend on his realised period 1 income as well as the value of his assets at that time. He will make these decisions on the basis of maximising his expected discounted lifetime utility:

$$\Lambda^*(W_0, W_1, \ldots, W_N) = \max_{\{C,\theta_i\}} \left\{ U(C_0) + \sum_{i=1}^{N} p_i\, U\,(C_i) \right.$$

$$\left. subject\ to\ \begin{cases} W_0 = C_0 + \sum_{i=1}^{N} \theta_i\, q_i \\ C_i = \theta_i + W_i,\ i = 1, N \end{cases} \right\} \quad (7.1)$$

where we assume that both the individual's rate of time preference and the risk-free interest rate are zero. The first constraint states that consumption at time 0 plus the market value purchases of securities at time 0 must equal the income the individual receives at time 0. The second set of constraints state that at time 1, the individual consumes the state i value of his portfolio of securities and his labour income if state i occurs. The term $\Lambda^*(W_0, W_1, \ldots, W_N)$ on the left-hand side of equation (7.1) is known as a *value function*; it shows the maximal value of the utility function at which the constraints are binding. When the risk-free interest rate is zero:

$$\sum_{i=1}^{N} q_i = 1 \qquad (7.2)$$

and the q_i can be interpreted as the *risk-neutral probability* of state i occurring.[4]

Cox and Huang (1989) show that the employee's optimisation problem in (7.1) can be rewritten in a complete markets setting as:

$$\Lambda^*(\bar{W}) = \max_{\{C, \theta_i\}} \left\{ U(C_0) + \sum_{i=1}^{N} p_i\, U(C_i) \text{ subject to} \right.$$

$$\left. \bar{W} = W_0 + \sum_{i=1}^{N} W_i q_i = C_0 + \sum_{i=1}^{N} C_i\, q_i \right\}$$

$$(7.3)$$

where the value function is a function only of $\bar{W}$, the time 0 value of human capital or, equivalently, the market value at time 0 of a portfolio of securities which perfectly replicates the income stream promised to the employee under the employment contract.[5]

In other words, in a complete market setting, the employment contract can be replicated perfectly in financial markets, so that the employee could sell his time 1 income on the financial markets at time 0, and use the money to buy a portfolio of securities which matches his desired future consumption in all time 1 states.

This implies that the income realised in different states and time periods has no effect on the employee's lifetime utility unless it changes the time 0 value of the employment contract, $\bar{W}$. If the employee's time 1 income is labelled a pension, it does not matter in a complete markets setting whether the pension is paid in risky securities or in safe securities, or even when it is paid (time 0 or time 1), since the employee

---

[4] If a security j pays Y_{ji} in state i in a year's time and has a current value V_{0j}, then the following relationship holds between *real-world probabilities* p_i and *risk-neutral probabilities* q_i when markets are complete:

$$V_{0j} = \frac{\sum_{i=1}^{N} Y_{ji}\, p_i}{(1+r_j)} = \frac{\sum_{i=1}^{N} Y_{ji}\, q_i}{(1+r)}$$

where r_j is the risk-adjusted return on security j and r is the risk-free return.

[5] Note the role of the risk-neutral probabilities in the constraint in (7.3).

can use market transactions to switch from any undesired risk exposure to any desired risk exposure. At the optimum, the employee's expected marginal utility of exposure to each risk will equal the market price of that risk. This will be the same for all employees and so there will be efficient risk sharing (Gordon and Varian, 1988).

The value function $\Lambda^* \left(\bar{W} \right)$ is a monotonically increasing function of $\bar{W}$ and does not depend on its distribution across securities or time periods. We can therefore write the inverse of this function as:

$$\bar{W} = \Lambda^{-1} \left(\Lambda^* \right) \tag{7.4}$$

The employer wishes to minimise the cost of paying the employee, subject to the employee achieving a minimum level of lifetime utility, otherwise the employer will not retain the employee who will instead seek a job elsewhere. In other words, the employer needs to pay at least as much as the employee's *reservation wage*, if he wants to retain the worker. The employer's optimisation problem is:

$$\Phi^*(\bar{W}) = \min_{\{W_i\}} \left\{ W_0 + \sum_{i=1}^{N} W_i \, q_i \text{ subject to } \bar{W} \geq \Lambda^{-1} \left(\Lambda^* \right) \right\} \tag{7.5}$$

Like the employee in a complete markets setting, the employer is indifferent to market risk: all that matters is $\bar{W}$, the market value at time 0 of a traded portfolio which perfectly replicates the income promised to the employee.

An optimal employment contract $\{W_0, W_1, \ldots, W_N\}$ is one which satisfies $\bar{W} = \Lambda^{-1} (\Lambda^*)$. There are an infinite number of such contracts in a complete markets setting, and both employer and employees are indifferent to all of them, whatever their attitude to risk.

These results are an extension of Sharpe (1976), who showed that pension funding and investment policy have no effect on firm value in complete markets, and Blinder (1981), who showed that pensions and wages are perfect substitutes in complete markets.

7.3.2 Incomplete Markets

In reality, markets are not complete. Some risks cannot be traded, there are restrictions on the long and short holdings of securities in portfolios, and there are transactions costs associated with changing the composition of portfolios. For example, workers cannot sell their pensions or their future wages. In the case of incomplete markets, the valuation of securities depends not only on the market price of those securities, but also on the preferences of market participants (especially their attitudes to risk). To determine the optimal allocation of pension risk, it is necessary to specify how employee and firm preferences for risk and return are established. If markets are incomplete, the optimal holding of a security might not be at the point where the expected marginal benefit equals the market price of the security.

Untradeable Risks

An untradeable risk is one which must be borne by those exposed to it, since it cannot be diversified away or completely transferred to a third party via an insurance arrangement; it is also known as an aggregate or systematic risk. Examples are wage risk and annuity price (interest rate) risk in the absence of deferred annuities. We consider the case in which such risks can be partially transferred from the employee to the employer.

Assume that at time 1, the employee's wealth will either fall by e_1, with probability π, or it will increase by e_2, with probability $(1 - \pi)$ and that the expected value of this shock is 0 and that it is uncorrelated with any other state of the world. The employee therefore cannot hedge the risk by altering his traded portfolio. Rather, he has to fully assume the risk, which means that his time 1 consumption will change by either e_1 or e_2, depending on circumstances.

Suppose the employer offers to insure part ($\alpha \in (0,1)$) of the risk faced by the employee, so that the employee's net exposure to the risk is $(1 - \alpha) e_i$.

The employee's objective function is now:

$$\Lambda^*(\bar{W}, \alpha) = \max_{\{C, \theta_i\}} \left\{ U(C_0) \right.$$

$$+ \sum_{i=1}^{N} p_i [\pi U(C_i + (1 - \alpha)e_1) + (1 - \pi)U(C_i + (1 - \alpha)e_2)]$$

$$\text{subject to } \left\{ \begin{matrix} \bar{W} = W_0 + \sum_{i=1}^{N} W_i q_i = C_0 + \sum_{i=1}^{N} C_i q_i \\ \pi e_1 + (1 - \pi)e_2 = 0 \end{matrix} \right\} \right\} \quad (7.6)$$

Total consumption at time 1 is hedgeable consumption in the ith state, C_i, plus the unhedgeable risk, e_i, less the insurance payoff from the employer, αe_i. The employee's budget constraint is still the same: the employee chooses hedgeable consumption subject to the market price of the portfolio which replicates his hedgeable consumption equalling the market price of the portfolio which replicates his hedgeable income; as in the complete markets case, he is not concerned about the individual components of the portfolio, just the total value. The second constraint states that the expected value of the shock is 0.

The existence of the risk might alter the employee's optimal consumption at time 0: if he is risk averse, he will consume less in the first period in case there is a negative shock in the second period.

Suppose the employer wishes to minimise the expected cost of the employee compensation package, but also dislikes a high variance for this cost. The employer's objective function is assumed to be:

$$\Phi^*(\bar{W}, \alpha) = \min_{\{W_i, \alpha\}} \left\{ W_0 + \sum_{i=1}^{N} W_i \, q_i + \frac{\gamma}{2}\alpha^2 \left(\pi e_1^2 + (1 - \pi)e_2^2 \right) \right.$$
$$\left. subject \; to \; \Lambda^* \left(\bar{W}, \alpha \right) \geq \Lambda^*_{MAX} \right\} \tag{7.7}$$

where γ is the employer's risk aversion parameter.

The employer will pay the worker no more than his reservation wage, so the optimal solution to equation (7.7) will lie somewhere along the worker's indifference curve, $\Lambda^*(\bar{W}, \alpha) = \Lambda^*_{MAX}$, which shows combinations of lifetime wages and insurance that give the same total utility. This is shown in Figure 7.1. The indifference curve is downward sloping, since the worker will demand a higher wage when $\alpha = 0$ and he has to bear all the risk than when $\alpha = 1$ and he bears no risk. By totally differentiating the indifference curve, we can find its gradient:

$$\frac{d\bar{W}(\alpha)}{d\alpha} = -\frac{\partial \Lambda^*}{\partial \alpha} \left/ \frac{\partial \Lambda^*}{\partial \bar{W}} \right. < 0 \tag{7.8}$$

where $\partial \Lambda^* / \partial \bar{W} > 0$, since the employee prefers more to less, and

$$\frac{\partial \Lambda^*}{\partial \alpha} \begin{cases} = 0 & \text{if } \alpha = 1 \\ > 0 & \text{if } \alpha < 1 \end{cases}$$

since the employee is averse to the untradeable risk.

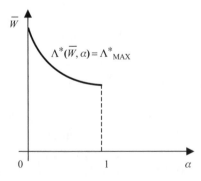

Figure 7.1 Employee's indifference curve
Source: McCarthy (2005). Reproduced by permission of the Controller of HMSO.

The optimum contract will occur at the combination of $\bar{W}$ and α which minimises the risk-adjusted cost, Φ^*, to the employer. This will be where the employer's objective function is tangent to the employee's indifference curve.

Along the employer's iso-cost curve:

$$\frac{d\bar{W}(\alpha)}{d\alpha} = -\gamma\alpha\left(\pi e_1^2 + (1-\pi)e_2^2\right) \leq 0 \qquad (7.9)$$

The gradient of the iso-cost curve depends on both the variance of the risk and the employer's degree of risk aversion.

If the employer is very risk averse, the gradient of the employer's objective function will be very steep and the optimal contract will result in the employee bearing all of the untraded risk (see Figure 7.2). If the employer is risk neutral ($\gamma = 0$), the optimal contract will involve the employer bearing all the risk (see Figure 7.3). If the employer's risk aversion lies somewhere between these two, the risk will be shared between employee and employer (see Figure 7.4). In incomplete markets, there may be an optimal sharing of risk between employee and employer, which depends on the relative risk aversions of the two parties.

A specific example of risk transfer is the full funding of the pension promise when there is a risk of employer insolvency. Interpret e_i as the risk of firm insolvency and failure to pay the promised pensions and α as the degree of funding of the pension scheme. Suppose employees are unable to hedge the long-term risk of employer insolvency. Hence an increase in α decreases the risk to which employees are exposed, but increases the employer's upfront employment costs and may well increase the likelihood of insolvency. Employees are averse to employer

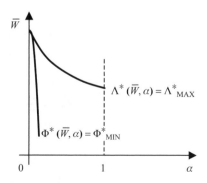

Figure 7.2 Employee takes all untraded risk
Source: McCarthy (2005). Reproduced by permission of the Controller of HMSO.

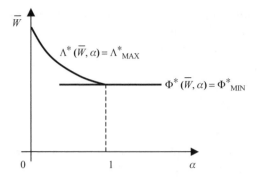

Figure 7.3 Employer takes all untraded risk
Source: McCarthy (2005). Reproduced by permission of the Controller of HMSO.

insolvency risk and will be willing to trade off lower wages for more secure future pensions in the form of increased funding of the pension scheme. Employers, however, are indifferent to the extra pension payments they would make if they stay in business long enough to make them, since these payments are perfectly hedged by firm income. The optimal pension funding position is shown in Figure 7.3: employers fully fund their pension plans.

This result differs from Sharpe's (1976) model, in which employees were indifferent to the funding status of the pension scheme, since they could fully replicate the pension payout by trading in options. In McCarthy's more realistic model, the cost of options is too high given the additional risk of firm default. Workers therefore need to be compensated

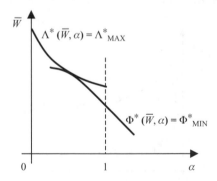

Figure 7.4 Employee and employer share untraded risk
Source: McCarthy (2005). Reproduced by permission of the Controller of HMSO.

for any pension default risk in the form of higher upfront wages. The employer can reduce costs by paying employees with fully-funded pensions.

Why should the employer agree to assume risks on behalf of the employee when no insurance company would be prepared to do so under the same circumstances?

One reason why an insurance company might refuse to assume this risk is moral hazard. Moral hazard arises in cases where buyers and sellers of insurance have different access to information and this creates incentives for the buyers to act in a way that imposes costs on the sellers. To avoid the time 1 risks, the worker would like to sell his time 1 wages at time 0 for an assured amount. But this would immediately reduce the incentive for the worker to work hard at time 1. Similarly, the employer will not be able to pay the employee with an unfunded pension promise, because this creates an incentive for them to default.

Employers might be in a better position than an insurance company to mitigate the effects of moral hazard because they have more information about the employee and this reduces information gathering and other transactions costs. By dealing with employees in a group, firms may be able to reduce transactions costs of pension provision to a level where firm provision becomes optimal.

A second reason is transactions costs, e.g., the costs of gathering information about individuals. If these are high relative to the size of the risk covered, the insurance company will not be prepared to assume the risk without charging such a high price that the demand for the insurance is zero. By dealing with employees as a group, transactions costs might be reduced to a level where it is optimal for a firm to insure its workers. Examples are group medical insurance and death-in-service benefits in a pension scheme.

Large employers are in a better position than small employers to bear the risks of their employees if these risks are independent of each other. The employer's objective function for an individual employee's wage contract becomes:

$$\Phi^*(\bar{W}, \alpha) = \min_{\{W_i, \alpha\}} \left\{ W_0 + \sum_{i=1}^{N} W_i \, q_i + \frac{\gamma}{2M} \alpha^2 \left(\pi e_1^2 + (1 - \pi)e_2^2 \right) \right.$$

$$\left. subject \ to \ \Lambda^*(\bar{W}, \alpha) \geq \Lambda^*_{MAX} \right\} \qquad (7.10)$$

where the factor $1/M$ reflects the diversification effect of the M employees on the variance of the average risk payout per employee. As M

increases, the employer becomes less risk averse with respect to the untraded risk and the optimal employment contract involves the employer assuming increasing amounts of it and in the limit all of it. An example is the individual mortality risk of employees.

However, some risks cannot be diversified across different individuals (since they are highly correlated with each other) or are large relative to the size of the capital markets, and in these cases not even the employer will be prepared to assume these risks on behalf of its employees. An example is long-term annuity price risk. Although a market in deferred annuities from insurance companies exists, insurance companies charge such a high price to insure this risk that few employees buy deferred annuities. Firms would not be able to offer them either at a lower price, since the risk is so large.

Portfolio Restrictions

Portfolio restrictions affect the ability of employees to trade securities to reach their optimal portfolio holdings. The classic example is limits on short positions in most assets, e.g., it is impossible in practice to borrow unlimited amounts. Similarly, employees are unable to sell their pension rights to third parties.

In the absence of these restrictions, individuals could adjust their private portfolios to offset the portfolio restrictions they face in their pension fund. The pension fund contains a particular asset mix which the individual cannot adjust. If there are no portfolio restrictions on the assets which employees hold outside their pension schemes, and the liquidity constraints employees face are non-binding (so that employees can borrow against their pensions to finance consumption, or the amount saved in the pension is lower than the optimal amount of savings the employees would choose if there were no pension scheme), then employees can trade assets outside their pensions to achieve an overall optimal asset allocation that includes the asset allocation in the pension scheme. The value of the compensation package is the same as in the complete markets case. Offering employees investment choice in their DC pension schemes would, in these circumstances, add little value to the compensation contract.

If, however, an employee cannot reach the optimum overall asset allocation by adjustments to his private portfolio then the complete markets result no longer holds. This could be because the private portfolio is too small relative to the pension, or because the pension fund's asset allocation is too far from the employee's optimum to make adjustment possible if there are restrictions on the employee's private portfolio. Now, the employee will no longer be indifferent between two different securities of equal market value contained in his pension fund.

The same holds if liquidity constraints bind: the employee will no longer be indifferent between pension compensation which cannot be borrowed against or sold to finance consumption, and cash compensation which can be consumed.

Transactions Costs

Transactions costs limit the extent to which the complete markets optimum can be achieved, e.g., the cost of determining the employment contract, the cost of understanding the pension scheme, and the cost of selecting and adjusting the asset allocation. The existence of transactions costs means that employees will no longer be indifferent between two different types of scheme. If the employer offers his employees a simpler pension scheme with lower transactions costs, he can lower his wage bill for each employee by the size of the transaction cost incurred in the previous, more complex pension scheme.

Taxation

If pension compensation is treated more favourably in terms of taxation than wage compensation, employees will prefer the former to the latter. The employer can lower costs by increasing the former and reducing the latter. So the benefits of the favourable tax treatment of employee pensions are shared between the employer and the employees.

A similar situation emerges in respect of the differential taxation of assets in the pension fund. For example, if domestic equities are more heavily taxed than bonds (as is the case in the UK), then it will be better to hold bonds in the pension fund than equities. This means that if there are costs to adjusting investment portfolios, employees will value pension compensation paid in bonds more highly than pension compensation paid in equities.

Externalities

By offering employees a specific type of pension, employers might accrue additional benefits not directly linked to the pension offered. This is known as an *externality*. One example of an externality associated with a pension scheme is longer job tenure. This reduces employer search costs and the disruption costs associated with job turnover. A final salary pension scheme, which benefits workers who have high salaries when they retire, provides an incentive for employees to work harder, get promotion and hence a higher salary. Similarly, an underfunded DB pension scheme, which makes employees unsecured creditors in the firm, might induce co-operative behaviour from employees, fearful of losing their jobs and pensions (Cooper and Ross, 2002).

Selection or Sorting Effects

The pension scheme can be designed to attract workers with desirable characteristics to the job being offered. Employees who value pensions more highly would value a compensation package with a pension more than workers who do not, and would therefore be more likely to be attracted to the job. If these workers have desirable characteristics (another example of an externality), then the pension scheme can be used to select workers with these characteristics.[6]

7.4   REDISTRIBUTION IN PRIVATE PENSION SCHEMES

Pension schemes also have different redistributional implications, involving transfers of pension wealth between different groups of people. Sometimes these transfers are unanticipated since they are the result of some surprise event. Sometimes they are the deliberate consequence of the design of the scheme, although, given the complexity of many scheme designs, this might not be well understood by scheme members or sometimes even by sponsors. We now give some examples.

An occupational DB scheme involves the following types of pension wealth transfers. Early leavers subsidise long stayers. Every time workers switch jobs they experience a *portability loss* in respect of their pension entitlement. This is because DB schemes are generally provided by specific employers and when a worker changes jobs they have to move to a new employer's scheme. When they do so, they will take a transfer value equal to the cash equivalent of their accrued pension benefits with them or leave a deferred pension in the scheme that they are leaving.

---

[6] Ippolito (1997) found that employers who matched contributions in DC pension schemes attracted workers who discounted the future less heavily and saved more. Employers found that these workers were more efficient.

Accrued benefits are valued less favourably if someone leaves a scheme than if they remain an active member of the scheme. This is because scheme leavers (whether they choose a transfer value or a deferred pension) have their years of service valued in terms of their leaving salary, whereas continuing members will have the same years of service as the early leaver valued in terms of their projected salary at retirement, which is likely to be higher; this is nothing more than the backloading of benefits.[7] Long stayers are therefore subsidised at the expense of early leavers. This is a deliberate consequence of the scheme's design and is intended to reward long and loyal service.

Blake and Orszag (1997) estimated the portability losses for a range of typical UK employees who change jobs about six times in a lifetime.[8] Table 7.1 shows that the portability loss lies between 25% and 30% of the full service pension (i.e., the pension of someone with the same salary experience but who remains in the same scheme all their working life). Even someone changing jobs once in mid-career can lose up to 16% of the full service pension. It is possible to reduce portability losses by, for example, indexing leaving salaries between the leaving and retirement dates to the growth in real earnings or by providing full service credits on transfers between jobs, but this is not common in the UK (except on transfers between different public sector occupational pension schemes).

Similarly, low flyers subsidise high flyers. Again this follows from the backloading of benefits in DB schemes. Take an extreme example. Suppose two workers have precisely the same salary experience for 39 years, but that one (the high flyer) gets a huge pay rise in his final year. The high flyer's pension will be considerably higher than the other's (the low flyer's) pension, yet he will have paid only slightly higher total contributions. The low flyer is subsidising the high flyer, compared with the case in which there is an equal split of the combined pensions. By a similar analogy, women (who tend to have lower final salaries than men) subsidise men in DB schemes. However, there is also a case in which men subsidise women. This is because women tend to live longer than men, so a woman retiring with the same final salary and hence pension as a man will on average draw the pension for longer.

In DC schemes, poor people subsidise rich people. This is because the rich are healthier than the poor and so live longer on average. If the annuities purchased with the DC fund are based on the average life

---

[7] See Table 1.1.

[8] Burgess and Rees (1994), Gregg and Wadsworth (1995).

Table 7.1 Portability losses from defined benefit schemes (percentage of full service pension received at retirement)

Worker type	Job separation assumptions[1]	Transfer value[2]	Deferred pension[3]	Defined contribution pension (employer-run)[4]	Personal pension (employer contributions)[5]	Personal pension (no employer contributions)[6]
Average UK worker (MFR assumptions realised)[7]	A	75	75			
	B	71	71			
	C	84	84	71	61	37
Average UK manual worker	A	75	88			
	B	71	86			
	C	84	96	78	66	45
Average UK non-manual worker	A	75	86			
	B	71	83			
	C	84	94	79	68	44

Notes:
[1] This table presents estimates of the size of the portability losses experienced by three different types of UK workers (based on typical lifetime earnings profiles) under three different sets of job separation assumptions: A – separates at ages 28, 29, 30, 40 and 57; B – separates at 26, 27, 30, 31, 38, 44 and 55; C – separates at 45. The loss is expressed in the form of a reduced pension compared with what each of the three workers would have received had they remained in a single scheme for their whole career.
[2] Leaving worker takes transfer value to new scheme.
[3] Leaving worker leaves deferred pension in leaving scheme.
[4] Leaving worker transfers into employer-run DC scheme.
[5] Leaving worker transfers into personal pension scheme where the employer also contributes.
[6] Leaving worker transfers into personal pension scheme where the employer does not contribute.
[7] The MFR (Minimum Funding Requirement) assumptions are the assumptions specified in the 1995 Pensions Act concerning future inflation, earnings growth and investment returns that were used by UK pension funds between April 1997 and December 2005 to determine the minimum contribution level needed to meet projected pension liabilities. The MFR was also used to calculate transfer values.
Source: Blake and Orszag (1997, appendix E, table 5.8, p. 74).

expectancy of the annuitants, they will be very good value for longer-lived richer people and poor value for shorter-lived poorer people. Similarly, if annuities are based on unisex annuity rates, men subsidise women.

7.5   PRIVATE SECTOR MARKET FAILURE AND THE COMPENSATING ROLE OF STATE PENSION SCHEMES

In this section, we consider some circumstances in which the private sector fails to achieve an optimal outcome and this gives rise to a potential role for state pension schemes.

Diamond (1977), Merton (1984) and Merton et al. (1987) argue that private sector pension arrangements can involve inefficient risk shifting (i.e., transference of risks) and this situation can be improved through additional public insurance. This result is based on standard risk diversification principles. Private pensions are a desirable but risky asset. The desire comes from the pension's ability to remove the risk of poverty in old age. But with private pensions, this risk is being traded for another: the risk that the company (in the case of occupational schemes) and the annuity provider (in the case of personal schemes) will become insolvent. A state pension is an alternative asset and one that is generally regarded as safer.[9] Therefore, diversifying across different types of pension scheme reduces total pension risk in the same way that diversifying across different financial assets reduces total portfolio risk. There are, of course, alternatives to a state pension in these circumstances, such as the mandatory requirement for companies to fully fund their pension scheme at all times or for publicly supported pension insurance.

Private pension arrangements require individuals to plan their retirement savings when young. But this is often easier said than done. Many people find retirement planning an extremely difficult and complex exercise. They suffer from myopia and cannot see ahead to a future of retirement that might involve extreme poverty. Feldstein (1985) explains this myopic behaviour in terms of individuals applying too low a weight to old age utility in their lifetime utility function. In addition, executing the retirement plan can also be difficult since it requires both discipline and sacrifice.[10] As evidence of myopic behaviour, Katona (1964) finds that individuals pay increased attention to events only when the realisation

---

[9] We will reconsider this statement later.

[10] This is examined in more detail in Chapter 8.

date approaches,[11] while Hammermesh (1984) and Bernheim (1989) show that individuals' forecasts of their retirement date become more accurate as the event approaches. But by then it is too late. Cagan (1965) argues that a mandatory social security system induces a *recognition effect*: forced to participate, individuals begin to recognise the need to provide for retirement income. Both Katona and Cagan argue that many individuals will not save enough for retirement without mandatory state pensions (i.e., the state has to take a paternalistic role).

A state pension scheme can also help to correct an explicit market failure, such as that arising in the private annuities market due to asymmetric information (see Eckstein *et al.*, 1985a,b; Townley and Broadway, 1988). Where individuals have private information about their survival probabilities, a free market in private annuities might not generate a Pareto-optimal outcome because of adverse selection. Under these circumstances, a mandatory social security system might Pareto-dominate the free market outcome.

7.6 RISKS IN STATE PENSION SCHEMES

An unfunded state scheme involves young workers paying the pensions of retired workers in the expectation that they will in turn receive a pension from the generation below them when they themselves retire. Unfunded schemes are very easy to run when the population is growing and each generation is larger than the previous one. They are also relatively easy to run when the population is constant over time. It is a very different matter when the population is systematically ageing or even worse declining over time.

The two principal risks in state pension schemes are *systematic demographic risk* and *political risk* (Diamond, 1977, 1997).

Systematic demographic risk occurs as a result of systematically increasing longevity and systematically declining fertility. In the UK, in the rest of Europe, and indeed most of the rest of the world, the population growth rate is slowing down (and in some countries is actually negative) and, due to advances in medical science, people are living longer. This is compounded by the fact that in most (but not all) countries, the fertility rate is declining. The combination of increasing longevity and declining fertility leads to a rapid ageing of the population[12] and, in turn, a *demographic timebomb*, the intergenerational risk that there will be

---

[11] He called this a *goal gradient effect*.
[12] See Table 6.1.

insufficient younger workers to pay the pensions of the large numbers of pensioners.

Demographic risks are particularly acute in Europe. In 1990, there was one pensioner in the UK for every four workers. By 2030, there is projected to be nearly two pensioners for every five workers.[13] It is worse elsewhere on the Continent. The worst case is Germany, where the ratio is projected to rise from one-in-five to one-in-two between 1990 and 2030. While, in all developed countries, there is a net flow of resources from the young to the old, the required increase in resources flowing between these generations is likely to be too large to be politically or socially sustainable. For example, in the case of Germany, contribution rates to the state pension scheme would have to rise from 23% of workers' incomes in 1995 to 42% by 2050, while the corresponding increase in the case of Italy would be from 43% to 68%.[14] The political risk facing state pension schemes will therefore be highly correlated with the demographic risk that they face.

Blake (2004) examined the political risk in the UK state pension system,[15] as measured by reductions in the internal rate of return (IRR)[16] as a consequence of policy changes that reduce scheme benefits. He divided political risk into three components: demographically induced, economically induced and pure political risk. Table 7.2 shows that the IRR on the original Basic State Pension (BSP) Scheme was 13.9% in real terms for married men (row 1) and 13.6% for single women (row 11). These very high rates of return, which are the same across all income ranges, are explained by the facts that the flat-rate contributions into the BSP Scheme were very low, just 2% of the Lower Earnings Limit or LEL (which equalled £3900 in 2002/03, making the cost of membership of the BSP just £78 in 2002/03), and that the resulting flat-rate pensions (£3926 for a single person and £6276.40 for a married couple in 2002/03) were payable for life (from age 60 for women and 65 for men) and uprated annually in line with national average earnings. The original SERPS pension, which was also uprated annually in line with earnings,

---

[13] World Bank (1994a).

[14] Chand and Jaeger (1996). See also World Bank (1994b).

[15] For a review of the UK state pension system, see Blake (2003a,b). The UK first-pillar state scheme is called the Basic State Pension Scheme. The second-pillar state scheme used to be called the State Earnings Related Pension Scheme (SERPS), but, in April 2002, became more generous to lower paid individuals and changed its name to the Second State Pension (S2P). All employees in the UK with earnings above the Lower Earnings Limit are 'contracted in' to SERPS/S2P unless they have 'contracted out' into an eligible private sector scheme.

[16] The internal rate of return is the discount rate that equates the present value of pension benefits with the present value of contributions.

Table 7.2 Political risk with the UK state pension scheme: real internal rates of return (%)

Type of member Earnings 2002/03 (£)	Low-paid 10,800	Average 24,600	High-paid 30,420
Male: 25-year-old, married			
1 *Original Basic State Pension Scheme: linked to earnings*	*13.857*	*13.857*	*13.857*
2 Revised Basic State Pension Scheme: linked to prices	10.900	10.900	10.900
3 *Original SERPS: linked to earnings*	*5.646*	*5.143*	*5.082*
4 Revised SERPS: linked to prices	4.931	4.401	4.337
5 Revised SERPS: accrual rate reduced to 20% of band earnings	4.259	3.728	3.663
6 Revised SERPS: lowering revaluation factor	3.421	3.421	3.421
7 Revised SERPS: spouse's pension reduced to 50%	2.014	2.014	2.014
8 Revised SERPS: raising the effective contribution rate	−0.639	1.303	1.303
9 SERPS replaced by S2P: flat rate	4.291	1.466	0.508
10 SERPS replaced by S2P: flat rate plus MIG and Pension Credit	6.232	3.290	2.368
Female: 25-year-old, single			
11 *Original Basic State Pension Scheme: retirement at 60*	*13.645*	*13.645*	*13.645*
12 Revised Basic State Pension Scheme: retirement at 65	11.725	11.725	11.725
13 *Original SERPS: retirement at 60*	*5.050*	*4.499*	*4.432*
14 Revised SERPS: retirement at 65	4.180	3.590	3.518

Note: The table reports real internal rates of return from membership of the first-pillar Basic State Pension Scheme and the second-pillar SERPS/S2P in their original forms and subsequent revised forms for a married male and a single female both joining the schemes at age 25 in 1978 at three different starting salaries equal to the Low Earnings Threshold or LET (denoted low-paid), the Second Earnings Threshold or SET (approximately equal to average earnings) and the Upper Earnings Limit for membership of SERPS/S2P (denoted high-paid), respectively for 2002/03: these salaries are assumed to grow annually in line with national average earnings. The male is assumed to be married to a female of the same age, the female is assumed to be unmarried and both are assumed to survive until at least their respective retirement ages. MIG = Minimum Income Guarantee.
Source: Blake (2004, table 1).

generated a lower, but nevertheless still high real rate of return which varied between 5.1% and 5.6% for married men (row 3) and between 4.4% and 5.1% for single women (row 13).

Most of the political risk to which the state pension scheme has been subject has been demographically induced, and the policy reforms have been designed to deal with the increasing dependency ratio. The change in the uprating of the BSP and SERPS/S2P from earnings to prices reduced the IRR by around 3 and 0.75 percentages points, respectively (rows 2 and 4). The combined effect of reducing the SERPS accrual rate, revaluation factor and spouse's pension (from 100% of the member's pension to 50%) was to lower the IRR on SERPS to just 2%, which is less than 40% of the original IRR (rows 5–7, cf row 3). Raising the state pension age for women from 60 to 65 reduces their IRR on the BSP and SERPS/S2P by about 1.9 and 0.9 percentage points, respectively (rows 12 and 14).

There has been one case of economically induced political risk involving the state pension scheme, and this has been the use of strong financial incentives to persuade people to contract out of SERPS/S2P into a private sector scheme. The government's aim was to reduce the level of state pension provision and hence the cost to the tax payer. The financial incentives have come in the form of age-related rebates on National Insurance contributions (NICs)[17] for contracting out of SERPS/S2P. These rebates have increased substantially over time. When SERPS first started in 1978, the combined employee and employer contracted out rebate was 7% for all workers with earnings between the Lower Earnings Limit (LEL) and Upper Earnings Limit (UEL).[18] In 2002, men aged above 51 with earnings between the LEL and Lower Earnings Threshold (LET) had a combined contracted out rebate of 21%. These increases in the contracted out rebate have raised the effective contribution rate for SERPS membership and, in the case of low-paid workers, have resulted in a negative IRR for SERPS membership, while, for higher-paid workers, the IRR for SERPS membership has been reduced to only 1.3% (row 8).

An example of pure political risk came with the replacement of the earnings-related SERPS with S2P by the Labour government in 2002. It is intended that the S2P pension will at some stage in the future become

---

[17] This is the name of the UK social security or payroll tax. When a worker contracts out of SERPS/S2P, he receives a rebate on his NICs which is transferred into his private second-pillar scheme.

[18] Workers with earnings below the LEL are not eligible to join SERPS/S2P, while SERPS/S2P benefits are capped on earnings above the UEL.

a flat-rate pension (offering at best only 40% of the LET). However, the contributions will still be earnings related. If this happens, the real IRR for high-paid workers, will be just 0.5%. Low-paid workers, on the other hand, natural supporters of the Labour Party, will have their IRR from S2P membership raised to 4.3%.

At the same time, the Labour government can be accused of political naiveté. In 1999, it introduced a Minimum Income Guarantee (MIG) for pensioners: by April 2003 the MIG was £100 a week for individuals and £154 for couples. In October 2003, it introduced an additional Pension Credit which enhances the pension of single pensioners up to £135 per week and couples up to £201 per week if they have additional income from other sources such as private pensions and savings. The plan is to uprate all these limits in line with national average earnings. This promise will become increasingly expensive to honour over time. This is because all pensions in payment are uprated in line with prices (capped at 2.5% p.a. for private sector pensions), and therefore over time larger and larger proportions of the retired population would become eligible for the MIG and Pension Credit. Row 10 of Table 7.2 shows why: the effect of the promise is to raise the real return on the state pension scheme to 6.2% for low-paid workers and to 2.4% for high-paid workers.

So political risk can be substantial even in a country with a stable political system such as the UK.

7.7   RISK SHARING IN STATE PENSION SCHEMES

So long as demographic risk is not systematic, one of the biggest benefits of a state pension system is its ability to hedge this demographic risk between generations. This is an example of *intergenerational risk sharing*. Brandts and De Bartolome (1992) argue that an unfunded pay-as-you-go (PAYG) system is Pareto-improving if individuals are uncertain which type of generation they will be born in, since the risks of becoming a member of a small generation of workers supporting a large generation of retirees and of becoming a member of a large generation of retirees being supported by a small generation of workers exactly offset.

Blinder (1981, pp. 61–62) makes the following case for social security:

We must not forget that the social security system was a child of the Great Depression. If we conceptualize the Great Depression as a terrible random event that severely damaged the economic well-being of several generations, then it makes sense to transfer income from generations yet unborn to generations that were damaged by the Depression. One way to do this was to start an unfunded social security system.

The people who retired in the early years of the social security system (say, those who reached 65 in 1940) were 54 or so when the Depression began. For them, the Depression represented a huge and irreparable loss of lifetime income. It is not something they could have been expected to have prepared for, nor subsequently made up for. The social security system made huge transfers to these people, who had contributed very little but drew substantial benefits.[19] It thus transferred some of their Depression losses to unborn generations. Was this bad social policy?

Moving down a generation or so, people who reached 65 in, say, 1960 were 34 when the Depression started – just entering their peak earning years. They too suffered huge losses of lifetime income, and received huge transfers from social security.

It takes a long time for the 'start up' period of a social security period to end. Even the cohorts that reached age 65 as late as 1970–1975 were victims of the Great Depression to a significant degree. These people were only 19–24 years old when the recession began, but were 29–34 when it ended. The incidence of unemployment must have been particularly severe for them, depriving them of work experience that would have been valuable in their subsequent careers. Most of these people also received large income transfers from social security. Only when the system is fully mature will intergenerational transfers stop. By this time, most people damaged by the Great Depression will have died, having received a lifetime wealth increment from social security.

Thus compensation for the Depression can provide a rationale for a public pension system and, in particular, for an unfunded public pension system.

Gordon and Varian (1988) develop a model of intergenerational risk sharing that exploits the fact that what is a *systematic risk* for one generation (as outlined by Brandts and De Bartolome, 1992, above) becomes an *idiosyncratic risk* across a series of generations. Whole generations can be subject to adverse outcomes. As Blinder powerfully shows above, one generation can experience a deep economic depression that not only results in that generation being poor when it is young, but also means that it is poor when it is old, since it has not been able to save enough for its retirement. Gordon and Varian examine various social devices to facilitate intergenerational risk sharing. One is the family and another is a social security pension system.

7.7.1   The Family

If there is *two-way altruism* within the family (parents are willing to help their children and children are willing to help their parents, via bequests and loans), then this potentially provides a device for intergenerational risk sharing. For example, suppose the parents belong to a generation that faces a depression and wish to maintain their standard of living, but

---

[19] This can be seen by examining the male generational accounts in Table 6.2.

do not have sufficient financial assets to draw upon. They might try to borrow funds to finance their consumption. The problem is that they lack collateral for the loan, and although their children might be willing to repay the loan, the parents cannot legally commit their children to do so. Further, every generation within the family that discovers it is a 'paying' generation has an incentive to renege on the family risk-sharing scheme whatever the preferences of the 'receiving' generation and whatever promises it made when it was young. This means that the scheme is *time inconsistent*, the incentive to stay in the scheme changes over time as the future evolves. Also, it is impossible to pre-commit generations of the family not yet born. For all these reasons, a family risk-sharing scheme is likely to break down.

7.7.2   Social Security Pension System

Base Case[20]

Gordon and Varian set up a simple two-period overlapping generations model with no population growth, implying that the model involves no systematic demographic risk. Each generation is identical except for its date of birth, and works when young and consumes when old. The government is assumed to have the power to precommit future generations. With an arbitrarily large number of future generations to share in any particular risk, such as a recession today, each generation will bear an arbitrarily small share in the outcome of any risky event (similar to the diversification principle in finance).

Workers receive a fixed wage W for a fixed amount of work when young. This wage is saved for retirement and earns a stochastic return e_t (which has a zero mean, a variance v, and is serially independent[21]), enabling the retired worker to consume $W + e_t$ when old. The expected utility of each generation is assumed to be a function of the mean and variance of the stochastic income:

$$\bar{\Lambda} = U(W) - V(v) \tag{7.11}$$

where $U' > 0, \ V' > 0$.

---

[20] The remainder of this section draws on lecture notes on the Gordon and Varian model prepared by Professor Irwin Collier of the Free University in Berlin.

[21] Variance is a measure of the dispersion of the actual return around the expected return, $E(e_t) = 0$, and is defined as $\text{var}(e_t) = E(e_t - E(e_t))^2$ where E is the expectations operator. Serial independence implies that $E(e_t - E(e_t))(e_{t-1} - E(e_{t-1})) = E(e_t e_{t-1}) = 0$.

The return is realised (i.e., the shock – or 'lottery' in Gordon and Varian's terminology – occurs) at the end of each generation's working phase and before retirement begins (i.e., in the mid-life of each generation). As the shock occurs, one generation dies and another (the grandchildren) are born. This means that there are never two generations alive both before and after a shock, and so it is not possible to share risks between generations through the market. However, because there are always two generations alive simultaneously, the government can transfer income from one to the other, based on the outcome of past events, and so raise the utility of all generations. In other words, the introduction of a social security system is Pareto-improving.

To illustrate this, suppose the government establishes a social security system financed on a *tax-transfer* basis in which each generation receives a *transfer* $e_{t-1}/2$ from the previous generation in period t and pays a *tax* $e_t/2$ to the next generation. This implies the risks are shared equally between the two generations. The total consumption available to each generation (except the first) is $W + (e_{t-1} + e_t)/2$ and its expected utility is higher than the case in which risks are not pooled (7.11):

$$\bar{\Lambda} = U(W) - V\left(\text{var}\left(\frac{e_{t-1} + e_t}{2}\right)\right)$$
$$= U(W) - V\left(\frac{\upsilon}{2}\right) > U(W) - V(\upsilon) \qquad (7.12)$$

The first generation does best, since it participates in only one single risky event:

$$\bar{\Lambda} = U(W) - V\left(\text{var}\left(\frac{e_1}{2}\right)\right) = U(W) - V\left(\frac{\upsilon}{4}\right) > U(W) - V(\upsilon)$$
$$(7.13)$$

This tax-transfer scheme is Pareto-improving since all generations experience an increase in expected utility.

The social security system can be designed to spread risks equally across N generations. The consumption of the generation born in $t-1$ is:

$$W + \sum_{i=0}^{N-1}\left(\frac{e_{t-i}}{N}\right) = W + \sum_{i=1}^{N-1}\left(\frac{e_{t-i}}{N}\right) + \left(\frac{e_t}{N}\right) \qquad (7.14)$$

where the second term on the right-hand side is the share of previous shocks to be absorbed by generation $t - 1$ and the final term is the share of the current shock to be absorbed. The expected utility of this generation is:

$$\bar{\Lambda} = U(W) - V\left(\text{var}\left(\sum_{i=0}^{N-1}\left(\frac{e_{t-i}}{N}\right)\right)\right)$$

$$= U(W) - V\left(\frac{\upsilon}{N}\right) > U(W) - V(\upsilon) \qquad (7.15)$$

As the risks are shared across a larger and larger number of generations, the total risk facing each generation falls. In the limit (as $N \to \infty$), the total risk falls to zero and the expected utility converges to $U(W)$. As Gordon and Varian (1998, p. 190) argue: 'What is a social risk at one date is idiosyncratic risk when pooled with the independent lotteries of many generations. Thus, almost all risks should be passed forward to future generations'. If populations are growing over time, this increases the 'incentive to share risk with the future'.

Complicating Factors

In reality, the only way to transfer wealth across generations is via changes in the capital stock (adding to it when outcomes are favourable, consuming capital when outcomes are unfavourable). But changes in the capital stock will change the rate of return on capital. Further, there is a lower bound on the size of the capital stock: it cannot become negative. These factors will limit the efficient degree of risk sharing. To account for these factors, we assume that each generation i born over the next N periods receives only a constant proportional allocation α_i of each shock. So α_i is the degree of risk sharing: the higher the α_i the greater the degree of risk sharing.[22]

We also assume that the objective of government policy is to maximise the expected utility (as of the date of the introduction of the social security programme) of the steady state generations, with all earlier generations receiving *ex ante* the same utility as if there were no programme. A steady state generation is one born N or more periods after the introduction of the programme. If the introduction of the social security programme raises steady state utility subject to constraints (and no transitional generation is made worse off), then the programme is Pareto-improving.

---

[22] Note the parallels with McCarthy's (2005) model in Section 7.3. In this case, we are examining risk sharing over N periods of time, while in McCarthy's model, we examined risk sharing over N states of the world in a single period of time or over M workers in a single period of time.

The consumption of each generation is now:

$$W + \sum_{i=0}^{N-1} \alpha_i e_{t-i} \tag{7.16}$$

and its expected utility is:

$$\bar{\Lambda} = U(W) - V \left(\upsilon \sum_{i=0}^{N-1} \alpha_i^2 \right) \tag{7.17}$$

The government's objective function is:

$$\max \left[U(W) - V \left(\upsilon \sum_{i=0}^{N-1} \alpha_i^2 \right) \right] \tag{7.18}$$

subject to:

$$\sum_{i=0}^{N-1} \alpha_i = 1 \tag{7.19}$$

The first-order conditions for a maximum are:

$$2\upsilon\alpha_i V' = \lambda, i = 1, \ldots, N \tag{7.20}$$

where λ is the Lagrange multiplier. This means that at the optimum:

$$\alpha_i = \alpha_j, \forall i, j \tag{7.21}$$

which, when combined with the constraint (7.19), implies that:

$$\alpha_i = \frac{1}{N} \tag{7.22}$$

That is, risks are shared evenly across the N generations. The social security programme is Pareto-improving, since the steady state generations are better off than without it. Early generations share in fewer risky events, so they are even better off.

Role of the Capital Stock in Transferring Risk to Later Generations

When a unit of capital is transferred from generation t to generation $t + 1$, generation $t + 1$ not only gains the extra capital, it also gains the marginal product of the capital. This means that generation $t + 1$ gets a larger lottery than generation t gives up.

The capital stock received by the first of the steady state generations equals (assuming no depreciation):

$$K_t = W + \sum_{i=1}^{N-1} \left(\frac{N-i}{N} \right) e_{t-i} \tag{7.23}$$

in the base case, but there is nothing to guarantee that this is positive. However, the main force keeping the capital stock positive is the high marginal product of capital when the capital stock is small. If the income earned by capital is $F(K_t) + e_t$ (where $F(\cdot)$ is the production function) and marginal product F' is positive and $F' \to \infty$ as $K_t \to 0$, then this will ensure that K_t stays positive.

Risk sharing is still Pareto-improving, as the following two-generation tax-transfer social security programme shows. Steady state consumption is:

$$W + \alpha e_{t-1} + F(W + \alpha e_{t-1}) + (1 - \alpha) e_t \tag{7.24}$$

and steady state expected utility is (where $E(\cdot)$ is the expectations operator):

$$\begin{aligned}
\bar{\Lambda} &= U\left[W + E(\alpha e_{t-1}) + EF(W + \alpha e_{t-1}) + E((1 - \alpha)e_t) \right] \\
&\quad - V\left[\mathrm{var}(W) + \alpha^2 \upsilon + \mathrm{var}(F) + 2E\,(\alpha e_{t-1} F) + (1 - \alpha)^2\,\upsilon \right] \\
&= U\left[W + EF(W + \alpha e_{t-1}) \right] - V\left[\alpha^2 \upsilon + E(F^2) \right. \\
&\quad \left. - (EF)^2 + 2E\,(\alpha e_{t-1} F) + (1 - \alpha)^2\,\upsilon \right]
\end{aligned}$$

$$\tag{7.25}$$

since:

$$E\,(\alpha e_{t-1}) = E\,((1 - \alpha)\, e_t) = \mathrm{var}(W) = 0 \tag{7.26}$$

and in the $V[\cdot]$ term use is made of the properties that:

$$\mathrm{var}(X + Y) = \mathrm{var}(X) + \mathrm{var}(Y) + 2\mathrm{cov}(X, Y) \tag{7.27}$$
$$\mathrm{var}(F) = E(F^2) - (EF)^2 \tag{7.28}$$

The first derivative of (7.25) with respect to α is:

$$\begin{aligned}
\bar{\Lambda}' &= U'E(F'e_{t-1}) - 2V'\left[\mathrm{cov}(F, F'e_{t-1}) \right. \\
&\quad \left. - (1 - 2\alpha)\upsilon + E\,(e_{t-1}F) + \alpha E\,(e_{t-1}^2 F') \right]
\end{aligned}$$

$$\tag{7.29}$$

using:

$$\frac{\partial EF}{\partial \alpha} = E(F'e_{t-1}) \tag{7.30}$$

$$\frac{\partial \operatorname{var}(F)}{\partial \alpha} = E(2FF'e_{t-1}) - 2(EF)E(F'e_{t-1})$$
$$= 2\operatorname{cov}(F, F'e_{t-1}) \tag{7.31}$$

$$\frac{\partial E(\alpha e_{t-1}F)}{\partial \alpha} = E(e_{t-1}F) + \alpha E\left(e_{t-1}^2 F'\right) \tag{7.32}$$

Evaluating equation (7.29) at $\alpha = 0$ gives $\bar{\Lambda}' = 2V'\upsilon > 0$ (since F is non-stochastic at $\alpha = 0$). Therefore, a small increase in risk sharing must raise steady state utility. Since the first generation also benefits from risk sharing, the introduction of a social security programme is Pareto-improving.

Solving the first derivative of utility with respect to α for α gives:

$$\alpha = \frac{1}{\left(2 + \frac{E(e_{t-1}^2 F')}{\upsilon}\right)} + \frac{\frac{U'}{2V'} \cdot E(F'e_{t-1}) - \operatorname{cov}(F, F'e_{t-1}) - E(e_{t-1}F)}{\upsilon \left(2 + \frac{E(e_{t-1}^2 F')}{\upsilon}\right)} \tag{7.33}$$

We need to sign the terms in equation (7.33). First:

$$\frac{E\left(e_{t-1}^2 F'\right)}{\upsilon} \geq 0 \tag{7.34}$$

since all the terms (including the marginal product F') are non-negative.

Second, the change in capital income as more risk is shared is negative:

$$\frac{\partial EF}{\partial \alpha} = E(F'e_{t-1}) \leq 0 \tag{7.35}$$

which follows because of the concavity of the production function F. Although $E(e_{t-1}) = 0$, the concavity of the production function means that a given fall in capital reduces output by more than the same increase in capital increases output. The expected value of the marginal product times the shock (e_{t-1}) will have a negative value because the biggest weight (probability times marginal product) now goes to the negative values of e_{t-1}. This is shown in Figure 7.5.

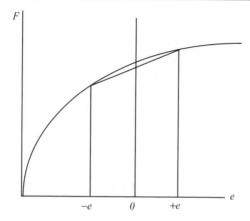

Figure 7.5   Explaining why $E(F'e_{t-1}) \leq 0$

Third:

$$\text{cov}(F, F'e_{t-1}) \geq 0 \tag{7.36}$$

and fourth:

$$E(e_{t-1}F) \geq 0 \tag{7.37}$$

These are proved by Gordon and Varian (1998) in an appendix. Intuitively, both follow from equation (7.35) and the concavity of the production function. For example, e_{t-1} and F in equation (7.37) need to be positively correlated for e_{t-1} to be negatively correlated with marginal product F' as in equation (7.35).

Equations (7.34)–(7.37) imply that $\alpha < \frac{1}{2}$ in equation (7.33), which means that the optimal degree of risk sharing is less than in the base case, where the optimal weight was $\alpha = \frac{1}{2}$ in the case of two generations; any higher level of risk sharing lowers mean capital income and raises its variance.

In the case of a linear production function $F(K_{t-1}) = rK_{t-1}$:

$$\alpha = \frac{1}{1 + (1 + r)^2} \tag{7.38}$$

As a result of the positive marginal cost of capital, the optimal $\alpha < \frac{1}{2}$.

Time Consistency of the Programme

Although the tax-transfer social security programme is optimal *ex ante*, there is no guarantee that it will be optimal *ex post*. At every future date, both generations alive will know the outcome of past shocks and one of those generations might realise that it would be better off without the programme. This generation might decide to repeal the programme. Since this possibility will be known to the original designers of the programme, any risk-sharing programme must take into account the possibility of future default in the initial design. In other words, the programme must be designed to be *time consistent*.

Gordon and Varian show that there is a very real likelihood that the programme will be repealed at some date in the future. An intergenerational risk-sharing programme transfers $P(e_t)$, say, from generation $t + 1$ to t as a function of the realisation of the random variable e_t. The younger generation has an incentive to participate in the programme if:

$$E_t U (W_{t+1} - P(e_t) + P(\tilde{e}_{t+1}) + \tilde{e}_{t+1}) \geq E_t U (W_{t+1} + \tilde{e}_{t+1})$$

$$(7.39)$$

where the tildes are used to make clear that the young generation does not know the size of the shock ($\tilde{e}_{t+1}$) it will face, but does know the size of the previous generation's shock (e_t).

But this constraint can only be satisfied (for all possible values of e_t) by a transfer programme in which $P(e_t)$ is a constant and hence provides no risk sharing. This can be proved by contradiction. Suppose that $P(e_t)$ is not constant, but takes a maximum value P_{MAX}. Then in order to satisfy the constraint (7.39) for $P(e_t) = P_{\text{MAX}}$, we must have:

$$E_t U (W_{t+1} - P_{\text{MAX}} + P(\tilde{e}_{t+1}) + \tilde{e}_{t+1}) \geq E_t U (W_{t+1} + \tilde{e}_{t+1})$$

$$(7.40)$$

which will only hold if $P_{\text{MAX}} = P(\tilde{e}_{t+1}) = P(e_t)$ is constant.

This appears to suggest that an intergenerational risk-sharing scheme is infeasible because of time inconsistency. However, Gordon and Varian show that a time-consistent tax-transfer social security programme can be designed. It requires certain conditions. The first is that there must always be transfers from the young to the old. The young need to *precommit* to the programme by paying for their benefits before receiving them. The second is that the generation that is tempted to repeal the programme must face a sufficiently large penalty for it that it decides it is not worth it, i.e., the *reputational risk* that it faces is too great. For example, if the transfers are debt-financed (rather than tax-financed), then repeal of the programme amounts to a repudiation of existing government debt. If the full costs of default, ζ, are such that:

$$E_t U \left(W_{t+1} - P_{MAX} + P(\tilde{e}_{t+1}) + \tilde{e}_{t+1} \right) \geq E_t U \left(W_{t+1} + \tilde{e}_{t+1} - \zeta \right)$$

$$(7.41)$$

then the programme can be made time consistent.

7.8   REDISTRIBUTION IN STATE PENSION SCHEMES

Blinder (1981) argues that one of the key features of a state pension scheme is that it allows for redistribution within a generation (i.e., *intra-generational risk sharing*). The benefit formula for most social security systems is redistributive. Individuals with lower lifetime earnings earn higher marginal and average returns from their social security contributions.

Private pension systems cannot redistribute income in a socially optimal manner. But it is appropriate to ask why any socially desired redistribution could not be achieved via a progressive taxation and transfer system, keeping social security distributionally neutral.

Blinder suggests two reasons. One is that poorer people have worse mortality and therefore need to get a higher return to achieve actuarial equity. Another is that social security is the only mechanism for redistributing lifetime income. All other redistributive mechanisms redistribute from those who are temporarily rich and give to those who are temporarily poor.

7.9   THE VIABILITY OF PAYG STATE PENSION SYSTEMS AND THE TRANSITION COSTS TO FUNDING

7.9.1   Viability

Systematically ageing populations and systematically declining fertility in developed countries have meant that PAYG state pension systems have become increasingly unviable (systematic demographic risk) and countries with high state pensions are looking at ways to reduce these pensions (political risk).[23]

---

[23] This is why a state pension system in a country with an ageing population is considerably riskier than most people believe.

To be viable over the long run, PAYG pension schemes require sufficient people in work, making sufficient contributions to pay for those who have retired. Technically, we need the sum of the growth rates in the working population and labour productivity (i.e., output per worker) to exceed the sum of the growth rates in the retired population and real pensions (for contribution rates not to rise).[24] This is equivalent to saying that the real growth rate in the national wage bill must exceed the real growth rate in the national pension bill. But in the UK, as in the rest of Europe, the population growth rate is slowing down (and in some countries is actually negative) and, due to advances in medical science, people are living longer. Thus the population is ageing dramatically, resulting in the so-called *demographic timebomb* that was mentioned above. A PAYG system *can* survive with increasing longevity: people need to work longer or pay higher contributions whilst in work. However, a PAYG system *cannot* survive in the long term with fertility rates below the replacement rate of the population (approximately 2.1 children per female in developed countries).

While the share of state pension costs as a proportion of GDP has been contained in the case of the UK over the next half century and actually falls in the case of Ireland, it is projected to grow substantially in other parts of Europe, rising by 61% in Italy, by 66% in Germany and more than doubling in the case of the Netherlands and Portugal. Estimates have been made of the size of unfunded state pension liabilities in Europe (calculated as the difference between the present values of promised future pension payments and expected future contributions).[25] Ireland has the lowest net liability (at 19% of GDP), closely followed by the UK (at 24%), while Sweden and Belgium have the highest net liabilities (at 132% and 153%, respectively). If these liabilities had been recognised as part of the national debt of each country and added to the official measure of national debt, then *no* member state of the EU would have satisfied one of the Maastricht criteria for participating in the Euro currency (namely that national debt must not exceed 60% of GDP)!

Labour productivity is not making up the shortfall caused by the declining population growth rate. There are a number of reasons for this. High labour productivity requires high capital per worker, but for most of the post-war period, net investment (gross investment *minus* depreciation) in the UK and in many parts of Europe has been negative; Europe

---

[24] Samuelson (1975).
[25] Roseveare *et al.* (1996).

has been consuming its own capital stock. The decline of the coal, steel and shipbuilding industries across Europe is clear evidence of this. On top of this and despite the headline stories of inward direct investment from abroad, capital is flowing out of Europe to the low-wage parts of the globe, such as the Far East and Latin America: during the 1980s and 1990s, outward direct investment from Europe was occurring at more than twice the rate of inward direct investment into Europe (as a proportion of GDP).[26]

Table 7.3 shows that unfunded pension schemes are *not* viable in the long run in *any* major country *if* real pensions grow in line with the growth rate in labour productivity. They are only viable in the long run if the real growth rate in pensions is zero; but this implies that pensioners will receive a constantly falling share of their country's resources.

If systematic demographic risk makes PAYG state pension schemes increasingly unviable (unless state pensions are constrained from growing in real terms or the effective working life is increased), then governments have little alternative but to transfer the burden of pension provision to funded pension schemes; and while these funded schemes could be in the public sector (as in the case of Sweden, for example), they are most likely to be in the private sector. Aaron (1966) showed the condition under which, in the long run, funded pension schemes are superior to unfunded schemes. It requires the real rate of return on the assets in funded schemes to exceed the real growth rate in the wage bill (which is equal to the 'rate of return' on a PAYG system). This condition appears to hold in the case of the UK and elsewhere (see Table 7.3), not least because pension funds are able to generate higher returns by investing in the fastest-growing economies of the world, rather than in Europe.

---

[26] Eltis (1994), see also Wolf (2006). Total investment in the Far Eastern economies of Japan, Korea, Taiwan, Singapore, Hong Kong, Indonesia, Malaysia and Thailand averaged 35% of GDP in 1990 compared with only 20% in the OECD economies; the growth rate in real GDP per capita averaged 5.5% in the Far Eastern economies between 1965 and 1990, and only 2.5% in the OECD economies (see World Bank, 1993). Asia receives 60% of world capital flows, Latin America 20%, Africa and the Middle East 4%, and Europe and North America between them only 16% (see *Financial Times*, 6 March 1997). Recent research has concluded that the 'Golden Age' of European economic growth between the early 1950s and mid-1970s, when per capita real incomes grew by an average of 3.8% p.a., will never be repeated. This growth was stimulated by a range of factors, such as post-war reconstruction, technology transfers from the USA (causing 'catch up' growth), structural change (as a result of a new accommodation between workers and employers), and an investment boom. The subsequent slowdown began with the oil crises of the 1970s, and continued with the rise of newly industrialising countries in the Far East and Latin America, the effect of technological change on unskilled labour, and the impact of information technology and international communications on the location of service industries, all factors leading to a permanent shift in comparative advantage away from Europe (see Crafts and Toniolo, 1996; van Ark and Crafts, 1996).

Table 7.3 The long-term viability of state pension schemes in different countries

Country	Growth rate in working population[1] (%)	Growth rate in labour productivity[2] (%)	Real rate of return on pension fund assets[3] (%)	Growth rate in retired population[4] (%)	Unfunded pension scheme viable:[5]		Funded pension scheme viable:[6]		Funded scheme superior to unfunded scheme?[7]
					If real pensions grow in line with productivity?	If real pension growth is zero?	If real pensions grow in line with productivity?	If real pension growth is zero?	
UK	0.0	2.1	6.3	0.7	No	Yes	Yes	Yes	Yes
Germany	−0.7	2.5	5.5	0.8	No	Yes	Yes	Yes	Yes
Netherlands	−0.3	2.1	4.3	1.2	No	Yes	Yes	Yes	Yes
Sweden	0.1	1.8	2.8	0.6	No	Yes	Yes	Yes	Yes
Denmark	−0.3	1.9	5.8	0.5	No	Yes	Yes	Yes	Yes
Switzerland	−0.2	1.5	2.2	1.1	No	Yes	Yes	Yes	Yes
USA	0.4	1.6	3.9	1.4	No	Yes	Yes	Yes	Yes
Canada	0.4	2.6	4.1	1.7	No	Yes	No	Yes	Yes
Japan	−0.6	4.1	2.9	1.4	No	Yes	Yes	Yes	Yes
Australia	0.5	1.8	4.2	1.9	No	Yes	Yes	Yes	Yes

Notes:

[1] Projected annual average growth rate in working population aged 15 to 64 between 1990 and 2050 (source: World Population Prospects: The 1994 Revision, United Nations, 1995).

[2] Annual average growth rate in real GDP per capita between 1967 and 1990, assumed to hold over the period 1990–2050 (source: Penn-World Tables, http://www.nber.org/pwt56.html).

[3] Annual average real return between 1967 and 1990, assumed to hold over the period 1990–2050 (source: Davis, 1995, table 6.15).

[4] Projected annual average growth rate in population over the age of 65 between 1990 and 2050 (source: World Population Prospects: The 1994 Revision, United Nations, 1995).

[5] Unfunded pension schemes are viable if the sum of the growth rates in the working population and labour productivity exceeds the sum of the growth rates in the retired population and in real pensions.

[6] Funded pension schemes are viable if the real return on pension assets exceeds the growth rate in real pensions.

[7] Funded schemes are superior to unfunded schemes if the real return on pension asset exceeds the sum of the growth rate in the working population and in labour productivity.

Source: Blake (2000, table 1).

There is also a good theoretical reason for supposing that, in long-run equilibrium, the average return on assets will exceed the growth rate in the wage bill (which, in turn, equals the growth rate in national income if the share of wages in national income is constant). This has to do with the *dynamic efficiency* of the economy. Saving via a pension fund helps the process of capital accumulation, which, in turn, improves the productivity of workers. However, it is possible to accumulate so much capital that the rate of return on capital assets falls below the growth rate in national income and the economy becomes *dynamically inefficient*: people could be made better off by saving less and consuming more. Dynamically inefficient economies are unlikely to be sustainable in the long run, since the owners of capital are likely to transfer their capital to economies offering higher returns.[27]

7.9.2 The Transition Deficit

Even if the move from an unfunded to a funded pension system is recognised as being desirable, there is a major transitional problem to solve. Existing pensioners in the unfunded scheme still have to be paid. With an unfunded system, pensions are paid from the contributions of those currently in work. If a funded pension system is introduced, the contributions from those in work will be invested in a fund and will no longer be available to pay the pensions of those who remain in the unfunded system. The introduction of a funded system creates what is known as a *transition deficit*. This has to be financed by extra taxation or by the issue of *recognition bonds* by the government (effectively a form of deferred taxation that formally 'recognises' the unfunded liabilities of the state PAYG system). In short, the next generation has to pay twice for its pensions: once in the form of direct contributions into its own pension fund and again in the form of extra taxation to pay for the previous generation's pensions.

Some people question whether, in a democracy, the transition generation would ever agree to make the switch, given that it is made worse off and that the future generations who would benefit from it are not in a position to vote on the matter. The issue boils down to whether the switch is Pareto-improving: could future generations compensate the transition generation for making the switch without making themselves worse off? The answer depends on the assumptions made.[28]

---

[27] Abel *et al.* (1989).
[28] The arguments in the next two paragraphs were first raised in Sections 4.2.4 and 4.3.5.

For example, Breyer (1989) (see also Geanakoplos *et al.*, 1998a,b) uses an infinite-horizon overlapping generations (OLG) model in which the labour supply of each worker is fixed exogenously and there is a perfect capital market trading a single financial instrument (essentially a government bond) with a real return (r) that exceeds the growth rate (g) in the population; because the labour supply is fixed, the real wage bill (measured in wage units) also grows at rate g. Suppose the government replaces the PAYG system by issuing recognition bonds equal to the value of the unfunded pension liabilities. Workers start paying into the new funded scheme, which invests in government bonds paying r. While this is higher than g, the rate of return in the unfunded scheme, workers also have to pay extra taxes to meet the interest payments on the recognition bonds. The maximum extra taxes that workers can pay is at the rate $(r - g)$, otherwise they would be worse off than under the PAYG system. With tax payments of just $(r - g)$ to pay the interest on the recognition bonds, the recognition bond debt will grow at rate g. But because the population is also growing at rate g, the recognition bond debt per worker will remain constant over time. However, the important point to note is that the recognition bond debt can never be paid off without making future generations worse off, since the tax rate would have to be higher than $(r - g)$ to pay off the debt in finite time. Therefore the switch to funding can never be Pareto-improving if the assumptions of this model are valid.

However, when the assumptions are changed, we can get a different outcome. Breyer and Straub (1993), for example, allow labour supply to be endogenous and respond to net wages. Since the payroll taxes (social security contributions) collected to pay PAYG pensions are usually proportional to earnings, this will distort labour supply decisions to such an extent that PAYG is no longer Pareto-efficient. Breyer and Straub show that switching to lump-sum payroll taxes can both remove labour supply distortions and raise sufficient revenue to pay off the recognition bonds in finite time, so that a switch to funding can lead to an intergenerational Pareto-improvement. Similarly, if the capital markets trade not only bonds, but also equity with a higher return than bonds $(r_E > r)$, then the switch to funding could also be Pareto-improving, since the tax payments to fund the recognition bond debt could be marginally higher than $(r - g)$ and the debt could be paid off in finite time and all future generations would be better off.

Geanakoplos *et al.* (1998a,b), however, argue that equity is riskier than bonds, and that, appropriately adjusting for risk, the return on equity does not exceed that on bonds. However, the absolute risk attached to a financial instrument is not the relevant measure of risk when considering a pension fund portfolio. Instead, what is relevant is surplus risk, the risk on the assets relative to that on the liabilities, since the assets in an optimal pension fund portfolio are chosen to match as closely as possible the returns and risks on the liabilities. Equity is a natural long-term matching asset for pension liabilities growing at the rate of real wage inflation, for the simple reason that the shares of labour and capital in national income are fairly constant over time (or at least do not trend in a significant way), and equity represents the ownership of capital. In contrast, fixed-income bonds are riskier than equity when liabilities grow with wage inflation. Pension funds gain the long-run equity risk premium ($r_E - r$) by investing in equities rather than bonds. Geanakoplos *et al.* (1998a,b) do concede that when there are capital market imperfections and the poor are constrained from holding equities, the investment of pension fund contributions by the poor in equities could be Pareto-improving.

As a final illustration, consider an overlapping generations model with a finite horizon; the burden of paying the transition deficit could be transferred like a hot potato to the last generation alive, since it pays into a pension fund but will not be in a position to draw it down.

There are other potential benefits from a switch to funding, as listed in Valdés-Prieto (1997), such as: positive externalities in the capital markets (e.g., greater capital market deepening), access to international risk diversification, more transparent fiscal accounting and greater insulation from political risk.

To illustrate the size of the potential benefits from a switch to funding, the Conservative government in the UK announced in March 1997 plans to privatise the state pension system from the turn of the century and to end its unfunded nature. All individuals in work would receive rebates on their social security contributions, which had to be invested in a personalised pension account. The initial costs in terms of additional taxation were estimated to be £160m in the first year, rising to a peak of £7bn a year in 2040. However, the long-term savings to the taxpayer from the end of state pension provision were estimated to be £40bn per year (all in 1997 prices).[29] In contrast, in Chile, the government financed the transition from an unfunded to a funded system in the early 1980s by issuing recognition bonds.

---

[29] *Basic Pension Plus*, Conservative Central Office, 5 March 1997. These plans were put on hold as a result of the Conservative government's defeat in the May 1997 UK general election.

7.10 CONCLUSIONS

Different types of pension scheme involve different types of risk and different ways of sharing those risks. As a consequence, there will be different types of redistribution of resources within the different schemes. What is a risk before an event has taken place becomes an act of redistribution afterwards.

A private pension scheme member faces replacement rate risk, investment risk, interest rate risk, longevity risk, inflation risk, political risk and portability risk. In personal defined contribution pension schemes, these risks are borne directly by the scheme member (with the exception of portability risk which is non-existent in such schemes). Some of these risks can be hedged: for example, longevity and inflation risks in retirement can be hedged by purchasing an index-linked life annuity. In occupational defined benefit pension schemes, these risks (with the exception of portability risk) can be shared between the employer and employee, but have traditionally been borne by the employer as scheme sponsor. Again, some of these risks can be hedged. For example, investment risk can be hedged using asset–liability matching and management. Other risks, such as the risk of employer insolvency, can be shared between employer and employee via the degree of funding of the pension scheme. A higher level of funding increases the likelihood of employer insolvency. Employees are averse to this and will be willing to trade off lower wages for more secure pensions in the form of increased funding in the pension scheme.

Private pension schemes involve complex transfers of wealth between different groups of people. For example, early leavers subsidise long stayers, low flyers subsidise high flyers, and women subsidise men.

The risks in unfunded, pay-as-you-go state pension schemes are principally demographic and political in nature. A state pension scheme becomes increasingly onerous to operate when the population is ageing systematically, which occurs when longevity increases and fertility falls below the replacement ratio. This is because, under these conditions, the national pensions bill grows at a faster rate than the national wages bill, and taxes on the working population have to continually increase to pay for the state pensions.

If demographic risk is idiosyncratic between generations rather than systematic, one of the biggest benefits of a state pension system is its ability to hedge this demographic risk between generations, i.e., intergenerational risk sharing. Gordon and Varian (1988) showed that the optimal degree of risk sharing depends on what happens to the capital stock, since the only way to transfer wealth between generations is via changes in the capital stock. Changes in the capital stock change the marginal productivity of capital. When a unit of capital is transferred from generation t to generation $t + 1$ as a result of a tax-transfer social security system, generation $t + 1$ not only gains the extra capital, it also gains the marginal product of the capital. This means that generation $t + 1$ gets a more valuable benefit than generation t gives up. This means that the optimal degree of risk sharing between these generations depends on the marginal product of capital and is therefore generally less than $1/2$. Time consistency is also an important factor in the design of an efficient risk-sharing programme, since the generation that discovers it is losing out might decide to repeal the programme, even though it accepted beforehand that the programme's risk-sharing objectives were desirable. The time consistency of the programme can be enforced through a combination of pre-commitment devices and exposure to reputational risk.

State pension schemes also allow for redistributions within one generation, i.e., intragenerational risk sharing. The lifetime benefits from social security systems to poorer people are typically greater than their lifetime contributions, while the opposite holds for richer members of society. Private pension systems cannot redistribute in this way.

Despite the potential benefits of a state pension system in terms of both inter- and intragenerational risk sharing, the systematic demographic risk that state pension systems face in developed countries means that they are not viable in the long run unless their benefits are severely curtailed or people have to work longer to earn them. The solution to this problem might be to switch away from PAYG to funding. In a dynamically efficient economy, in which the return on capital (which equals the return on a funded pension scheme) exceeds the growth rate in the population (which equals the return on an unfunded pension scheme), the switch might be Pareto-improving. However, the switch also creates a transition deficit, since the transition generation needs to pay twice for its pensions. The deficit can be funded through the tax system over a number of future generations, but whether the switch is Pareto-improving or not depends on both the form of the tax and how those future generations adjust their labour supply in response to the tax. If, for example, the tax is a lump-sum payroll tax then the distortions to labour supply are minimised and sufficient extra revenue can be raised to pay the transition costs.

QUESTIONS

1. What is welfare economics?
2. What is the difference between equity and efficiency?
3. What is meant by market failure and how can it be dealt with?
4. What is the condition for efficient risk sharing?
5. Explain how a social security system can be interpreted as a risk-sharing device.
6. What is moral hazard and how can it be mitigated?
7. What is adverse selection and how can it be mitigated?
8. Explain the difference between idiosyncratic and aggregate risks and the implications for risk sharing.
9. What are the main risks in private pension schemes?
10. How are the risks in personal defined contribution pension schemes shared or hedged?
11. Explain the importance of life annuities in personal pension schemes.
12. How are the risks in occupational defined benefit pension schemes shared or hedged?
13. Why is portability risk usually a greater risk for an occupational pension scheme member than a personal pension scheme member?
14. What is asset–liability matching and management?
15. What is the difference between a complete and an incomplete market?
16. Why is the composition of an employee compensation package of wages and pensions irrelevant in a complete market?
17. What are the main types of market incompleteness?
18. What is a value function?
19. Why are the attitudes to risk of employer and employees irrelevant when markets are complete, but critical when they are not?
20. When there are untradeable risks (such as the risk of employer insolvency), how is the optimal compensation package of wages, pensions and risk sharing established?
21. Why might an employer agree to assume risks on behalf of an employee when no insurance company would be prepared to do so under the same circumstances?
22. How might portfolio restrictions influence the value of the employee compensation package?
23. What role do externalities and selection effects play in the design of compensation packages?

24. Examine some of the kinds of redistribution of pension wealth that take place in occupational pension schemes.
25. Examine the different types of redistribution of pension wealth between men and women that take place in occupational pension schemes.
26. How can the state pension system mitigate market failure in private sector pension provision?
27. What are the two main risks in state pension schemes?
28. What are the conditions for the long-run viability of a PAYG pension scheme?
29. How has political risk affected the UK state pension scheme?
30. What is intergenerational risk sharing?
31. What is two-way altruism?
32. Why is the family not an efficient risk-sharing machanism?
33. How does efficient intergenerational risk sharing work in a tax-transfer social security system?
34. What happens to the total risk facing each generation as the number of generations included in a tax-transfer social security system increase?
35. How do changes in the capital stock affect the optimal degree of intergenerational risk sharing in a tax-transfer social security system?
36. How can a tax-transfer social security system be made time consistent?
37. What is intragenerational risk sharing?
38. How can a social security system be used for intragenerational risk sharing?
39. What conditions are needed for a PAYG state pension system to be viable in the long run?
40. Are PAYG state pension systems in developed countries currently viable? If not, why not? And if not, what needs to be done to make them viable?
41. Under what condition is a funded scheme superior to an unfunded scheme and what is the relationship between this condition and the dynamic efficiency of the economy?
42. Why does the switch from an unfunded to a funded pension system create a transition deficit?
43. How can a transition deficit be financed?
44. Under what conditions will the switch from an unfunded to a funded pension system be Pareto-improving?
45. What are the potential benefits from a switch to funding?

REFERENCES

Aaron, H.J. (1966) The social insurance paradox, *Canadian Journal of Economics and Political Science*, **32**, 371–374.

Abel, A., Mankiw, N.G., Summers, L. and Richard, J. (1989) Assessing dynamic efficiency, *Review of Economic Studies*, **56**, 1–19.

Arrow, K. (1964) The role of securities in the optimal allocation of risk bearing, *Review of Economic Studies*, **31**, 91–96.

Bernheim, D. (1989) The timing of retirement: a comparison of expectations and realisations, in Wise, D. (ed.), *The Economics of Ageing*, University of Chicago Press, Chicago, pp. 335–358.

Blake, D. (2000), Does it matter what type of pension scheme you have?, *Economic Journal*, **110**, F46–F81.

Blake, D. (2003a) *Pension Schemes and Pension Funds in the United Kingdom*, Oxford University Press, Oxford.

Blake, D. (2003b) The UK pension system: key features, *Pensions*, **8**, 330–375.

Blake, D. (2004) What is a Promise from the Government Worth? Measuring and Assessing Political Risk in State and Personal Pension Schemes in the United Kingdom, Pensions Institute Discussion Paper 0409 (http://www.pensions-institute.org/workingpapers/wp0409.pdf).

Blake, D. and Orszag, M. (1997) The Portability and Preservation of Pension Rights in the UK, Report of the Director General's Inquiry into Pensions, Volume III, Office of Fair Trading, October (http://www.pensions-institute.org/reports/oft191c1.pdf).

Blinder, A. (1981) *Private Pensions and Public Pensions: Theory & Fact*, W.S. Woytinsky Lecture No. 5, Institute of public Policy Studies, University of Michigan.

Bodie, Z. (1990) Pensions as retirement income insurance, *Journal of Economic Literature*, **28**, 28–49.

Brandts, J. and De Bartolome, C. (1992) Population uncertainty, social insurance and actuarial bias, *Journal of Public Economics*, **47**, 361–380.

Breyer, F. (1989) On the intergenerational Pareto efficiency of pay-as-you go financed pension systems, *Journal of Institutional and Theoretical Economics*, **145**, 643–658.

Breyer, F. and Straub, M. (1993) Welfare effects of unfunded pension schemes when labor supply is endogenous, *Journal of Public Economics*, **50**, 77–91.

Burgess, S. and Rees, H. (1994) *Lifetime Jobs and Transient Jobs: Job Tenure in Britain 1975–91*, Centre for Economic Policy Research, London.

Cagan, P. (1965) *The Effect of Pension Plans on Aggregate Savings: Evidence from a Sample Survey*, NBER Occasional Paper, No. 95, Columbia University Press, New York.

Chand, S.K. and Jaeger, A. (1996) *Ageing Populations and Public Pension Schemes*, Occasional Paper No. 147, International Monetary Fund, Washington, DC.

Cooper, R. and Ross, T. (2002) Pensions: theories of underfunding, *Labor Economics*, **8**, 667–689.

Cox, J. and Huang, C.-F. (1989) Optimal consumption and portfolio policies when asset prices follow a diffusion process, *Journal of Economic Theory*, **49**, 33–83.

Crafts, N. and Toniolo, G. (eds) (1996) *Economic Growth in Europe since 1945*, Cambridge University Press, Cambridge.

Davis, E.P. (1995) *Pension Funds*, Oxford University Press, Oxford.

Debreu, G. (1959) *Theory of Value*, Johan Wiley & Sons, New York.

Diamond, P. (1977) A framework for social security analysis, *Journal of Public Economics*, **8**, 275–298.

Diamond, P. (1997) Insulation of pensions from political risk, in Valdés-Prieto, S. (ed.), *The Economics of Pensions: Principles, Policies and International Experience*, Cambridge University Press, Cambridge, pp. 33–57.

Eckstein, Z., Eichenbaum, M. and Peled, D. (1985a) Uncertain lifetimes and the welfare enhancing properties of annuity markets and social security, *Journal of Public Economics*, **26**, 303–326.

Eckstein, Z., Eichenbaum, M. and Peled, D. (1985b) The distribution of wealth and welfare in the presence of incomplete annuity markets, *Quarterly Journal of Economics*, **100**, 789–806.

Eltis, W. (1994) The re-establishment of European competitiveness, *International Bank Credit Analyst*, June.

Feldstein, M. (1985) The optimal level of social security benefits, *Quarterly Journal of Economics*, **100**, 303–320.

Finkelstein, A. and Poterba, J. (2002) Selection effects in the market for individual annuities: new evidence from the United Kingdom, *Economic Journal*, **112**, 28–50.

Friedman, B. and Warshawsky, M. (1990) The cost of annuities: implications for saving behavior and bequests, *Quarterly Journal of Economics*, **105**, 135–154.

Geanakoplos, J., Mitchell, O.S. and Zeldes, S.P. (1998a) Would a privatized social security system really pay a higher rate of return?, in Arnold, R.D., Graetz, M.J. and Munnell, A.H. (eds), *Framing the Social Security Debate: Values, Politics, and Economics*, Brookings Institution Press, Washington, DC, pp. 137–157.

Geanakoplos, J., Mitchell, O.S. and Zeldes, S.P. (1998b) *Social Security Money's Worth*, Working Paper 6722, National Bureau of Economic Research, Cambridge, MA.

Gordon, R. and Varian, H. (1988) Intergenerational risk sharing, *Journal of Public Economics*, **37**, 185–202.

Gregg, P. and Wadsworth, J. (1995) A short history of labour turnover, job tenure, and job security, 1973–93, *Oxford Review of Economic Policy*, **11**, 73–90.

Hammermesh, D. (1984) Life-cycle effects on consumption and retirement, *Journal of Labor Economics*, **2**, 353–370.

Ippolito, R. (1997) *Pension Plans and Employee Performance: Evidence, Analysis and Policy*, University of Chicago Press, Chicago.

Katona, G. (1964) *Private Pensions and Individual Savings*, University of Michigan – Survey Research Centre, Ann Arbor, MI.

Kotlikoff, L. and Spivak, A. (1981) The family as an incomplete annuities market, *Journal of Political Economy*, **89**, 372–391.

McCarthy, D. (2005) The Optimal Allocation of Pension Risks in Employment Contracts, Research Report 272, Department for Work and Pensions, Leeds.

Merton, R. (1984) On the role of social security as a means for efficient risk-bearing in an economy where human capital is non-tradeable, in Bodie, Z. and Shoven, J. (eds), *Financial Aspects of the United States Pension System*, University of Chicago Press, Chicago.

Merton, R., Bodie, Z. and Marcus, A. (1987) Pension plan integration as insurance against social risk, in Bodie, Z., Shoven, J. and Wise, D. (eds), *Issues in Pension Economics*, University of Chicago Press, Chicago, pp. 147–174.

Mitchell, O., Poterba, J., Warshawsky, M. and Brown, J. (1999) New evidence on the money's worth of individual annuities, *American Economic Review*, **89**, 1299–1318.

O'Brien, C., Fenn, P. and Diacon, S. (2005) *How Long do People Expect to Live?*, Centre for Risk and Insurance Studies, Research Report 2005-1, Nottingham University Business School.

Roseveare, D., Leibfritz, W., Fore, D. and Wurzel, E. (1996) *Ageing Populations, Pension Systems and Government Budgets: Simulation for 20 OECD Countries*, Economics Department Working Paper No. 168, OECD, Paris.

Samuelson, P. (1975) Optimum social security in a life-cycle growth model, *International Economic Review*, **16**, 539–544.

Sharpe, W. (1976) Corporate pension funding policy, *Journal of Financial Economics*, **3**, 183–193.

Townley, P. and Broadway, R. (1988) social security and the failure of annuity markets, *Journal of Public Economics*, **35**, 75–96.

Valdés-Prieto, S. (1997) Financing a pension reform toward private funded pensions, in Valdés-Prieto, S. (ed.), *The Economics of Pensions: Principles, Policies and International Experience*, Cambridge University Press, New York, pp. 190–224.

van Ark, B. and Crafts, N. (eds) (1996) *Quantitative Aspects of Post-war European Economic Growth*, Cambridge University Press, Cambridge.

Wolf, M. (2006) There is something rotten in the welfare state of Europe, *Financial Times*, 1 March, p. 17.

World Bank (1993) *The Far East Asian Economic Miracle*, Oxford University Press, Oxford.

World Bank (1994a) *World Population Projections 1994–5*, World Bank, Washington, DC.

World Bank (1994b) *Averting the Old-Age Crisis*, Oxford University Press, Oxford.

8
Behavioural Pension Economics

Up till now, we have assumed that the individuals involved in pension planning over their lifecycle are well-informed rational economic agents who make decisions in a way that maximises their utility or welfare. Such individuals are assumed to be able to 'interpret and weigh information presented regarding options offered by employers and governments, appropriately evaluate and balance these choices, and then make an informed decision based on a weighing of the alternatives' (Mitchell and Utkus, (2004).

However, in recent years, social scientists working in the field of behavioural economics (which combines economics, finance, psychology and sociology) have found that although individuals do try to maximise their personal welfare, there are limits to the extent that they are able to do this.

In reality, individual decisions are subject to:

- *Bounded rationality* (Simon, 1955) – certain types of problem are too complex for individuals to solve on their own.
- *Bounded self-control* (Mullainathan and Thaler, 2000) – individuals lack the willpower to execute their plans.
- *Bounded self-interest* (Mullainathan and Thaler, 2000) – while individuals do seek to maximise their personal welfare, they turn out to be much more co-operative and altruistic than predicted by economic theory.

The recognition of these limits on optimising behaviour has begun to change our understanding of individual economic and financial decision making, especially long-term consumption and savings decisions such as those involved in accumulating and decumulating assets in a pension scheme. Here we examine the lessons of behavioural economics for the accumulation and decumulation phases in pension schemes.[1]

---

[1] The analysis follows closely Mitchell and Utkus (2004). See also Barberis and Thaler (2003).

8.1   THE ACCUMULATION PHASE

8.1.1   The Savings Decision

Saving for the rational economic agent is the result of a trade-off between consuming income today and deferring some of it to a future date. The lifecycle model (LCM) assumes that individuals rationally plan their consumption needs over their lifetime. When they are young, individuals are typically net dissavers, taking out loans to buy houses and increase current consumption (i.e., borrowing from the future). In middle age, they begin the accumulation phase of their pension scheme, becoming net savers and purchasers of financial assets. When they retire, the decumulation phase of their pension scheme begins and a new period of dissaving begins; the financial assets in the pension scheme are sold to finance old-age consumption. The overall objective is to smooth consumption over the lifecycle in a way that maximises lifetime expected utility.

The Problem of Complexity

The retirement savings decision in the LCM needs accurate forecasts of lifetime earnings, asset returns, interest rates, tax rates, inflation and longevity. Very few people have the skills to do this and to subsequently save enough for retirement by the age of 65 (Moore and Mitchell, 2000; Mitchell *et al.*, 2000). As a consequence, many people experience a significant fall in living standards in retirement (Bernheim *et al.*, 2001; Banks *et al.*, 1998). All this comes as no surprise to behaviouralists.

The Problem of Self-control

Behaviouralists explain the inadequate preparation for retirement in terms of *lack of willpower* or *bounded self-control*. People might want to save for retirement, but are unable to do so (Thaler and Shefrin, 1981). The same problem faces smokers or those who want to lose weight. They understand the benefits of implementing a particular plan, and might even start such a plan, but are unable to sustain the plan long enough to achieve the goal.

Why do some people find it difficult to save for retirement? One explanation is that individuals' short-term discount rates or rates of time preference are higher than their long-term discount rates (Thaler, 1981; Laibson *et al.*, 1998). Thaler argues that people show a high level of patience when it comes to long-term decisions: 'If I can receive an apple in 100 days and two apples in 101 days, I'll be happy to wait the extra

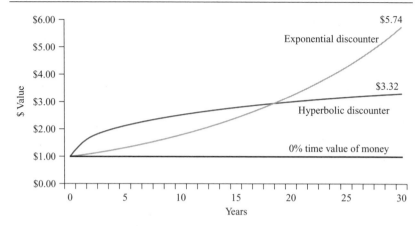

Figure 8.1   Exponential versus hyperbolic discounters: growth of $1 over time
Source: Mitchell and Utkus (2004, Figure 1). Reproduced by permission of Oxford University Press

day for another apple'. But when the decision is immediate, patience evaporates: 'I'd rather have an apple today than wait for two tomorrow'.

Conventional time value of money calculations involve *exponential discounting* in which the discount rate is constant over time. With a constant discount rate of 6%, an *exponential discounter* will value one dollar saved today as worth $5.74 in 30 years' time (Figure 8.1). The savings become more valuable as the investment horizon increases.

However, the different valuations applied to the short-term and long-term valuation of apples above is consistent with *hyperbolic discounting*. A *hyperbolic discounter* uses a high short-term discount rate and a lower long-term discount rate. Such a person treats one dollar saved as growing more rapidly in the short term and less rapidly in the long term. There are therefore decreasing benefits to increasing the investment horizon. Similarly, they overvalue current risks, and overdiscount future risks.

Since a hyperbolic discounter overvalues the present and undervalues the future, they have a self-control problem when it comes to retirement: they overconsume today and undersave for the future. There is a wide gap between individual desire and actual behaviour, as a survey of 10,000 employees at a single firm conducted by Choi *et al.* (2001a) discovered: 68% said their retirement savings rate was 'too low'. They knew that they *should* be saving around 14% of earnings, but were actually only saving about 6%. So the problem is not lack of awareness, but inability to take appropriate action.

Decision theorists argue that decision making has two dimensions: a primitive or emotional dimension and an advanced or cerebral dimension (Weber, 2004). Correspondingly, there are two dimensions to risk: *dread risk*, the fear of a catastrophe, and *uncertainty risk*, the fear of the new or unknown. Retirement risks are low in these two dimensions: there is neither a sufficient sense of catastrophe nor of great uncertainty for most people to frighten them into preparing for retirement and overcoming their self-control problem. To overcome the effects of hyperbolic discounting, it is necessary to merge conceptual and affective reasoning.[2] To achieve this, individuals might need to replicate the experience of poverty in retirement by living on a small fraction of current income for a while.

They then need to employ *commitment devices* that support permanent changes in behaviour (cf Laibson, 1997; Laibson *et al.*, 1998). A simple example that encourages long-term savings behaviour is payroll deduction of contributions. This is based on a commitment device called 'pay yourself first'.[3] This is common in US 401(k) pension plans, but not in Individual Retirement Accounts. Participation rates are 27% in the former and only 6% in the latter (in 1997). Withdrawal restrictions, by creating a psychological and financial barrier to accessing the funds, also act as a commitment device.

Ameriks *et al.* (2003) and MacFarland *et al.* (2004) found that workers with a strong 'propensity to plan' had a greater commitment to retirement savings. Only half the population are 'planners', however. The rest are just not interested in financial and retirement planning.

Framing and Default Choices

Individuals can also be influenced by *decision framing*. The response of rational economic agents will not depend on how a problem is posed. But this does not appear to be true for most people, as the case of *positive election* versus *automatic enrolment* in pension schemes illustrates.

---

[2] Conceptual reasoning is influenced by thoughts, ideas or notions formed in the mind, while affective reasoning is influenced by emotions.

[3] Beginnersinvest.about.com explains 'pay yourself first' as follows: 'When you set down to pay your bills, the first check you write should be to yourself. Decide on an amount you can commit to for at least six months and immediately pay that "bill" by depositing the money into your brokerage, mutual fund, or retirement accounts. You must do this even if you cannot afford it! Then, pay your other bills as usual. If you find that you do not have enough money to cover all the expenses, write down the amount you are short and then find a way to raise the money. If this means you have to recycle cans, switch to an off-brand cereal, work a few extra hours, or cancel your magazine subscriptions, do it.'

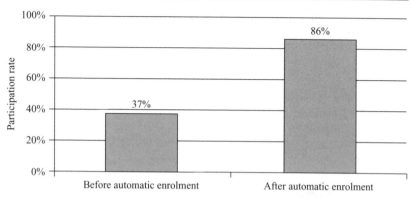

Figure 8.2 Decision framing: the impact of automatic enrolment in scheme participation rates
Source: Mitchell and Utkus (2004, Figure 2). Reproduced by permission of Oxford University Press

With positive election, workers have to actively join the scheme; the default option is to do nothing. Under automatic enrolment, a new worker is automatically enrolled in the pension scheme at a set contribution rate, unless he actively opts out. Madrian and Shea (2001) show that participation rates differ dramatically depending on which option is the default option. In the case of a large US corporate, scheme membership rose from 37% to 86% for new workers following the introduction of automatic enrolment (Figure 8.2). This appears to suggest that workers do not have firm views about their long-term savings desires but that preferences can be influenced by how a question is asked.

Automatic enrolment illustrates the significance of the *default option* in decision making. When faced with difficult choices, individuals often employ *simplifying heuristics* (shortcuts or simple rules of thumb). One simple heuristic is to choose the default option on the grounds possibly that someone else must have thought that it was a good idea.

However, although a default option, such as automatic enrolment, might have a positive effect in one dimension (increasing participation), it might not do so in all dimensions. Automatic enrolment does not actually increase total pension savings (Choi *et al.*, 2001b). This is because a number of individuals who would have been willing to make higher contributions than the default also accept the default contribution rate. The higher participation rate is broadly cancelled out by the lower average saving rate.

Table 8.1 The problem of self-control: divergence between desired and actual behaviour

Action	Planned change%	Actual change%
Enrol in 401(k) plan	100	14
Increase contribution rate	28	8
Change fund selection	47	15
Change fund allocation	36	10

Source: Choi *et al.* (2000a, table 6).

Inertia and Procrastination

The automatic enrolment example illustrates another common feature of human decision making, *inertia* or *procrastination*. Once enrolled, members tended not to alter either the contribution rate or the investment fund chosen by the employer as the default (Choi *et al.*, 2003). Members tended to behave passively, taking 'the path of least resistance' and making the easiest, rather than the best, decisions (Choi *et al.*, 2001b). All this is inconsistent with rational economic decision making.

Choi *et al.* (2001a) illustrate the 'desire versus action' conundrum by comparing workers' attitudes following a retirement planning seminar with subsequent behaviour. All workers said they would join the company 401(k) pension plan, but after six months, only 14% had done so. A similar pattern held for other decisions (see Table 8.1).

Choice Overload and Herding

Standard economic theory argues that people are better off the more choices they have. But when it comes to choice of investment fund for pension contributions, Sethi-Iyengar *et al.* (2004) argue that there can be *choice overload*. Confronted with too much choice, many people feel overwhelmed and end up not participating at all in the scheme. They are simplifying the decision by following the worst default heuristic of all: 'don't decide, don't join the plan'.

Duflo and Saez (2004) show that saving decisions are often influenced by the behaviour of peers. There is *herding behaviour*: a worker will join if other workers are also joining.

Save More Tomorrow Plans

These behavioural traits have been exploited to design pension schemes that increase long-term pension savings. The classic example is the

Save More Tomorrow (or *SmarT*) plan (Thaler and Benartzi, 2004). The scheme member agrees to start or increase savings on a regular basis not now but on a future significant date, such as the date of the next pay rise or the anniversary date of joining the company.

The plan deals with a number of behavioural traits:

- It accepts individuals have self-control problems and benefit from using a precommitment device.
- It utilises inertia, since, once signed up, workers typically do not cancel the payroll deduction facility.
- It recognises hyperbolic discounting by deliberately delaying the start date for implementing the plan (save more tomorrow not today), since hyperbolic discounters seriously underestimate the impact of this future commitment.
- It exploits *money illusion*,[4] since, if the savings plan starts on the day of the pay rise and the increase in the contribution rate is equal to the pay rise (say 3%), then additional pension contributions are being made without a fall in take-home pay.

The SmarT plan was tested at a 300-employee firm. The workers were offered financial advice, which most took. The financial adviser said that contribution rates should increase by 5% from the current 3.5%. Around 80 workers followed that advice. However, 160 workers started a SmarT plan which involved annual increases of 3%. After 4 years, their contribution rate had risen to 13.6% (Figure 8.3).

There are some striking lessons:

- The savings decision needs to be reframed to include defaults which automatically increase saving rates on a regular basis.
- Commitment devices, inertia and money illusion need to be exploited to deal with the problem of self-control facing hyperbolic discounters.

8.1.2   The Investment Decision

When it comes to making decisions about how to invest pension contributions during the accumulation phase, rational economic agents would be expected to invest in portfolios consistent with *modern portfolio theory*

---

[4] When individuals suffer from money illusion, they are unable to distinguish fully between nominal (i.e., money) values and real (i.e., inflation-adjusted) values. In the example here, the pay rise (mostly) compensates for inflation, yet because there is no fall in take-home pay, workers do not feel they are being made worse off by joining the pension plan. In reality, their real take-home pay has fallen by 3%.

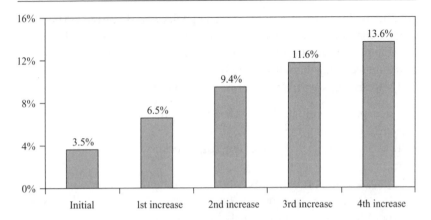

Figure 8.3 The impact of commitment devices and inertia: savings rates in SmarT plans
Source: Thaler and Benartzi (2004). Reproduced by permission

(MPT) (see, e.g., Blake, 2000, ch.13). MPT characterises investment portfolios in terms of their expected or mean return and their volatility or variance. For risk-averse investors, a higher mean is a good thing, while a higher variance is a bad thing. Such investors trade off risk for additional return. The greater the risk aversion, the higher the additional return needed in order to assume more risk. Investors will choose from portfolios of risk assets along the *efficient frontier*, those offering the highest level of expected return for a particular level of risk. Investors will select portfolios of assets rather than individual securities, since this is a way of diversifying and hence minimising risk. In an efficient capital market, individuals will be compensated for bearing systematic or undiversifiable risk but not diversifiable risk, since this can be reduced very easily at low cost. MPT has been used to justify low-cost and highly diversified index funds, and if MPT is valid large numbers of investors should be observed holding such funds.

MPT also justifies *time diversification*[5] as well as diversification across assets. Investors should switch into less volatile assets as the

---

[5] When time diversification is effective, asset return volatility falls as the length of the investment horizon increases. For time diversification to be effective, asset returns must exhibit the property of mean reversion. This implies that asset returns can deviate, sometimes quite substantially, from long-term averages (in other words, volatility can be high in the short term), but that eventually they adjust back to long-term average growth paths (in other words, volatility is much lower in the long-term).

investment period comes to an end and the fund is needed for spending (e.g., on the retirement date). Often simple rules are proposed, such as '100% minus the investor's age in equities'.

Studies of real-world investor behaviour do not show much support for MPT being implemented in practice. The median US investor holds a portfolio containing just two securities, whilst amongst the richest investors, the median holding is just 15 securities, far less than is needed to eliminate diversifiable risk (Polkovnichenko, 2003). Similarly, there is excessive DC pension fund investment in the sponsor's own shares. While this is not permitted in the UK, where the maximum level of self-investment is 5%, such restrictions do not hold in the USA. Mitchell and Utkus (2003) found that 11 million 401(k) plan members held more than 20% of their assets in their employer's stock, with 5 million of these holding more than 60%. This is extremely risky, since if the employer goes bust (as in the case of Enron), the plan member loses not only his job, but also much of his pension fund.

Behaviouralists have put forward a number of reasons for these investment puzzles.

Lack of Firm Preferences

The same lack of firm preferences in respect of the savings decision also appears to impact on the investment decision. Pension scheme members appear to have relatively weak preferences for the portfolio they choose (Benartzi and Thaler, 2002). In an experiment in which members were given a choice between holding their own portfolio, the portfolio of the median member of their scheme and the portfolio of the average member, 80% preferred the median to their own and many would have been happy with the average portfolio. Only 21% still preferred their own original portfolio. This is indicative of a herding instinct in investment bahaviour, where it is comforting to be at or near the average of the peer group of co-members.

These findings again come as no surprise to behaviouralists, who argue that many individuals do not make decisions on the basis of firm preferences. In many cases, preferences only become apparent at the time a decision needs to be made, and will depend on the conditions and information available at the time. Such preference forming is said to be *situational*. This leads to frequent *preference reversals*. Individuals, having selected their own portfolio, can find themselves in situations where they are happier with another choice.

Framing Effects

Framing effects are also important in investment decision making. Experiments have been conducted on the effect of investment menu design on investment choices made in DC pension schemes. The results of the experiments show that the menu design has a bigger influence on investment choice than the actual risk and return characteristics of the investments themselves.

Benartzi and Thaler (2001) conducted an experiment in which pension scheme members were invited to choose an investment mix from a choice of two different funds. One group was offered a stock fund and a bond fund. A second group were offered a stock fund and a balanced fund. A third group was offered a bond fund and a balanced fund. The most common strategy for all groups was to select an equal 50:50 mix of the two funds offered. Yet the underlying asset allocation and risk characteristics of this mix was dramatically different for each group. The equity weightings for the three groups were 54%, 73% and 35%, respectively.

As the number of funds offered in the experiment increased, a *1/N rule* seemed to emerge, with allocations spread equally across the number of funds offered, irrespective of the risk characteristics.

Benartzi and Thaler (2002) conducted a different experiment on DC pension scheme members involving three different menus with up to four funds: A (low risk) to D (high risk). The first menu contained A, B and C; the second menu B and C; and the third menu B, C and D. When it came to ranking C and B, which were in all three menus, C was preferred to B by 29% of those offered the first menu, 39% of those offered the second menu, and 54% of those offered the third menu. So C was most liked when it was the middle choice and least liked when it was listed as an extreme. This suggests scheme members follow the *naïve heuristic* of picking the middle option and avoiding extremes, rather than selecting on the basis of the return and risk characteristics of the underlying investments.

Thaler and Benartzi (1999) show that investment decisions can be affected by how information is presented. In an experiment where the information shown to pension scheme members was the 1-year return on US equities, the average allocation to equities was 63%. In another experiment where information on the less volatile 30-year return was presented, the average allocation to equities jumped to 81%.

What these experiments indicate is that the investment menu choice is an *opaque frame*, which pension scheme members are unable to see through to observe the return and risk characteristics of the underlying investments. Given their lack of firm preferences, they can easily be influenced by the framing effects of an investment menu.

Anchoring Effects, Inertia and Procrastination

Mitchell and Utkus (2004) show the significance of anchoring effects on investment decision making. *Anchoring* is the idea that the initial conditions used to justify a decision remain important over time, however irrational this might be. Figure 8.4 shows the 2003 equity allocations of the 2.3m members of 401(k) pension schemes operated by the Vanguard Group as a function of entry date into their scheme. Members who first enrolled during the equity bull market in the second half of the 1990s continued to allocate 70% of their 2003 contributions to equities. Those who started their schemes in 2003, after a 3-year slump in equities, only allocated 48%. It is unlikely that the newer entrants will be significantly more risk averse than the late 1990s entrants to explain these large differences.

This behaviour is consistent with the significant *inertia* and *procrastination* in investment decision making by pension scheme members documented by Madrian and Shea (2001) and Choi *et al.* (2001b). Fewer than 10% of Vanguard scheme members alter their contribution allocations each year.

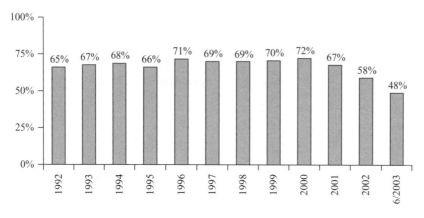

Figure 8.4   Anchoring and adjustment: current (2003) equity contributions by plan entry date (% contribution allocated to equity investments)
Source: Mitchell and Utkus (2004). Reproduced by permission of Oxford University Press

The Excessive Investment in Employer Stock

Mitchell and Utkus (2003) report that 11 million 401(k) scheme members hold at least 20% of their fund in their own company's shares, and 5 million hold at least 60%. This clearly violates the principle of risk diversification underlying MPT. One justification for why employers encourage this is that it provides an incentive for employees to work harder.

However, Mitchell and Utkus show that from a behavioural viewpoint, these large concentrations in company shares are the result not only of incentive effects, but also of computational or behavioural errors. Employees appear to suffer from *risk myopia* in respect of their own company's shares. This is shown by a 2003 Vanguard Group survey (reported in Mitchell and Utkus, 2003), which was conducted after the collapse of Enron in which employees lost their jobs and their pension funds, which had all been invested in Enron shares. Two-thirds of scheme members regard their employer's shares as less risky than, or equally risky as, a well-diversified equity fund, despite the greater volatility of the former. This is inconsistent with MPT.

Benartzi (2001) examined pension investments in employer shares and also found that scheme members concentrated on returns and ignored volatility. In particular, they forecast returns by extrapolating their company's shares' historic performance. Good past performance led to the pension fund being overweight in the employer's shares and vice versa. Weightings were also affected by whether the employer matched employee contributions with company shares; this is called an *endorsement effect*.

So again we see evidence of the framing effect of the sponsor's scheme design decision matters. If the employer offers matching contributions in the form of company shares rather than cash, employees increase their own weighting in company shares.

Reliance on Past Performance

Another anomaly is that past performance determines asset allocations in DC pension schemes rather than expected future returns and risk as anticipated by MPT (e.g., Choi *et al.*, 2004; Huberman and Sengmueller, 2003; Poterba *et al.*, 2003; Purcell, 2002). Two behavioural factors have been put forward to explain this.

The first is the *representativeness heuristic* identified by Tversky and Kahneman (1974). Offered a short series of random numbers, individuals will often try to identify a pattern in these numbers. Similarly, when making decisions, people often try to impose some order or structure on the information they use.

The classic example of this is to examine the investment performance of the top-performing mutual fund manager over the last 3 years, say, and draw the conclusion that his pre-eminent position is due to skill, whereas an equally and possibly more likely explanation is that his position is due to pure chance, since a 3-year track record is insufficiently long to identify genuine skill.

The *representativeness bias* might be caused by a framing effect. Rather than use a wide frame to assess skill versus luck, such as the population of all mutual fund managers, the individual investor might adopt a narrow frame, such as the 3-year track record of a single fund manager. As a consequence, what in reality might be a random outcome could be interpreted as a logical sequence.

The second is an *availability heuristic*. Confronted with a complex decision, individuals often use whatever information is readily at hand. In the example above, investors rely on past performance probably because it is freely available from newspapers and websites and is used despite the small print warning that 'past performance is no guide to future performance'.

These two heuristics might help to explain the *return chasing phenomenon*[6] observed in mutual fund purchase decisions (Patel *et al.*, 1991).

Prospect Theory

An alternative to the mean–variance optimisation of MPT as a decision rule for investment choice is prospect theory, developed by Kahneman and Tversky (1979). They argue that individuals maximise a non-linear value function as in Figure 8.5. This optimisation problem differs from standard utility maximisation in two important respects. First, individuals judge how their decisions affect incremental gains and losses to their wealth, rather than their total wealth (as required by standard utility theory). Second, individuals treat gains and losses differently: losses have a much more negative impact on welfare than the same dollar gain has on improving welfare. The *gain function* (to the right of the origin) is

---

[6] This is where mutual fund investors rush into funds whose recent past performance has been exceptional, irrespective of these funds' future prospects.

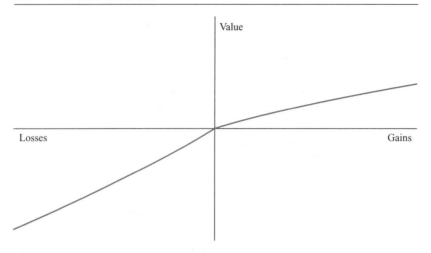

Figure 8.5   Prospect theory value function
Source: Mitchell and Utkus (2004). Reproduced by permission of Oxford University Press

concave, but the *loss function* (to the left of the origin) is convex and has a much steeper slope. In experiments, Kahneman and Tversky found that the index of loss-aversion is about 2.5. This implies that a typical individual would not be willing to take part in a fair game unless the potential gain was 2.5 times the potential loss.

Kahneman and Tversky called this alternative to MPT *prospect theory*, and it has powerful implications for investment behaviour. Investors will be risk averse for a realised gain and will act to lock in this gain prematurely (called the *disposition effect* by Shefrin and Statman, 1985). However, they will be risk seeking (i.e., gamble) in an attempt to avoid a certain loss. Further, actual behaviour will depend on the particular sequence of gains and losses and how these have been incorporated into current perceptions.

Mitchell and Utkus (2004) offer the following illustration: 'Suppose an individual wins $100. If offered a reasonable chance to win more money or lose the $100, many people would decline the additional gamble, because of the risk of forfeiting the $100 sure gain. But if offered a choice to win more money while preserving a meaningful part of the $100 gain, many people take the risk..... On the loss side of the equation, after losing $100, many people will accept a gamble that entails losing significantly more than $100 in an effort to recoup the $100 loss.'

This suggests that when it comes to gains, many investors switch from risk-averse to risk-seeking behaviour if they feel they are risking someone else's money (e.g., accumulated earnings from prior bets): this is known as the *house money effect*. When it comes to losses, in addition to risk-seeking behaviour, a *breakeven effect* also operates. Recognising they face a certain loss, many investors take on additional risk in an attempt to recover their investment and break even. This is particularly observed in falling stock markets, where losses are perceived as temporary and another bet will enable the losses to be recovered. This contrasts with rational economic behaviour, which predicts that realised losses should be ignored on the grounds that they are sunk costs.

Kahneman (2003) argues that prospect theory is important for understanding investment decision making in three ways: overconfidence in the domain of gains, combined with premature realisation of investment gains; a policy of loss avoidance in the domain of losses; and narrow framing effects or mental accounting magnify these features.

Overconfidence

A key finding of behavioural economics is the tendency for individuals to be overconfident about the future and make excessively optimistic forecasts. Overconfidence in decision making, as a consequence of an inflated view of one's skill and ability, is a widespread phenomenon in a wide range of spheres, especially in business and investments. At the same time, people can be much more critical of the skills and abilities of others.

This overconfidence is in part caused by a tendency to underestimate the impact of chance in determining future outcomes and to subsequently overestimate the degree of control an individual had over these outcomes; and the stronger the feeling of control, the more powerful the feeling of confidence.

While overconfidence might be the beneficial source of business risk taking, it can also induce suboptimal behaviour that in the field of investing, for example, is inconsistent with MPT. One illustration of this is reported by Barber and Odean (2001), namely excessive trading in equities. In their study, they found that typical US brokerage account holders had a turnover rate of 75% p.a. The 5-year average return of active traders was 11.4%, compared with an overall market return of 17.9% p.a., and a return on low-turnover accounts of 18.5% p.a. Further, men traded 45% more than women.

De Bondt (1998) also found evidence that rich male investors experience overconfidence and emphasise personal investment skills. Most of these investors showed a high degree of confidence about their stock picking ability, and dismissed MPT factors such as diversification. Goetzmann and Kumar (2001) show that although individual investors might own portfolios containing a variety of equities, these portfolios tend not to be genuinely diversified, but consist of securities from highly correlated sectors.

Loss Aversion and the Disposition Effect

Loss aversion explains why investors are unable to 'cut their losses' and keep loss-making positions in the hope that they will recover their original investment. Odean (1998) reports that investors who hold on to loss-making positions underperform the market in the following year by 1%. He also found that investors sold their winning positions too quickly, i.e., failed to 'run their profits', and subsequently underperformed the market over the next year by 2%. This is a consequence of the disposition effect. The net effect of these two behavioural traits was therefore 3% p.a.

Narrow Framing or Mental Accounting

Kahneman (2003) reports that overconfidence and loss aversion are exacerbated by *narrow framing* effects, also known as *mental accounting*.

Mental accounting is the set of cognitive operations individuals seem to use to keep track of and evaluate financial transactions (Kahneman and Tversky, 1984, 2000; Thaler, 1985, 1999; Barberis and Huang, 2001). One feature of mental accounting is the assignment of specific activities to specific accounts. Expenditures are grouped into categories (e.g., housing, food, holiday savings, etc.) and spending in these categories is often limited by implicit or explicit budget constraints. Mental accounting plays a key role in understanding investor attitude and response to risk.

Small-scale risk aversion seems to result from a tendency to assess risk in isolation rather than in a broader context (i.e., the investor is 'thinking small'). If small-scale, better-than-fair gambles were assessed in a broader context, individuals would be more likely to accept them. Many individuals refuse to accept a coin-tossing gamble where heads wins $200 and tails loses $100. However, if the gamble is rephrased in terms of a $200 increase in the individual's housing equity if the coin shows heads and a $100 reduction if tails, then more people are likely to take part (Rabin and Thaler, 2001).

Investors also often act myopically in evaluating sequences of investment opportunities. For loss-averse investors, myopia can result in the sequence looking less attractive (e.g., because of short-term mental accounting losses) and might lead to the rejection of an investment programme (e.g., a retirement savings plan invested in equities) that would otherwise be accepted. Benartzi and Thaler (1995) called this *myopic loss aversion* (MLA). A symptom of MLA is excessive (i.e., very frequent) monitoring of the performance of the investment programme, even by long-term investors. If all investors behave in this way, it can have real consequences for the economy. If investors concentrated on the long-term returns on equities, they would recognise that the long-term risk on equities was no greater than that on bonds and would accept a correspondingly low equity risk premium. Instead, they focus on short-term volatility and the associated frequent mental accounting losses, and demand a substantial equity risk premium in compensation. Gneezy and Potters (1997) confirm using an experiment that the more frequently returns are evaluated, the more risk averse investors will be. Another symptom of MLA is overinsurance against small-scale, low-risk events, such as extended warranties on household appliances (Rabin and Thaler, 2001).

Benartzi and Thaler (1995) showed that, while a MLA investor would reject a single small-scale, better-than-fair gamble such as the coin-tossing gamble of $200 winnings versus a $100 loss, he would be prepared to engage in a series of such gambles (i.e., the investor switches to 'thinking big'), so long as each gamble in the sequence was not individually monitored. To avoid the risk that the investor withdraws from the sequence of gambles in response to early mental accounting losses, a commitment device is needed. An example of this would be a standing order for the premiums to a personal pension scheme, rather than an annual invitation to send a cheque to the scheme provider. The scheme provider should also report the performance of the scheme's assets to the scheme member no more frequently than annually. This too would help to sustain commitment. It would also help to avoid the overconfidence that would emerge in the investor if the early sequence of gambles fortuitously showed net winnings. However, Langer and Weber (2004) have shown using experiments that, of the two key factors influencing MLA, the period of commitment is more influential than the feedback frequency.

8.2   THE DECUMULATION PHASE

A rational lifecycle financial planner entering retirement plans to run down his accumulated financial assets so as to maximise the utility of his retirement consumption. A range of risks are involved, however: longevity risk, inflation risk, health risks and capital market risks, and these risks can lead to consumption being lower than anticipated.

8.2.1   Longevity Risk

Longevity risk is the risk of running out of resources before dying. This risk can be eliminated by purchasing a life annuity at retirement. Panis (2004) shows that annuitants are more satisfied in retirement than those without annuities.

However, given the choice, most people do not choose to buy annuities with the lump sums they have accumulated from their DC retirement plans. In the past, members of DB plans took their accrued entitlement in the form of a pension at retirement. Now, in the USA, 75% of company pension payouts are in the form of lump-sum payments (McGill *et al.*, 2005). This means that increasing numbers of people are failing to hedge the longevity risk they face.

A number of explanations have been offered for this:

- People tend to underestimate how long they will live after retirement (two-thirds in a survey by MetLife, 2003; see also Drinkwater and Sondergeld, 2004).
- People also usually have a state pension, which implies some insurance against longevity risk.
- In a world of low interest rates, annuity rates are also low, so annuities appear to offer poor value for money.
- The cost loading of the annuity provider reduces the return compared with a pure investment (yet the evidence indicates that the *money's worth* of annuities is high; e.g., Mitchell *et al.*, 1999; Finkelstein and Poterba, 2002).
- People might have a strong bequest motive and are concerned about future long-term care costs, and this might be combined with the behavioural trait of loss aversion: individuals are concerned that they might die shortly after buying the annuity and the lump sum used to buy the annuity is no longer available to make bequests. (To address such concerns, some insurers offer annuities combined with life assurance, long-term care and disability benefits.)

The extent of annuity aversion is shown by Warner and Pleeter's (2001) study of the behaviour of 65,000 US soldiers made redundant in 1992 following the end of the Cold War. They were offered an early retirement package involving either an annuity or a cash lump sum. The return on the annuity ranged from 17.5% to 19.8%, compared with a return on government bonds of 7%. Yet 52% of the officers and 92% of the ranks elected to take the lump sum over the annuity, thereby foregoing $1.7 billion in economic value.

8.2.2 Inflation and Capital Market Risk

Inflation reduces the real value of investments paying fixed-income returns, such as level annuities. Inflation risk can be hedged by purchasing indexed annuities. However, if inflation is expected to be 3% p.a., an indexed annuity will have a starting payment that is 30% below that of a level annuity. It will take 11 years for the cash payments on the two annuities to equalise, and 19 years in total for the total payments on the indexed annuity to exceed that of the level annuity. Given the choice, few people choose the indexed over the level annuity.

A different alternative to a level annuity is an investment-linked annuity, with a high weighting in equities. Equities are regarded as a good long-term inflation hedge. However, Brown et al. (2000) show that equities have been a poor inflation hedge in the USA, at least in the short to medium term.

The possible behavioural explanations for why people choose the lump sum over the annuity are:

- *Overconfidence* – many people underestimate how much they need to live on after retirement.
- *Lack of self-control* – some people actually spend all their retirement savings within a few years of retirement.
- *The framing effect* – choices can be framed in a way that causes people to overvalue the 'large' lump sum and undervalue the 'small' annuity.
- *Poor financial literacy* – most people are not sufficiently competent to manage the drawdown of their investments in old age (Dus et al., 2004).

To deal with the self-control problem, pension scheme providers could offer an annuity as the default option, rather than a lump sum.

8.3   CONCLUSIONS

Mitchell and Utkus (2004) argue that behavioural economics provides the following lessons:

1. *Behavioural research challenges some of the most central assumptions of decision making.*

    It shows, contrary to the standard economic model, that workers are not rational lifecycle financial planners in respect of their pension schemes because of:

    - Self-control problems over savings and hence need commitment devices.
    - Overdiscounting of the future and overvaluation of the present, which require the need for precommitment programmes for pension savings.
    - A divergence between desire and action, which requires the default option to be appropriately designed.
    - Weak or uncertain preferences about the basic questions of how much to save or how much risk to take, can again be influenced by the default.
    - A poor understanding of risk, as evidenced by an overemphasis on past performance, overconfidence about the future, a concentration on gains and losses, and the preference for lump sums over longevity risk-eliminating annuities.

    This is confirmed by a study by Bernheim *et al.* (2001). They found, using the Panel Study of Income Dynamics and the Consumer Expenditure Survey, that the average replacement ratio in retirement is around 64% in the USA. However, there is considerable variation around this figure, even among households with similar socioeconomic characteristics. Lifecycle theory explains this variation in terms of differences in time preference rates, risk tolerance, exposure to uncertainty, and relative tastes for work and leisure at advanced ages. These factors have testable implications concerning the relation between accumulated wealth and the shape of the consumption profile. Bernheim *et al.* found little support for these implications. The data are instead consistent with rule-of-thumb, mental accounting or hyperbolic discounting theories of wealth accumulation.

2. *Scheme design drives participant decision.*

    As a result of default, framing and inertia effects, investment and saving decisions are heavily influenced by the design of the pension scheme. Similarly, behaviour can be altered by merely changing the default structures. Of particular importance are the design decisions selected by the employer on automatic enrolment, automatic saving and default investment funds. Thaler and Sunstein (2003) argue that what is needed is a strategy of *paternalistic libertarianism*, where individuals can be offered some choice, but the choices are predetermined by a paternalistic plan designer.

3. *The current design of DC schemes does not encourage pension savings.*
   This follows because workers are told that:

   - Saving is optional (since joining the scheme is an active decision).
   - The need to increase saving is optional (again this requires an active decision).
   - Risk is a bad thing rather than something that is a necessary feature of a balanced investment portfolio (since the default fund is generally a low-risk, fixed-income fund).

4. *Current work-place financial education is inappropriate.*
   Employers are keen for workers to join the pension scheme (as this enhances their reputation as socially responsible employers), but they also want to limit the costs they face (in terms of higher matching contributions) and any potential liability for the member's investment decision. The current model of providing information to employees assumes that workers are rational economic planners, but this is not the case.

An alternative model is that desired behaviour must come about before education (Selnow, 2004). The defaults are needed to induce the correct behaviour. Then, education is used to explain the defaults. In other words, behavioural economics suggests a reversal in the causality of education.

These lessons generate four scheme design choices:

1. *Much depends on the default choices in defined contribution plans.*
   Behavioural traits such as inertia, procrastination and lack of decision-making willpower can actually be used to increase pension saving. This is how Save More Tomorrow schemes work: automatic enrolment of all workers, planned annual contribution increases, and default funds that constitute optimal portfolio choices, e.g., balanced portfolios with age-related switching to bonds as retirement approaches (i.e., lifestyling). The passive decision maker can therefore

depend on the scheme design to achieve the best possible pension outcome. Financially skilled workers can reject the default and make their own preferred choices.

2. *Simplified menu design in retirement plans could be very useful.* It is clear that 'choice overload' in investment menus can have a negative impact on scheme participation. What is needed instead is a limited menu of core choices, and, separate from the main menu, an expanded range of options for more sophisticated investors.

3. *New approaches are needed to help workers and retirees better manage company stock risk.* The behavioural finding concerning excessive investment in the employer's equity in US 401(k) pension schemes suggests that the only effective solution is to limit the level of self-investment, as in the UK.

4. *Sensible plan design includes default choices at retirement.* Behavioural research suggests that the framing of the annuity or lump-sum decision can be improved. Account should also be taken of worker understanding of mortality and investment risks. This research suggests that the annuity should automatically be the default option in DC schemes, as it is in DB schemes.

QUESTIONS

1. Why in recent years have behavioural economists begun to question the validity of the lifecycle model?
2. What is meant by bounded rationality?
3. What is meant by bounded self-control?
4. What is meant by bounded self-interest?
5. Explain the difference between exponential and hyperbolic discounting.
6. Why do hyberbolic discounters find it hard to save for retirement?
7. How can the problem of hyperbolic discounting be overcome?
8. What are commitment devices? Give an example.
9. What is decision framing?
10. Explain the significance of default options, using an example.
11. How can inertia and procrastination be used constructively to increase pension savings?
12. What is choice overload?
13. Explain herding behaviour.

14. Why are Save More Tomorrow plans so smart?
15. Modern portfolio theory does not appear to be implemented in practice by many investors. How do we know this?
16. How do we know investors often lack firm preferences?
17. How do we know framing effects are important in investment decision making?
18. What is the $1/N$ rule?
19. Explain the role of anchoring effects, inertia and procrastination in investment decision making.
20. What explains the excessive investment in employer stock by pension plan members?
21. What is the representative heuristic?
22. What is the availability heuristic?
23. What are the key propositions of prospect theory?
24. What is the disposition effect?
25. What is the breakeven effect?
26. Prospect theory is important for understanding investment decision making in three ways. What are they?
27. Why do investors sometimes suffer from overconfidence?
28. What implication does loss aversion have for investors with loss-making positions?
29. What implication does the disposition effect have for investors with winning positions?
30. What is mental accounting?
31. How does mental accounting help us understand investor attitude and response to risk?
32. What is myopic loss aversion?
33. What are some of the symptoms of myopic loss aversion?
34. What mechanisms can be used to overcome myopic loss aversion?
35. Why do so many pension plan members fail to hedge longevity risk when they retire by failing to purchase a life annuity?
36. What are the key lessons of behavioural economics for improving pension plan design?

REFERENCES

Ameriks, J., Caplin, A. and Leahy, J. (2003) Wealth accumulation and the propensity to plan, *Quarterly Journal of Economics*, **118**, 1007–1047.

Banks, J., Blundell, R. and Tanner, S. (1998) Is there a retirement-savings puzzle? *American Economic Review*, **88**, 769–788.

Barber, B. and Odean, T. (2001) Boys will be boys: overconfidence and common stock investment, *Quarterly Journal of Economics*, **116**, 261–292.

Barberis, N. and Huang, M. (2001) Mental accounting, loss aversion, and individual stock returns, *Journal of Finance*, **56**, 1247–1292.

Barberis, N. and Thaler, R. (2003) A survey of behavioral finance, in Constantinides, G., Harris, M. and Stulz, R. (eds), *Handbook of the Economics of Finance*, Elsevier, Amsterdam, pp. 1053–1128.

Benartzi, S. (2001) Excessive extrapolation and the allocation of 401(k) accounts to company stock, *Journal of Finance*, **56**, 1747–1764.

Benartzi, S. and Thaler, R. (1995) Myopic loss aversion and the equity premium puzzle, *Quarterly Journal of Economics*, **110**, 73–92.

Benartzi, S. and Thaler, R. (2001) Naive diversification strategies in retirement saving plans, *American Economic Review*, **91**, 79–98.

Benartzi, S. and Thaler, R. (2002) How much is investor autonomy worth?, *Journal of Finance*, **57**, 1593–1616.

Bernheim, B.D., Skinner. J. and Weinberg, S. (2001) What accounts for the variation in retirement wealth among U.S. households?, *American Economic Review*, **91**, 832–857.

Blake, D. (2000) *Financial Market Analysis*, John Wiley, & Sons Chichester.

Brown, J., Mitchell, O. and Poterba, J. (2000) The role of real annuities and indexed bonds in an individual accounts retirement program, in Campbell, J.Y. and Feldstein, M. (eds), *Risk Aspects of Investment-Based Social Security Reform*, NBER, University of Chicago Press, Chicago, pp. 321–360.

Choi, J., Laibson, D., Madrian, B. and Metrick, A. (2001a) Defined Contribution Pensions: Plan Rules, Participant Decisions, and the Path of Least Resistance, NBER Working Paper 8655.

Choi, J., Laibson, D., Madrian, B. and Metrick, A. (2001b) For Better or For Worse: Default Effects and 401(k) Savings Behavior, NBER Working Paper 8651.

Choi, J., Laibson, D., Madrian, B. and Metrick, A. (2003) Passive Decisions and Potent Defaults, NBER Working Paper 9917.

Choi, J., Laibson, D., Madrian, B. and Metrick, A. (2004) Employee investment decisions about company stock, in Mitchell, O. and Utkus, S. (eds), *Pension Design and Structure: New Lessons from Behavioural Finance,* Oxford University Press, Oxford.

De Bondt, W. (1998) A portrait of the individual investor, *European Economic Review*, **42**, 831–844.

Drinkwater, M. and Sondergeld, E. (2004) Perceptions of mortality risk, in Mitchell, O. and Utkus, S. (eds), *Pension Design and Structure: New Lessons from Behavioural Finance*, Oxford University Press, Oxford.

Duflo, E. and Saez, E. (2004) Implications of information and social interactions for retirement saving decisions, in Mitchell, O. and Utkus, S. (eds), *Pension Design and Structure: New Lessons from Behavioural Finance,* Oxford University Press, Oxford.

Dus, I., Maurer, R. and Mitchell, O. (2004) Betting on Death and Capital Markets in Retirement: A Shortfall Risk Analysis of Life Annuities versus Phased Withdrawal Plans, Pension Research Council Working Paper 2004–1.

Finkelstein, A. and Poterba, J. (2002) Selection effects in the United Kingdom annuities market, *Economic Journal*, **112**, 28–50.

Gneezy, U. and Potters, J. (1997) An experiment on risk taking and evaluation periods, *Quarterly Journal of Economics*, **112**, 631–645.

Goetzmann, W. and Kumar, A. (2001) Equity Portfolio Diversification, NBER Working Paper 8686.

Huberman, G. and Sengmueller, P. (2003) Company Stock in 401(k) Plans, Columbia University Working Paper.

Kahneman, D. (2003) The Psychology of Risky Choices, address before the Investment Company Institute, May 2003, Washington, DC.

Kahneman, D. and Tversky, A. (1979) Prospect theory: an analysis of decision under risk, *Econometrica*, **47**, 263–291.

Kahneman, D. and Tversky, A. (1984) Choices, values and frames, *American Psychologist*, **39**, 341–350.

Kahneman, D. and Tversky, A. (2000) *Choices, Values and Frames,* Russell Sage Foundation and Cambridge University Press, Cambridge, MA.

Laibson, D. (1997) Golden eggs and hyperbolic discounting, *Quarterly Journal of Economics*, **112**, 443–478.

Laibson, D., Repetto, A. and Tobacman, J. (1998) Self control and saving for retirement, *Brookings Papers on Economic Activity*, **I**, 91–196.

Langer, T. and Weber, M. (2004) Does Commitment or Feedback Influence Myopic Loss Aversion? An Experimental Analysis, University of Mannheim Discussion Paper.

MacFarland, D., Marconi, C. and Utkus, S. (2004) 'Money attitudes' and retirement plan design: one size does not fit all, in Mitchell, O. and Utkus, S. (eds), *Pension Design and structure: New Lessons from Behaviioural Finance*, Oxford University Press, oxford.

Madrian, B. and Shea, D. (2001) The power of suggestion: inertia in 401(k) participation and savings behavior, *Quarterly Journal of Economics*, **116**, 1149–1187.

McGill, D., Brown, K., Haley, J. and Schieber, S. (2005) *Fundamentals of Private Pensions*, 8th edn., Oxford University Press, Oxford.

MetLife (2003) *The MetLife Retirement Income IQ Test: Findings from the 2003 National Survey of American Pre-Retirees*, Metlife Mature Market Institute, New York, June.

Mitchell, O. and Utkus, S. (2003) Company stock and retirement plan diversification, in Mitchell, O.S. and Smetters, K. (eds), *The Pension Challenge: Risk Transfers and Retirement Income Security*, Oxford University Press, Oxford.

Mitchell, O. and Utkus, S. (2004) Lessons from behavioural finance for retirement plan design, in Mitchell, O. and Utkus, S. (eds), *Pension Design and Structure: New Lessons from Behavioural Finance,* Oxford University Press, OXford.

Mitchell, O., Poterba, J., Warshawsky, M. and Brown, J. (1999) New evidence on the money's worth of individual annuities, *American Economic Review*, **89**, 1299–1318.

Mitchell, O, Moore, J. and Phillips, J. (2000) Explaining retirement saving short-falls, in Mitchell, O.S. Hammond, B. and Rappaport, A. (eds), *Forecasting Retirement Needs and Retirement Wealth*, University of Pennsylvania Press, Philadelphia, PA, 139–166.

Moore, J. and Mitchell, O. (2000) Projected retirement wealth and saving ade-quacy, in Mitchell, O.S. Hammond, B. and Rappaport, A. (eds), *Forecasting Retirement Needs and Retirement Wealth*, University of Pennsylvania Press, Philadelphia, PA, pp. 68–94.

Mullainathan, S. and Thaler, R. (2000) Behavioral Economics, NBER Working Paper 7948.

Odean, T. (1998) Are investors reluctant to realize their losses?, *Journal of Finance*, **53**, 1775–1798.

Panis, S. (2004) Annuities and retirement satisfaction, in Mitchell, O. and Utkus, S. (eds), *Pension Design and Structure: New Lessons from Behavioural Finance*, Oxford University Press, Oxford.

Patel, J., Zeckhauser, R. and Hendricks, D. (1991) The rationality struggle: illustrations from financial markets, *American Economic Review*, **81**, 232–236.

Polkovnichenko, V. (2003) Household Portfolio Diversification, working paper presented at the Rodney White Center for Financial Research conference, Household Portfolio Choice and Financial Decision-Making, March.

Poterba, J., Rauh, J., Venti, S. and Wise, D. (2003) Utility Evaluation of Risk in Retirement Saving Accounts, NBER Working Paper 9892.

Purcell, P. (2002) The Enron Bankruptcy and Employer Stock in Retirement Plans, *CRS Report for Congress*, US GOP, Code RS21115.

Rabin, M. and Thaler, R. (2001) Anomolies – risk aversion, *Journal of Economic Perspectives*, **15**, 219–232.

Selnow, G. (2004) Motivating retirement planning: problems and solutions, in Mitchell, O. and Utkus, S. (eds), *Pension Design and Structure: New Lessons from Behavioural Finance*, Oxford University Press, Oxford.

Sethi-Iyengar, S., Huberman, G. and Jiang, W. (2004) How much choice is too much? Contributions to 401(k) retirement plans, in Mitchell, O. and Utkus, S. (eds), *Pension Design and Structure: New Lessons from Behavioural Finance*, Oxford University Press, Oxford.

Shefrin, H. and Statman, M. (1985) The disposition to sell winners too early and ride losers too long: theory and evidence, *Journal of Finance*, **40**, 777–790.

Simon, H. (1955) A behavioral model of rational choice, *Quarterly Journal of Economics*, **69**, 99–118.

Thaler, R (1981) Some empirical evidence on dynamic inconsistency, *Economics Letters*, **8**, 201–207.

Thaler, R. (1985) Mental accounting and consumer choice, *Marketing Science*, **4**, 199–214.

Thaler, R. (1999) Mental accounting matters, *Journal of Behavioural Decision Making*, **12**, 183–206.

Thaler, R. and Bernartzi, S. (1999) Risk aversion or myopia? Choices in repeated gambles and retirement investments, *Management Science*, **45**, 364–381.

Thaler, R. and Bernartzi, S. (2004) Save more tomorrow: using behavioural economics to increase employee saving, *Journal of Political Economy*, **112**, S164–S187.

Thaler, R. and Shefrin, H. (1981) An economic theory of self-control, *Journal of Political Economy*, **89**, 392–406.

Thaler, R. and Sunstein, C. (2003) Libertarian paternalism, *American Economic Review*, **93**, 175–179.

Tversky, A. and Kahneman, D. (1974) Judgment under uncertainty: heuristics and biases, *Science*, **185**, 1124–1131.

Warner, J. and Pleeter, S. (2001) The personal discount rate: evidence from military downsizing programs, *American Economic Review*, **91**, 33–53.

Weber, E. (2004) Who's afraid of a poor old age? Risk perception and risk management decisions, in Mitchell, O. and Utkus, S. (eds), *Pension Design and Structure: New Lessons from Behavioural Finance*, Oxford University Press, Oxford.

Index